Advance Praise for EcoKids

Finally a book that helps parents nurture their children into holistic environmental thinking from an early age and lights the way to instilling a profound reverence for the Earth. In the tradition of Aldo Leopold, with *EcoKids*, Dan Chiras brings us practical ways to environmentally inspire our children by example — an absolute must read if we're to provide stewardship for future generations.

— JOHN SCHAEFFER, founder and president of Real Goods and the Solar Living Institute

In *EcoKids* Dan Chiras focuses on touching the hearts and minds of our youth, for the future of the world depends on what they feel, think, and believe. Most importantly he has given parents the tools by which they can raise children who truly care for the Earth. It's a must read — long overdue.

— DENNIS WEAVER, actor, founder of Institute of Ecolonomics

EcoKids is an excellent resource for environmentally conscious parents who want to teach their children what it means to be a responsible citizen of the Earth. Nurturing a love of the environment, along with proper instruction on environmental protection are can help parents instill in their children a lifetime of conscientious action. It should go without saying that our future depends on it.

— MARTY STOUFFER, host of "Wild America"

EcoKids encourages and empowers children, parents, and educators to respect and restore nature and to live environmentally sustainable lifestyles. I believe this book will help preserve endangered habitats, bring new vigor to the field of environmental protection, and help create the strong, unshakable environmental ethic the world so desperately needs.

— DAVID WANN, coauthor *Affluenza: The All-Consuming Epidemic*

EcoKids

Raising Children Who Care for the Earth

Dan Chiras

NEW SOCIETY PUBLISHERS

Cataloging in Publication Data:
A catalog record for this publication is available from the National Library of Canada.

Copyright © 2005 by Dan Chiras.
All rights reserved.

Cover design by Diane McIntosh.
Cover image by Nicholas Halpin, www.eyeswideopen.ca

Printed in Canada.
First printing May 2005.

Paperback ISBN: 0-86571-533-5

Inquiries regarding requests to reprint all or part of *EcoKids* should be addressed to
New Society Publishers at the address below.

To order directly from the publishers, please add $5.00 shipping to the price of the
first copy, and $1.00 for each additional copy (plus GST in Canada). Send check or
money order to:

New Society Publishers
P.O. Box 189, Gabriola Island, BC V0R 1X0, Canada
1-800-567-6772

New Society Publishers' mission is to publish books that contribute in fundamental
ways to building an ecologically sustainable and just society, and to do so with the
least possible impact on the environment, in a manner that models this vision. We are
committed to doing this not just through education, but through action. We are acting on our commitment to the world's remaining ancient forests by phasing out our
paper supply from ancient forests worldwide. This book is one step towards ending
global deforestation and climate change. It is printed on acid-free paper that is 100%
old growth forest-free (100% post-consumer recycled), processed chlorine free, and
printed with vegetable based, low VOC inks. For further information, or to browse
our full list of books and purchase securely, visit our website at: www.newsociety.com

NEW SOCIETY PUBLISHERS   www.newsociety.com

TABLE OF CONTENTS

This book is dedicated to my friend Chance Ruder in appreciation for all he has done to protect and enhance wildlife and create a humane, sustainable future. I sleep better at night just knowing you are out there "fighting" the good fight with love, compassion, insight, wit, and wisdom.

ACKNOWLEDGMENTS

Like all of my books, this work was made possible in part because of the experiences and generous advice of many others, individuals who have studied and practiced parenting. I have gained valuable insights on the subject by studying the writings of Betsy Taylor at the Center for a New American Dream; Marie Sherlock, author of *Living Simply with Children*, Susan Vogt, author of numerous books, including *Raising Kids Who Will Make a Difference*; Foster Cline and Jim Fay, authors of *Parenting with Love and Logic*; Steve Van Matre, author of *Earth Education*; Phillip Hoose, author of *It's Our World, Too!*; and many others.

I am also deeply grateful to the many people who responded to my questionnaires, recounting experiences in their lives that helped forge their environmental commitment. This group includes Doug Seiter, Jim Schley, Clarke Snell, Ianto Evans, Simmons Buntin, Kelly Hart, Bill Baker, Lois Arkin, Chris Walker, Dave Wann, Louis Hornyak, Scott Reuman, Ed Evans, Mary Golden, Robyn Lawrence, Carolyn Roberts, G. Winter, Jessica Creveling, Mike and Cindi Whitehead, Sally Meyer, Chas Ehrlich, Belle Star, Miyaca Dawn Coyote, Charles Fletcher, Bim Krumhansl, Michael Smith, Chris Magwood, Hannah Silverstein, James Plagmann, Michael Reynolds, Shay Solomon, Rob Roy, and Claudia Brown. Their insights have helped give shape to this book. Thanks to all of you for your time and thoughtful responses.

I would also like to express my appreciation to my dear friends Chris and Judith Plant at New Society Publishers who took a chance on this book. I would also like to thank the dedicated staff at New Society Publishers, including Heather Wardle, who helped create the wonderful cover of this book; my copyeditor Murray Reiss for his thoughtful, expert editing; and Sue Custance for her expert design and layout.

The loftier the building, the deeper
must the foundation be laid.
— Thomas A. Kempis

*I expect to pass through life but once. If therefore, there
be any kindness I can show, or any good thing I can do to
any fellow being, let me do it now, and not defer or
neglect it, as I shall not pass this way again.*
— William Penn

Introduction

MY PATH TO SUSTAINABLE LIVING

The deteriorating state of the environment was the last thing on my mind during the first twenty years of my life — in the 1950s and 1960s. First, environmental concerns were only just starting to make the front pages of American newspapers. Second, I was pretty oblivious to the issues of the day. I had my mind on other things like swimming in the creek that ran behind our house, taking care of my fancy pigeons, baseball, school, and farm work.

More than oblivious, I was clueless. Even at Scout camp, in the deep rich deciduous forests of the Adirondack Mountains in upper New York State, during my early teens I struggled through the soil and water conservation merit badge class. I was bored, frankly, and unaware of what all of the fuss was about. The merit badge counselor, who seemed so passionate about his subject, a guy we called "Nature Boy" behind his back (I'm ashamed to say), was the butt of our youthful snobbery. We couldn't wait until class was over.

Those who know me realize that somewhere along the road from my oblivious youth to adulthood, something profound must have taken place, something that changed me so deeply that I turned my back on a potentially lucrative career in medicine (sorry Dad) in favor of a fulfilling, but clearly less financially profitable, and often disheartening environmental career.

What was it? What "lightning" bolt from the heavens struck me so compellingly that I devote nearly every waking minute of my days to the protection of this tiny piece of real estate in the vast expanse of space?

Actually, it was not a single high-voltage bolt of inspiration that rocked my world, but a series of seeds sown during my early life — various events and discoveries — that individually had little effect, but cumulatively conspired over a period of many years to create in me a deep and resolute devotion to environmental protection.

One of the first lightning bolts occurred when I was a teenager. The Scout troop I belonged to was hiking along a remote section of the Appalachian Trail. I'm not even sure where we were. I think we were in Connecticut.

As our troop trudged happily along, our homemade wooden pack frames creaking with each step, we suddenly entered an unusual patch of forest, a remnant of the eastern old-growth forest — miraculously spared from the saw. This part of the forest was unlike the younger forests that we had been tromping through all day. It consisted of trees so tall that I strained my neck to see their top branches. The leaves of these monstrous trees intercepted nearly all sunlight, creating a cool, dark environment.

Although I did not know that we were in an old-growth forest, I could feel the magnificence and grandeur of these stately trees that had stood for hundreds of years against all sorts of weather. I felt a stirring in me, the closest thing I've ever had to a religious experience. My spirit rose for a few minutes, and then plunged as we exited into the hot, sunny neighboring forests, no doubt harvested within the past forty years.

The experience was over in a flash, but I was changed forever.

Unbeknownst to me, a small seed had been sown in my heart and in my mind.

Our troop hiked on to our camping spot, several miles farther along the trail.

No one said a word about our brief encounter with that ancient remnant of the old-growth forest that once carpeted much of the nation's eastern half.

Deep inside, the seed remained, like the memory of a loved one's touch or a smile from a loving grandparent.

When I first heard the term old-growth forest in my twenties and read articles outlining the threats to them and the dire need to protect them from further clearcutting, I needed no convincing. My brief encounter left no doubt in my mind that the ancient forests were a treasure to be safeguarded, not an amenity to squander for short-term profit.

My love for this small remnant of ancient forest has translated into a lifetime of unyielding sympathy for venerable old-growth forests. Over the years, it has stirred me to write dozens of letters to congressional representatives, US presidents, and conservation groups, lobbying for their protection. It has also helped me learn to use wood wisely or avoid wood use entirely (hence the reason my home is constructed largely from straw bales and rammed earth tires).

But truthfully, this experience did not convert me overnight to an environmental sympathizer.

There were other experiences and lessons I learned along the way that forged my devotion to and respect for the natural world. Years earlier, while I was in grade school for instance, I remember watching a television program with my family. The show was a biography of some great person. (I am embarrassed to say that I can't recall who it was now.) The narrator commented that throughout his life, this remarkably accomplished individual sought "to leave the woodpile a little fuller."

It was a cold wintry night, which somehow contributed to the power of this analogy. What a novel idea, I thought. It was as if that notion became imprinted on my consciousness. Life isn't just about what we get; it's about what we do for others, what we leave behind.

Years of being a Boy Scout brought that lesson home over and over again. I saw grown men giving their time to take us camping or hiking or to teach us canoeing. My dad volunteered at the district level. I can still see him trotting off in his Boy Scout uniform. He looked a little silly, well very silly, to be truthful, but I was proud of him for giving his time so generously, and still am. He set a good example for a lifetime of giving to others for which I am eternally grateful.

A few years later, as a member of a Scout troop, I found an immediate outlet to give to others by assuming the role of teacher and leader. I taught many a boy how to tie his knots and perform dozens of other skills we learned in Scouts. Teaching has been a role I've assumed ever since, not for financial gain, but to satisfy a deep desire to give back, to leave the woodpile a little fuller, and to share my love and enthusiasm for knowledge.

Another profound influence occurred in high school, quite a few years after my brief encounter with the old-growth forests of the Appalachian Trail. At my father's insistence, my family was living in rural upstate New York on a 13-acre (5.2 hectare) site in the country. (He was adamant about bringing us up in the country, a fact for which I remain eternally grateful.)

Our property was bordered by a dense, wide marsh that crackled with the cacophony of red-winged black birds. Through the marsh ran a slow-moving creek that was our playground. We fished for bluegills, bullheads, and carp, rowed our boat in search of turtles, and swam in the warm waters day after glorious summer day. We never experienced boredom.

Several years after we moved in, though, the creek that meandered toward our property and through deciduous forests and lush farm fields of beans and wheat upstream from us, turned foul almost overnight.

Why?

Many miles away upstream, a Duffy-Mott factory that ground apples into applesauce had, for reasons we never discovered, decided to disgorge huge amounts of organic waste into the stream all at once.

The organic detritus from the factory migrated downstream, rotting in the shallow waterway, depleting oxygen, and choking out all fish life. It put an abrupt end to our summer afternoons on the "crick" — as the local farmers called it. The creek became so odoriferous that year, we had to hold our noses as we passed by the smelly waterway on the school bus.

In the years that followed the initial release the stench gradually subsided, but the plant nutrients the company had released into the creek stimulated massive growth of algae and aquatic vegetation. In short order, the creek became choked with tangles of vegetation so thick that it was difficult to row our boat. Each time we tried to row through the creek, or fish — reeling in balls of weeds with our line along with bluegills and sunfish — we cussed the factory that created this disaster.

The pollution of the stream upset me, but not enough to make me do anything. I was pretty easygoing about things over which I had no control. Unlike my boyhood friend John Bower, who wrote a poem to memorialize the event and read it at an assembly to crucify the perpetrators, I simply shrugged my shoulders in youthful resignation.

Still, another seed was planted.

This one serves as a personal reminder of how one thoughtless act can have devastating consequences on the environment, and how it can upset the lives of many for years to come. Today, when I hear about a stream being polluted, it is not some abstract event. I think about the fish that perished in our stream when the plant matter rotted in the fall, using up all the oxygen. I think about the rancid smell that pervaded our nostrils, and the many people affected by this event. This indelible event lingers in my mind, so that stories of stream pollution in distant rivers are painfully real to me, dredging up old memories and old anger.

In 1968, at the age of 17, I left for college in the Midwest. Tucked away in the quaint and quiet town of Manhattan, Kansas, at Kansas State University, a hotbed of political apathy, I remained sheltered from the real world for four years. I spent my time studying organic chemistry, zoology, cell biology, embryology, human anatomy, and the like to prepare for a career in medicine. While I pored over my notes and reading assignments, memorizing everything I could in the library, protests over the war in Vietnam reached a fevered pitch. If the truth be known, I did follow the war, but political activism did not suit my studious nature. Even though concerns over the state of the environment were stirring among the general public, I was pretty oblivious to the world around me. I was eyeing a career in medicine.

But fate (if you believe in such things) had other plans for me.

During my senior year, on a trip home to see my parents, I decided to stop in at Northwestern University Medical School in Chicago to talk with the dean about my application. As I neared Chicago, however, I passed some factories in Gary, Indiana. Huge clouds of black smoke poured from the stacks, darkening the sky.

"My God," I murmured, and turned to leave the area, disgusted.

"How could anyone in their right mind pour so much filth into the air we breathe?" I wondered.

Even though evidence of acid rain and other forms of air pollution had not yet been brought into public attention, and I had never studied pollution and its environmental impacts, it just seemed intuitively wrong to me that we should release so much junk into the air we breathe.

At that moment, another seed was sown, a seed of doubt. For a moment, something vague passed through me; a question as to my career choice. Maybe, I mused for a moment, medicine wasn't the correct route. Maybe there was a "bigger patient" to heal.

But the thought quickly passed. I'd never heard of anyone making a career out of environmental protection. K-State didn't even offer a course on the subject.

The next year, my dream of a career in medicine crumbled. The admissions office at Northwestern University Medical School apparently lost my application and the only other school I had applied to (UCLA) turned me down. Being an out-of-stater, I stood about as much chance of getting into UCLA as a trout surviving opening day in the cool waters of the rivers in Naples, NY, when anglers line the banks elbow to elbow.

So I changed my plans. I enrolled in a Ph.D. program in reproductive physiology at the University of Kansas School of Medicine in Kansas City. I was fascinated by the subject and hoped to matriculate in the medical school a few years into my doctoral program. As an M.D./Ph.D. I could teach and do research at a major medical school.

Clearly, despite my jarring experience in Gary, Indiana, I was unable — or unwilling — to give up my dream of a career in medicine, and I had no data to suggest that I could make a living "saving the planet."

As a graduate student, I immersed myself once again in course work, absorbed in the intricate details of the human body. But again, fate would deal me different cards. A couple of years later, after completing my course work, I began my research. With a bit more free time on my hands, stories on the nightly news about pollution and other environmental ills began to captivate my attention. I began to read books such as Paul Ehrlich's *The Population Bomb*. The draw toward environmental protection grew ever stronger.

Feeling torn between a career in medicine and my growing concerns for the environment, I found some release by reshaping my modest existence to create a more environmentally responsible lifestyle. In 1971, at age 21, for example, I started recycling, a practice I continue today. Since then, I have recycled every can, bottle, newspaper, and piece of cardboard that has entered my home. Back then, I even volunteered to take neighbors' recyclable materials along with me. You will still find me picking up cans and bottles along the road on evening walks or in parking lots. When on business trips, I devotedly cart home cans, bottles, and even paper napkins from restaurants — rather than throw them away.

As a graduate student, I drove a small, energy-efficient car, a VW bug. I usually walked wherever I needed to go, and I began writing a column on the environment for the student newsletter, merging my two greatest loves, writing and the environment. I even began spending weekends backpacking in the Ozarks of southern Missouri.

In the last year of my Ph.D., I applied to the medical school program and was accepted. A few weeks later, and after much painful deliberation, I turned the offer down. I took three weeks off to backpack in Colorado, as if looking for vindication of my decision. In southwestern Colorado, I strapped on my pack and headed into the San Juan Mountains. There, I photographed wildflowers and gazed out upon magnificent rocky peaks, reveling in the minute and the magnificent and everything in between. Nature's beauty filled my heart.

While hiking high in the mountain country, I came across an ancient clearcut, ravaged by erosion and still struggling to heal. I knew at that moment that I had made the correct decision. Somehow, I knew I had to be a part of larger healing, a process much more important than attending to patients whose arteries were clogged with cholesterol from eating too many Big Macs. I needed to be a part of a broader, perhaps more essential, healing.

Upon completing my Ph.D., I was offered a teaching and research position in the biology department at the University of Colorado in Denver, which I gladly accepted. There I taught courses I'd been trained for — cell biology, microanatomy, reproductive physiology, and endocrinology. In my spare time, however, I began to study a wide range of environmental issues now appearing on America's (and my) radar screen. I began teaching courses on environmental pollution as an overload to my regular course work, so as not to aggravate the department chair who had hired me as a biologist, not an environmental science instructor.

The more I read, the more serious the problems appeared, and the more certain I was that I'd found both a cause and a career. It's not often we can meld our loves so seamlessly.

From this point, I went on to a career as an environmental educator, writer, public speaker, and consultant. Every book I've read, every newscast I've seen, every polluted sky I've viewed has deepened my resolve to fight for the environment and a better future for all, and to live a life that is consistent with my values.

Since then, I've published 21 books, most of them on some aspect of environmental protection or sustainability, including several best-selling college textbooks. I've published several hundred articles, also principally focused on building a sustainable future. I lecture widely these days to audiences all over the country, and teach workshops on passive solar heating and passive cooling as well as natural building. I also consult on green building and other aspects of sustainability.

Today, I'm living a dream, pondering and writing about — and hopefully helping to solve — the environmental nightmare humankind has created. I'm raising two children to care for the Earth. We live in a state-of-the-art environmental home, powered by solar and wind energy and constructed from many recycled and environmentally friendly materials.

One lesson I've learned from my own journey, when it comes to raising children to care for the Earth, is that a great many factors may forge one's commitment to the environment. Don't expect a single inspirational bolt of lightning to change your child, to electrify his or her passion and commitment. Although there are exceptions to the rule, the vast majority of the people I interviewed, when researching this book, were influenced by a variety of factors: parents, teachers, experiences, reading, and classes in high school or college.

Becoming a parent for the first time can, in and of itself, be a powerful stimulus for change. Mary Golden, an aspiring green architect from Rochester, New York, for instance, confided in me, "Having my daughter was probably the most head-turning event in making lifestyle and career changes. It suddenly became very important to me to work and to live in a way that supported life, protecting the environment for her and other people's kids."

Several people I interviewed believe that they were environmentally oriented from early on. "I think I was born an environmentalist. Ever since I can remember, environmental protection has resonated with me," notes James Plagmann, a Colorado-based architect who is building a successful business designing environmentally friendly homes. Even so, his life of environmental commitment has been shaped by many outside forces, including important books, television coverage of environmental issues, school projects, college teachers, and influential architects.

Others stumbled upon it in the most unusual way. Ed Evans, my junior high school chemistry teacher, noted, "In my second year of teaching, my boss told me that I would teach Earth science. I fought this suggestion but was forced to give in." He had no background in Earth science. "I had to teach myself the course as I went along, and by the time that first year was over, I was hooked on appreciating our planet. And I could fire up the kids, too!" Ed went on to nearly 35 years of inspirational teaching, helping many students understand and develop a passion for the environment and environmental protection.

So be patient and hopeful. Plant seeds. Provide your child with many opportunities to foster his or her innate love for nature. Provide opportunities to develop a deep understanding of the importance of the environment to our lives, and the lives of all people and all other living things. And be sure to breed hope by helping them see how their actions — combined with those of others — can truly change the world for the better. Yes, if everyone lit just one little candle it would be a brighter world!

And don't forget to live consistently with your values.

Set a good example and hope they're watching, listening, and learning to be people who will make a huge difference in their own lives, leaving the woodpile much fuller than when they arrived.

ABOUT THIS BOOK

This book contains advice on raising children who care for the Earth, derived from my own experience as a father of two boys, from numerous other adults I've interviewed, and from experts in the field. My hope is that this information can help you steer your children to a life of environmental responsibility.

As you shall soon see, this book also contains background information on key environmental issues and other topics to help you become a more informed parent and teacher. It is my belief that if you understand the issues, values, and ecology, you'll be more effective.

In this book, I've also included numerous inspiring stories — typically short pieces on kids who are making a difference. You may want to read them aloud to your family. For further inspiration and ideas on actions people can take to create a sustainable future, I've included short case studies I call "Models of Sustainability." These case studies highlight what businesses and governments are doing to help build a sustainable future. They also provide additional background information on some of the most pressing environmental concerns.

At the end of each chapter, you'll find a list of family activities to help drive home the key ideas presented in this book. Finally, at the very end of the book is a resource guide, a list of important books, magazines, videos, organizations, and websites that could help you and your family reach your full potential.

*You cannot escape the responsibility
of tomorrow by evading it today.*
— Abraham Lincoln

1 CHANGING THE WORLD ONE CHILD AT A TIME

To many people in our society, the word *environment* is a four-lettered word. Just mention the word in some crowds and you'll likely be dismissed as a "bleeding heart liberal" or a "tree hugger."

Those inclined to ridicule you and your desire to protect the environment do so, in large part, because they view environmental protection efforts as subversive to human progress. Those on the extreme right, in fact, hold the mistaken notion that environmental protection undermines the economy that puts food on our tables and shelter over our heads and big screen TVs in our living rooms.

The anti-environmental faction sees environmental protection not only as an impediment to economic progress but as a threat to our way of life. Moreover, some critics of environmentalism view it as a form of elitism. Environmentalists, they say, pursue a narrow agenda designed to save pretty places for backpackers and bird watchers. Protecting the environment puts hard-working men and women out of work. They lose their jobs and their families suffer deeply because of the environmental protection efforts of elitists. The backbone of the economy, the labor force, they contend, endures hardship while economically valuable land and its resources are set aside to protect our playgrounds.

It's too bad our schools and the media haven't tried to correct this dangerous misconception. If they had mounted a successful campaign to educate people on the true underlying value of the environment, detractors might be able to see that by actively opposing environmental protection, they are, figuratively speaking, shooting themselves and their children — and their children's children — in the feet. They might realize that their environmental ignorance and resultant disdain for environmental protection that translates into environmentally contemptuous policies may benefit them in the very short term, but will foreclose on their own future and the future of subsequent generations, ultimately making it harder and harder for people to live a decent life and make a decent living.

All ignorance toboggans into know and trudges up to ignorance again: but winter's not forever, even snow melts; and if spring should spoil the game, what then?

— e.e. cummings

Robert Goodland, an ecological economist, writes that the "environment is the source of all our resources and the sink for all our waste." That is to say, everything around us comes from the environment. Every bit of food we eat, every piece of clothing we wear, and every drop of water we drink comes from the Earth and its once-rich ecosystems. Even synthetics such as plastics and nylon come from the environment — in this case, from chemicals extracted from crude oil, which was geologically manufactured from the remains of ancient marine algae. Moreover, the light shining from incandescent light bulbs in the living rooms of many households comes from coal, fabricated in the Earth's thick crust from ancient plants. These plants trapped solar energy several hundred million years ago in the Carboniferous era, then were deposited along swamps where they were buried by sediment. Over time, heat and pressure transformed the plant matter into coal. When we burn this black, carbon-rich fuel, we release the ancient solar energy. The energy liberated at power plants lights our homes and powers our computers and runs our washing machines.

Forests, fields, rivers, and oceans are the source of the resources that make our lives possible. They are also the source of most money in the human economy. Today and every day, our lives and our economy are dependent on a sound environment.

Too bad detractors don't get that point.

As a parent, you can make sure your children don't grow up ignorant of this essential fact.

Ecosystems, as you'll see in Chapter 3, also supply us with many free services — like clean air and protection against flooding and insect control. These benefits are free to us, until we destroy them. Then we either suffer or spend millions trying to replicate what nature once offered gratis.

There's another point that's important to realize. The environment serves as a repository for all of our waste — not just garbage, but sewage and a wide assortment of toxic pollutants from factories, power plants, homes, and cars. The soil, the water, and the air are a dumping ground for human wastes. Unfortunately, the soil is also the source of our food and fiber. Waterways provide the water we drink and bathe and swim in. The atmosphere provides the air we breathe.

Polluting the common resources we need for survival is clearly not one of our better ideas. It's a bit suicidal. However, all species do it. Pollution is inevitable. But we humans produce so much waste that it often exceeds the ability of the ecosystems we live in to assimilate or dilute the wastes to harmless levels. It's too bad detractors don't understand the pollution we produce has dangerous backlashes, for example, the violent weather and flooding we're experiencing very likely resulting from global warming due to the excessive production of greenhouse gases from cars, factories, homes, jets, and so on. (At this writing, in the summer of 2004, the United States is about to be clobbered by its fourth major hurricane of the season.) Again, this is a fact you can help your children realize. We pollute and destroy natural systems at our own peril.

Forests, fields, rivers, and oceans are the source of the resources that make our lives possible. They are the source of most money in the human economy, too. Today and every day, our lives and our economy are dependent on a sound environment.

So, not only are we dependent on the environment to supply our resources and get rid of our wastes, we're treating it with disregard for possible repercussions. Herman Daly once wrote that "most nations are treating the Earth as if it were a corporation in liquidation." We are rapidly selling off its assets to the highest bidders. Are these claims exaggerated?

ECOTRENDS: ARE WE ON A SUSTAINABLE COURSE?

In over 30 years of studying environmental issues and tracking environmental trends, I've seen significant progress in many areas. In the United States, for example, recycling has increased dramatically. Nationwide, 31 percent of our waste is now recycled. Soil conservation efforts are paying off too. Soil erosion has dropped dramatically thanks to historic legislation that has taken highly erodible land out of production. Nationwide, Americans have become more efficient in their use of resources such as water and energy. Factories produce less hazardous waste and huge tracts of wilderness have been set aside for protection.

Unfortunately, there are many signs that paint a troubling picture. In a nationwide study I performed a few years ago, for example, I found that trends in such areas as carbon dioxide emissions, population growth, energy consumption per capita, industrial energy production, transportation, destruction of farmland, and loss of wildlife habitat showed significant movement away from sustainability. On balance, the negative trends offset the positive ones by a 3 to 1 ratio. All in all, the trends suggest quite strongly that we're living and conducting business on the planet in an unsustainable fashion.

To get an idea of how significant our impacts are, consider the impact of human activity on just one day, a technique my colleague David Orr, an Oberlin College environmental studies professor, likes to use to give his audiences a realistic view of what's happening to the planet — and us.

A study of environmental trends suggests quite strongly that we're on an unsustainable course.

On a typical day on planet Earth, says Orr, we destroy 140 to 180 square miles (363 to 466 square kilometers) of tropical rainforest. That's a two-mile wide, 70-mile long (3.2 kilometer wide, 112 kilometer long) swath of land, cleared of its diverse and colorful biological garment to provide timber and to make room for mines, roadways, farms, and new towns. To date, over three million square miles (7.7 million square kilometers) of tropical rainforest have been lost to development. That's an area half the size of the United States.

On a typical day, the world's nations pump more than 15 million tons (13.5 million metric tons) of carbon dioxide into the atmosphere, largely from the combustion of fossil fuels, gasoline, coal, oil, and natural gas. For well over 100 years, scientists have known that carbon dioxide is a greenhouse gas. That is, it traps heat radiating from the Earth's surface somewhat like the glass in a greenhouse. Scientists have known that a little bit of carbon dioxide is good for us; in fact, it's required to create temperatures hospitable to life on Earth. If carbon dioxide were missing from the Earth's atmosphere, our planet would be 50°F (27.5°C) cooler than it is today. Very few, if any, life forms could exist in the frozen wasteland.

While small quantities of carbon dioxide are good for us, too much can cause serious overheating. The heat excess carbon dioxide traps is kept from escaping into the vast expanse of outer space. Abundant evidence suggests that the accumulation of carbon dioxide and other greenhouse gases is now causing the Earth's surface temperature to spiral upward like that of a patient with an uncontrollable fever.

While many readers know that the world has suffered from perpetual hot spells in the past couple of decades, few realize how significant it is. At this writing in 2004, 17 of the hottest years in 100 have occurred since 1980. While heat spells are not uncommon, having so many swelteringly hot years in a row is extremely unlikely. It is statistically quite improbable. Recent studies show that the 1990s and 2000s represent the hottest period on Earth in the past 2000 years.

Global warming is not just making the Earth's surface hotter, it is dramatically altering the climate, influencing rainfall patterns that result in costly floods. While some areas are wetter, others suffer searing and devastating droughts. Forest fires are breaking out with great regularity, even in tropical climates. Who knows what this is costing us in lives lost each year? In the summer of 2003, France suffered 20,000 deaths, mostly among the elderly, in a summertime hot spell. In Colorado, where I live, the US Forest Service posted a fire warning in January! Who knows what this wacky weather is costing our society, but the price tag is surely in the tens of billions of dollars each year.

On a single day, Orr tells us, scientists estimate that the planet loses approximately 100 species. Most of the losses occur as rainforests topple, as coral reefs die — largely due to warming seas but also due to pollution and sediment — and as wetlands are cleared to make room for humans. While species do become extinct naturally, modern extinction is occurring at a greatly accelerated pace. In fact, we're losing species approximately 30 times faster than through natural extinction. Moreover, the face of extinction has changed. During natural extinction, many species disappeared, but they were typically replaced by evolutionary offshoots, new species that emerged from the old. In modern extinction, species are wiped out completely, without a trace — that is, without a new lineage. Modern extinction is forever. John Ryan of the Worldwatch Institute summed up the situation best: "Difficult as it is to accept, mass extinction has already begun, and we are irrevocably committed to many additional losses."

On a typical day, 70 million tons (63 million metric tons) of topsoil are lost from the world's farmlands. To put this into perspective, that rate of erosion results in a loss of 24 billion tons (21.6 billion metric tons) per year. Over a decade, that's 240 billion tons (216 billion metric tons) — equivalent to approximately one half of the topsoil on US farms.

While we systematically tear apart the Earth's rich biological tapestry, let our soils wash away, and pollute the air, water, and land, the human population — which depends on the Earth and its declining ecosystems — continues its inexorable expansion. On a typical day, nearly 250,000 — one-quarter of a million — people are added to the planet's population. That's a quarter of a million new residents, each needing food, water, shelter, and clothing — all derived from the environment — to survive.

And tomorrow, it all starts over again.

CHANGING THE WORLD ONE CHILD AT A TIME

I saw a bumper sticker the other day on a Toyota Prius, one of the new energy-efficient, clean-burning hybrid cars. It read, "I don't know where we're going, but what's this hand basket I'm in?"

The idea that crises have both negative and positive aspects is captured in a word the Chinese have for crisis, wei-chi. The first part of the word means "beware, danger." The second part, however, has a very different implication. It means "opportunity for change."
— Peter Russell,
The Global Brain.

Surely, if you study the trends seriously for any length of time it is difficult to avoid the feeling that we humans are heading straight over a cliff.

Nonetheless, many think that trend need not be our destiny.

We have a chance to heed the signs, to make mid-course corrections.

The changes must begin with each of us. We adults can't wait for generations of children to clean up the mess. The longer we dally and the further we drift off our once-sustainable course, the more difficult it will be for our children to repair the damage and restore the Earth.

We must begin now.

It is also imperative that parents, teachers, and others train our children now to work with us and to eventually take over for us. It is imperative that we help create kids with ideals, values, and a serious commitment to live environmentally sustainable lifestyles. That's what this book is about. It's a guide for parents who want to help out by leaving behind a living legacy — children — who *will* make a difference.

Generations of environmentally responsible children are needed to make the changes in our lives and our economy. Inevitably, some of our children will become leaders. Some of them will grow up to replace today's environmental leaders. Some will lead influential environmental organizations that help shape thinking, policy, and action in profound ways here and abroad. Others may play equally important roles as teachers in public schools or colleges and universities.

Others may become writers or news reporters. Still others may become influential scientists or even eminent politicians who lead the charge. This book has some advice for parents, teachers, and others to encourage our youth to follow an environmental career path.

But not all children need take an active role in education, writing, and governance. Not everyone needs to become an activist. Indeed, the vast majority of our offspring will not aspire

We can't wait for generations of children to clean up the mess. The longer we dally and the further we drift off our once-sustainable course, the more difficult it will be for our children to repair the damage and restore the Earth. We must begin now.

to such heights. It makes no difference. Far more important than a few good leaders are generations of good planetary citizens; that is, kids who become adults who use energy and other resources efficiently, and who recycle and buy recycled products. We need children who, when they grow up, opt to build solar homes or install solar electric panels on their energy-efficient homes made of straw bales and other environmentally friendly materials. We need children who will eventually grow their own food or buy organic produce from local farms, and who will compost kitchen and garden waste and use natural fertilizers and pesticides in the garden and yard. We need citizens who support the restoration of the Earth's endangered ecosystems and who, as adults, take responsibly their right to have children.

Moreover, we need doctors, lawyers, accountants, and business people who run environmentally sound businesses. We need copy shop owners and grocery store managers who ensure that their operations are carried out in an environmentally sustainable fashion. We need manufacturers who produce products in environmentally sound ways. You, as a parent, can help ensure this solid base of support for a sustainable society.

I hope the ideas in this book help.

I'm also hoping that this book will help parents teach their children to adopt environmentally responsible lifestyles now — refraining from the highly consumptive buying habits of their peers, turning off lights, helping with the family's recycling, using energy and water sparingly, biking or walking to school or to friends' houses rather than insisting on a ride from mom or dad.

While there are several books on raising children who care about and take action on social issues — kids who work to promote peace and eradicate poverty, homelessness, and hunger — I, also, will spend a little time on the subject. I do so because creating a sustainable world requires more than simply living within the means of the planet. It means creating a just and peaceful global society where basic needs are met and where people live free from harm and are able to participate in their governance. Without these, there is no chance of achieving environmental goals. In countries torn by civil strife, as a rule, the environment will suffer. Sustainability has no chance of flourishing.

Not all children will need coaxing and teaching from mom and dad. Some are naturally empathic, that is, naturally inclined to feel a connection to the natural world. Several people I interviewed for this book indicated they felt an early affinity for wild places and the species that inhabit them. Such children may become the catalysts of changes within our families. This book is dedicated to one such child, Chance Ruder, who lives in San Antonio, Texas. His story is told in Chapter 8.

If you have such a child, my advice is to get out of his or her way. Be supportive and learn as much as you can from them. Although their reasoning may not always be sound, their hearts are in the right place. Following their hearts can lead you along a path of transformation that has profound effects on you and the rest of your family.

AVOIDING GLOOM AND DOOM

In Sweden, thousands of residents have rallied around sustainable development and have made many important strides in using energy efficiently, converting to renewable energy sources, building with environmentally friendly materials, conserving water, and preventing pollution. In fact, entire cities and towns have made a concerted shift toward sustainable lifestyles and a sustainable economy. They are called ecomunicipalities and are described in the book *The Natural Step for Communities*, by Sarah James and Torbjörn Lahti.

Although Sweden and many other European nations are far ahead of the United States when it comes to environmentally friendly attitudes, lifestyles, and businesses, the key to success in creating change rested, in large part, on educational efforts, particularly efforts to explain the impacts humans were having on the environment and how unsustainable our lives really were. Success with your children may also hinge on similar lessons. That is to say, you may need to present dramatic evidence of the need before you can expect children to accept the idea that we all need to live more environmentally sustainable lifestyles. You can do so, for instance, by describing the trends mentioned earlier in this chapter.

However, it is important, indeed essential, not to let your children become mired in gloom and doom. Such feelings may lead to a sense of despair and helplessness. Children may feel as if there is no hope. Hopelessness, in turn, may lead to disempowerment and, ultimately, to inaction. Inaction, of course, will get us nowhere, and the only ones who will gain are the doctors who prescribe and the pharmaceutical companies that manufacture antidepressants — and, oh yes, the forces that stand in the way of sustainability.

KIDS WHO ARE MAKING A DIFFERENCE
STUDENTS HEAT SCHOOL WITH ROTTING GARBAGE

Science students in Maryland Heights, Missouri, launched an ambitious program that could start a trend in the United States and abroad. Their project: to capture methane, a combustible gas released from rotting garbage in a nearby landfill, to heat their school.

Today, thanks to the efforts of a handful of students and a local businessperson, all 117 classrooms and two gymnasiums at Pattonville High are heated by methane from rotting garbage. Pattonville High is believed to be the first school in the United States heated by waste gas.

The methane, piped to the school by a 3600-foot (1100-meter) pipeline from the 85-acre (35-hectare) landfill, is burned in the furnace in place of natural gas. Thus, it not only puts waste to good use, it helps reduce their dependence on a finite fossil fuel. (The school is not entirely heated by methane. Some natural gas is needed for the cafeteria and other operations, but the use is minimal.)

What makes this all the more exciting is that the landfill operators used to burn off the waste gas. Even more exciting is that this project, which cost $175,000, saves the school $40,000 a year in heating bills. The savings paid the capital costs in fewer than five years. The principal of the school, Tom Byrnes, said, "The methane gas is there. It's a matter of burning it off or using it productively."

The US Environmental Protection Agency (EPA) estimates that 750 landfills in the United States could be tapped to generate gas. If only half of them were tapped, it would cut the emissions of thousands of tons of carbon dioxide each year. According to the EPA, this would be equivalent to removing 12 million cars from the road. Obviously, landfill waste gas is not the only answer to creating a sustainable future, but it can help.

New regulations require that landfills with more than 2.75 tons (2.5 metric tons) of trash be tested for gaseous emissions. If emissions exceed a certain level, the new Clean Air Act amendments require the operator to install a system to collect and burn off the gas, to prevent possible explosions caused when the gas reaches certain levels. If methane can be put to good use, say proponents, it should be.

Adapted with permission from Daniel D. Chiras, *Environmental Science: Creating a Sustainable Future*, 6th ed., Jones and Bartlett, 2001.

AVOIDING THE PARADOX OF INCONSEQUENCE

While we are on the topic, years ago I "discovered" an unusual psychological trap that parents and educators must be aware of. I dubbed it the "paradox of inconsequence" in one of my very first environmental books, *Beyond the Fray: Reshaping America's Environmental Movement*.

The paradox of inconsequence unfolds like this: As we go about our daily lives, many of us realize that there are serious environmental problems. However, for most of us, our role in creating the problems seems insignificant. We reason that we're just one of around 300 million Americans or nearly 6.5 billion world citizens. Therefore, what we do is insignificant, of infinitesimal proportion. "Why fret about our actions?" we ask. "It makes no difference." Freed from responsibility by the inconsequence of our own action, we drive gas-guzzling cars, fail to recycle, leave lights on, let the hose run longer than we should, buy the latest electronics, and consume as if there were no end in sight. "Why not? What difference does it really make? We're just one of millions."

Ironically, this logic creates many of the world's environmental and resource problems. That is to say, millions of people all thinking their part is insignificant — and then acting accordingly — are largely responsible for many of the modern environmental problems. It is one key reason why countries like the United States are on an unsustainable course. Our seemingly insignificant contributions, however, do add up. They create problems of epic proportions: millions of tons of carbon dioxide dumped into our atmosphere each day and millions of tons of hazardous waste from factories that produce the long list of consumer goods, and so on and so on.

> *Each snowflake in an avalanche pleads not guilty.*
> — Stanislaus Lee

Writer Stanislaus Lee put it best when he said, "Each snowflake in an avalanche pleads not guilty."

But the ironies don't end here.

The sense of inconsequence that creates our problems also keeps us from solving them.

How so?

Quite simply: The logic that spawns our problems keeps many people from changing. "Why bother?" they ask, "My contribution to solving the problem is so insignificant. If I turn out my lights or use water efficiently or drive the speed limit or use public transport, my sacrifice won't amount to a drop in the ocean."

So why act?

Why do anything?

And so it goes: The logic that creates massive environmental problems and our sense of inconsequence, also keep us from solving them. Instead we rely on governments and business to solve them for us. We expect new laws or regulations to change behavior and new technologies to rescue us.

Although government and business can help, we can't rely on them to solve our problems. In fact, because of short-term thinking both entities may work at cross purposes, engaging in activities that force us further off a sustainable path. Surely, if we're going to successfully steer back onto a sustainable course, we need their help, but we need to address pressing issues from the bottom up, too. And guess who's on the bottom?

We are.

And our children are.

And their children, and so on.

Generations of responsible citizens can change the world.

You and your children can be a part of the transformation, a positive force for the betterment of society.

THE IMPORTANCE OF POSITIVE EXAMPLES

To avoid gloom and doom and the crippling paradox of inconsequence, our children need to see and feel and be a part of positive solutions. While a hike through a clear-cut or a visit to the city dump can help them realize the enormity of our problems, it's just as important, maybe even more important, to take them on a tour of a recycling center so they can see for themselves the tens of thousands of tons of recycled cans, bottles and newspapers on their way back into the production cycle. Take them on a tour of a sustainably harvested forest or visit a sustainable farm or two. Take them to stores like Boulder, Colorado's Planetary Solutions, which sells environmentally friendly building materials, to see the options. Take them to tour homes built by green builders. Take them to alternative wastewater treatment plants that clean up sewage using aquatic plants and capture the wastes for reuse. Encourage schools to tour wind farms. Tour the National Renewable Energy Laboratory in Golden, Colorado.

Create positive experiential connections, not just theoretical associations.

Be a positive example, too. Recycle, install energy-efficient lights, and grow your own food or participate in community-supported agriculture. Add up the savings to help your children see that their small part really counts. You can track your changes by joining or forming an EcoTeam. Discussed in more detail in Chapter 7, EcoTeams are groups of neighbors or friends who get together once a month for a period of six months. During each of their monthly meetings, EcoTeam members focus on one area, such as household waste, energy, water, or transportation. Using a workbook published by Global Action Plan, the nonprofit organization that created this program, neighbors discuss ways to cut back on waste and energy use, and each family comes up with its own plan. The actions are tallied and converted into real savings in resource use, pollution, and, of course, money.

Another option, discussed in Chapter 6, is to log on to the Center for a New American Dream's website, <www.newdream.com>. Here, you can set up your own personal workspace where you keep track of changes you and your family are making. The online calculator tallies the environmental impact of your actions. The Center also keeps a running total of all of the impacts of changes made by those who've logged on to their site. You can get a copy of their book, *More Fun Less Stuff: Starter Kit* to guide you through the process. It also contains worksheets that allow you to keep track of your changes and the impacts of these changes.

You might want to get a copy of Phillip Hoose's book, *It's Our World, Too! Stories of Young People Who Are Making a Difference.* It's full of stories that may inspire your young ones.

One of the important points made in Marie Sherlock's *Living Simply with Children* is to be upbeat about the choices you make. As Sherlock observes, "When we take action that says we believe individuals can make a difference, our kids absorb that message and are empowered by it." Many of the people I interviewed for this book expressed a similar sentiment. Louis Hornyak, whose frugal parents came from Hungary, noted that they once "recycled the wood and nails from an entire demolished house and then used them to build fences and other structures. They never threw anything away! Never."

MODELS OF SUSTAINABILITY:
GLOBAL WARMING AND WHAT ONE COMPANY IS
DOING TO ADDRESS THIS ISSUE

Each day the Earth is bathed in sunlight. Approximately one-third of the sunlight striking the Earth and its atmosphere is reflected back into space. The rest is absorbed by the air, water, land, and plants. Sunlight absorbed by surfaces is converted into heat. This heat is slowly radiated back into outer space.

Scientists have long known that certain chemicals in the atmosphere such as carbon dioxide and water vapor can upset this process. Carbon dioxide molecules, for example, absorb heat and reflect it back to Earth. It and other pollutants act like the glass in a greenhouse. The phenomenon is therefore called the greenhouse effect.

The greenhouse effect helps maintain the Earth's surface temperature. Without it, the Earth would be at least 50°F (10°C) cooler than it is today. Most life forms could not exist, including humans.

Unfortunately, many greenhouse gases are produced from human activities. When we drive our cars or heat our homes or use electricity supplied by a power plant to light our homes or power our TVs, we are producing carbon dioxide that is heating up the Earth.

Greenhouse gases typically come from natural sources, too, but human sources are the greatest concern. That's because emissions from natural sources have remained fairly constant over the past 100 years while emissions from human sources have increased dramatically. Carbon dioxide emissions, for instance, have climbed over 30 percent in the past 100 years largely as a result of the combustion of fossil fuels — coal, oil, natural gas, and gasoline. They have also increased as a result of deforestation, clearing forests to make room for farms, cities, towns, and roads, and to provide wood and wood products. Why? Plants, like trees, take up carbon dioxide from the atmosphere and convert it into plant matter. As trees are stripped from the land, the Earth's capacity to absorb carbon dioxide decreases. Atmospheric levels increase.

Many scientists believe that the increase in greenhouse gases is responsible for rising global temperatures, known as global warming, which we have witnessed since 1960. Numerous scientific studies suggest that the increase in the Earth's temperature is affecting the planet. It may be changing rainfall patterns and may be responsible for an increase in severe storms. In other words, it could be affecting global climate. Consequently, most scientists prefer the term global climate change over global warming.

Rising global temperature also affects natural ecosystems, agriculture, sea levels, insurance rates, and our economy. Further increases, which are likely to occur if we don't take actions, could result in a dramatic increase in global temperature and even more dramatic and costly changes in our climate. Scientists predict that sea levels will increase 20 inches (50 centimeters) from 1990 to 2100. The rise in sea levels would result from melting of glaciers and the land-based Antarctic ice pack and an expansion of the seas resulting from warmer temperatures.

Rising sea levels would threaten coastal cities throughout the world. Today, over half the world's population lives in coastal cities and towns. In fact, over 40 of the largest cities in the world are in coastal regions. Even a modest increase in sea levels would flood coastal wetlands, low-lying farm fields, wildlife habitat, and cities. The rise in sea levels would also worsen the damage from storms.

Less developed nations would also suffer enormously if the oceans rise. Low-lying island nations, many of them tropical resort places, already losing land to rising seas could be entirely submerged.

Shifting rainfall patterns and drought could cause devastating losses to farmers and reduce our food supply. They could also result in more devastating forest fires. These changes could also have devastating effects on wildlife and could cause the spread of diseases that currently affect people only in warm, tropical climates.

Progressive companies throughout the world are taking steps to help protect us against global warming. One leader in this effort is Applied Energy Services (AES) of Arlington, Virginia, a power company that burns coal to make electricity. In 1988 it announced plans to help finance the planting of 50 million trees in Guatemala to offset carbon dioxide emissions of fossil fuel power plants it planned to build. AES also wanted the project to improve the economic conditions of communities currently affected by deforestation and preserve endangered plant and animal species.

AES has also taken steps to offset pollution from a coal-fired power plant on Oahu, Hawaii, that came online in 1992. Instead of planting trees, though, AES helped to protect a forest in Paraguay from destruction. AES agreed to donate up to $2 million for the purchase and preservation of the 143,000-acre (58,000-hectare) Mbaracayu forest.

Located in eastern Paraguay, the Mbaracayu is one of South America's few remaining tracts of dense, humid sub-tropical forest. The area is vital to the survival of many species. It includes 19 distinct plant communities, at least 300 bird species, and threatened and endangered animals including tapirs, jaguars, giant armadillos, peccaries, the rare bush dog, king vultures, and macaws. The forest is the traditional hunting and gathering area for the Ache tribe. AES is partner in this project with the Nature Conservancy and a Paraguayan group that promotes sustainable development. AES has continued its carbon-offset programs with power plants in Oklahoma and Florida.

Individuals and businesses throughout the world can help reduce global carbon dioxide levels by planting trees, recycling, walking, bicycling, or riding a bus to school or work instead of using the car, by building smaller, more energy-efficient homes; by insulating existing homes, by using energy-and water-efficient appliances or doing some things by hand (for example, mixing by hand rather than using an electric mixer, or drying clothes on a line rather than using a dryer). When the time comes to buy appliances, choose the most energy-efficient ones available. New energy-efficient refrigerators, the leading user of electricity in our homes, can cut electrical demand from 1200 kilowatt-hours per year to 240. Using renewable energy can also dramatically reduce carbon dioxide.

THE WORLD OUTSIDE YOUR HOME

As I researched this book, I surveyed dozens of people who live environmentally friendly lifestyles, many of whom serve the cause in their professional lives. In my survey, I asked this group of dedicated individuals to describe the factors that influenced their life choices. While parents were influential in the majority of the individuals (70 to 80 percent) I queried, I was pleasantly surprised to discover that high school and college teachers also helped to shape young people's values and commitment.

Teachers can play a supportive role in some instances, or may be the prime influence in others. Interestingly, teachers were among the top three influences in shaping lives of environmental compassion and commitment — on a par with parents and slightly more important than experiences in the out-of-doors. One person I interviewed when working on this book was Jim Schley, a Vermont writer, editor, artist, and sustainable living practitioner. Jim was fortunate enough to be one of the late Donella Meadows's students at Dartmouth. Donella was an eloquent and thought-provoking teacher who led the world in shaping our understanding of limits to growth. Through her teachings, she also inspired many students to adopt careers and lives dedicated to environmental protection.

Doug Seiter, who lives in Denver, Colorado, and works for the Department of Energy's green building program says, "There was perhaps no greater influence on my connection with nature than my third grade teacher, Miss Leeka. She is the one who connected me with a variety of classroom 'pets' in the form of spiders, snakes, and a collection of fossils and inanimate objects from the natural world." Miss Leeka and a number of influences such as camping trips with his family and important books have inspired Doug to adopt a lifestyle and a career dedicated to caring for the Earth. What is more, his legacy is being passed on to his children. "We have two children, both of whom were raised in an environment of awareness of environmental responsibility," says Doug. "They both share the values, if not our passion, for environmental responsibility. One of our daughters has shown great interest in pursuing a career in environmental building."

The lesson in all of this is that you're not alone. Environmentally conscious teachers, scout leaders, ministers, friends, and a host of other individuals your children will interact with can have a positive influence. Some, they'll meet randomly; others they'll seek out or attract, almost magically. You can help steer your kids toward them, for example, by suggesting they enroll in environmental science in high school and college or by suggesting that they join the school's ecology club. If your child is in Boy Scouts, you might suggest they do the environmental science or natural resource conservation merit badges.

PLANET CARE: THE ULTIMATE FORM OF SELF-CARE

What we do to the planet, we do to ourselves. When we pollute the air, we pollute our own air supply. When we defile the water, we jeopardize our water supply and our own health. When we drive a species to extinction, we diminish the beauty and diversity we enjoy. You get the idea.

Planet care is the ultimate form of self-care. What we do for the planet — the acts of kindness that reduce pollution, species extinction, and resource depletion, and the improvements we make in restoring ecosystems — we also do for ourselves. Some people view these acts as sacrifice, that is, giving up the things they like or depend on.

I like to encourage individuals to think differently about environmental protection. Instead of thinking about sacrifices you need to make, that is, giving *up* things, it is important to think about our actions as giving *to*. Rather than give up, we are giving to ourselves, to future generations, and the millions of species that share this planet with us, creating a cleaner, healthier, richer world. We're not detracting from our lives, we're making them richer. We're better people for it. We live conscientiously and responsibly, in some cases, so that others may live well, too.

Planet care is the ultimate form of self-care.

You might like to have this conversation with your kids. It will help shape their philosophy early in life.

With this information in mind, we now turn our attention to a critical part in raising children who care for the Earth, fostering love. As Charles Dickens once wrote, "Love is the truest wisdom."

FAMILY ACTIVITIES

Below is a list of possible activities for children of various ages. You will very likely need to tailor some of these activities to your children, simplifying them for younger children, for instance.

1. Log on to <www.airhead.org> and look up their emissions calculator. Work with your family to determine your environmental impact.
2. Obtain a copy of the *EcoTeam Workbook* or *More Fun Less Stuff* and study it with your child. Determine if you would like to follow the recommendations.
3. Log on to the website of the Center for a New American Dream, <www.newdream.com>. Set up your own personal workspace where you track changes you and your family are making — and the reductions in your impact.
4. Read the "Kids Who Are Making a Difference" piece in this chapter aloud to your children. Be sure your spouse joins in. Discuss the project and other projects they could start at school or in the community.
5. Read the "Models of Sustainability" piece in this chapter aloud to your family and discuss it. Be sure they understand global warming and global climate change. Make a list of its impacts. Make a list of things your family could do to reduce their contribution to global climate change.
6. While on a trip or after dinner, make a list of all the ways the environment benefits you and your family.

The heart is wiser than the intellect
— J.G. Holland

2 FOSTERING LOVE FOR NATURE

D ave Freeman and Eric Frost run a nonprofit group called Wilderness
Classroom. Headquartered in Western Springs, Illinois, this organization offers school children throughout the United States an opportunity to join these two young men on their wilderness adventures, for example,
canoeing the entire 2,350 mile (3,760 kilometer) length of the Mississippi River
or trekking through 550 miles (880 kilometers) of Canadian wilderness using
skis, sled dogs, and toboggans along old fur-trapper trade and travel routes.
They have even tramped through Costa Rica's pristine rainforest.

School children don't actually don backpacks and strap on cross-country skis
or hop in canoes and paddle alongside the young educators on their lengthy
adventures, lasting from six to twelve weeks. They join them through cyber-
space. Each day, Eric and Dave connect with classrooms throughout the United
States that subscribe to their service via laptop computers. Dave and Eric offer
insights on ecology, history, and natural resource conservation, and help to foster an appreciation of wilderness. School children are treated to pictures of
moose tracks in Canada or exotic butterflies of the tropical rainforest. They can
ask questions to deepen their knowledge. All in all, it's a grand adventure for kids
who might never get to travel in the wilds.

Exciting as this new high-tech way of bringing wilderness to city kids may
be, in order to create a population of children who understand, appreciate, and
love nature we're going to have to dispense with the satellite-transmitted images
on the flat screens of computer monitors and get kids get outside. We need to

help them experience nature first hand — get their hands and feet and shirts and pants dirty, as it were. They need to see, feel, and breathe nature, not experience it vicariously through a computer monitor or television screen.

Why?

LOSING NATURE: LIFE IN SUBURBAN AND URBAN NEIGHBORHOODS

Each year, the human population becomes more and more urbanized. That is to say, each year a higher percentage of the population of the more developed countries, ours included, is choosing to live in and around cities — in urban centers and concentric rings of suburban development. Despite the hordes of people that are moving to the country to seek the good life, on balance we're become a more "citified" population, content with suburbs and cities and all that they have to offer.

While the urban/suburban living arrangement has definite advantages (for example, it means less countryside succumbs to development) this trend does come with a price tag. The most significant, but widely unappreciated, cost of our increasingly urbanized lives is that more and more of us are growing up deprived of any meaningful contact with nature.

The closest most kids these days get to nature is a romp in the leaves on our pesticide-treated, artificially fertilized, manicured lawns with robins chirping overhead. The closest glimpse of the natural world that we get is an English sparrow or a rock dove, commonly referred to as one of those Adamn pigeons, dining on French fries spilled by some hurried commuter. Or, if we're really lucky, we might glimpse an occasional flock of geese winging north or south on its annual migration. Nature shows have become our wild experience. Sitting safely on our couches in our air-conditioned homes, we can see nature without the bugs and without shedding a drop of sweat. Direct contact is out of the question. For the most part, our world of nature is one of squirrels precariously skittering about on overhead phone lines or, in some instances, cockroaches scurrying from the kitchen light. The wild has been ironed out of the fabric of most people's existence.

> *For the most part, our world of nature is one of squirrels precariously skittering about on overhead phone lines or, in some instances, cockroaches scurrying from the light. The wild has been ironed out of the fabric of most people's existence.*

So what?

Without meaningful contact with nature, wild places become an abstraction — something "out there," something we may be lucky enough to visit someday, but will most likely experience only through magazines or television programs or classroom lectures. No wonder so many people see nature as something separate from themselves.

Without meaningful contact with the natural world many of us will persist in believing in the separateness of humans and nature. That is, we will continue to embrace the false belief that we are independent from the natural world. The rift between humans and nature will only deepen. More to the point of this chapter, without meaningful contact with nature, there can also be no emotional connection to — no empathy for — other living things. Without meaningful contact, love for nature cannot set seed, grow, and blossom.

Without a connection to nature, protecting it will seem to have little to do with our everyday lives. Without love for nature, there is no hope for humankind. All in all, we have a dismal track record when it comes to protecting what we can't see, feel, or love. We may even revile what seems foreign.

Developing an environmental ethic in our children may not be possible without significant time spent in nature. Almost every committed environmental supporter I interviewed for this book, some of whom are prominent individuals in the environmental movement, considered experiences in nature early in life a major influence in their lives.

Lois Arkin, who helped create an environmentally friendly community in the heart of Los Angeles, which you'll read about in Chapter 7, lists "growing up around fields and forests" as a major influence in shaping her life of environmental and social responsibility.

When asked what shaped his values and commitment to the environment, Kelly Hart, a green building devotee who lives in Crestone, Colorado, noted, "Our family spent a lot of time exploring the wilderness around our home in Idaho." Kelly lives in an environmentally friendly home, drives a solar-powered vehicle, has created several videos that promote sustainable architecture, and runs an important green-building website, <www.greenhomebuilding.com>. His daughter has received a degree in environmental science and has worked for many years with a nonprofit environmental organization.

Simmons Buntin, who lives in a state-of-the-art solar community in Tucson, Arizona, and promotes environmentally friendly building noted that, "growing up in the Sonoran desert and in Central Florida's subtropical forests and having the opportunity to explore the wilderness" were key influences in his life.

Chris Walker, an instructional designer for environmental education in Davenport, Iowa, said, "My dad was a furniture maker and had a great reverence for trees and wood. He would sit in a boat in the slough of the Mississippi River and quietly take in as much as he could of this special world." His love and respect for nature obviously rubbed off. Chris and her husband Sam have raised their children to care about the environment. "We took our children camping in Iowa and in Colorado and showed them the peace and wonder of the plains, the Mississippi River, and the mountains. Our children grew up with boundaries on using resources and now understand why and respect that." She and Sam are now busily teaching their grandchildren the same lessons and values.

Charles Fletcher from Nederland, Colorado leads wilderness-trip rite-of-passage programs for gay men. He cites "wilderness experiences" as a key influence in shaping his life.

Miyaca Dawn Coyote from Shelburne Falls, Massachusetts, who works with children to promote a connection with the Earth, lists, "a twelve-day float trip on the Colorado River that majorly rearranged my assumptions and my internal make up!" as one of her prime influences. She also adds "Nature club trips, hikes, camp outs, canoe trips, plus photography in my twenties."

As I'll point out later, however, we don't need to travel to remote wilderness areas and backpack for two weeks with our children to introduce them to nature. However, we *will* need to get off the sofa, turn off the TV, and leave our homes to find some meaningful connections.

NATURE AS TEACHER AND HEALER

In his book, *Nature as Teacher and Healer*, James Swann argues that nature is a powerful healing force and a great teacher. As for healing, nature provides solace to the harried mind. By escaping into nature — even for a short afternoon stroll — we can heal our troubled souls. Nature is a place for reflection and insight, which also heals. It is a place to be still, to relax, and to simply enjoy the little things — a soft breeze, the gentle caress of sunlight, and a breath of clean air. It is also a place to exercise vigorously, to create a healthier body and mind.

The power of nature to heal has been demonstrated in scientific studies. One study of hospital patients, for example, showed that systolic blood pressure dropped 10 to 15 points when patients were exposed to paintings of serene landscapes. In addition, it's been shown that patients heal more rapidly when placed in rooms where they can see trees and other natural scenes outside their windows, compared to patients in rooms that overlook other buildings. They also need less pain medication. Imagine the benefits of direct contact.

You don't have to be sick to benefit from nature, however. Studies show that office workers whose desks face windows with a nature view are less stressed and report in sick less often than those whose offices offer inferior views.

Nature is also a teacher. If we observe carefully, there are lessons everywhere. William Shakespeare put it best when he wrote, "And this our life, exempt from Public Haunt," by which he means nature, "finds tongues in trees, books in the running brooks, sermons in stones and good in everything." Many others have waxed poetic about the teachings of nature. The poet Wordsworth wrote in "The Tables Turned":

And hark!
How blithe the throstle sings!
He, too, is no mean preacher;
come forth into the light of things,
let nature be your teacher

Thomas Paine, author of *Common Sense*, which helped stir Americans to fight for their independence from England, wrote "Man must go back to nature for information."

What can nature teach us? For one, nature demonstrates the grand answers for living sustainably on the Earth — for those who take the time to observe and reflect on nature's successes. I wrote a book about the subject, called *Lessons from Nature: Learning to Live Sustainably on the Earth*. In it I show how simple lessons we can learn from the broad-scale workings of nature can provide insight that could help us create an enduring human presence. After all, having persisted for over three billion years, nature is the master of sustainability. I'll share those ideas with you in Chapter 3.

But I am not the first nor will I be the last to draw on nature for inspiring ideas. The most recent is biologist and author Janine M. Benyus, who wrote a book entitled *Biomimicry: Innovation Inspired by Nature*, which shows ways that humans can utilize ideas from nature's designs to fashion products in our world that might work better, last longer, and perform more satisfactorily with less environmental impact. As an example, abalones produce shells that are twice as hard as the best ceramic, and make them at ocean temperature without toxic chemicals, unlike the

> *Nature demonstrates the grand answers for living sustainably on the Earth — for those who take the time to observe and reflect on nature's successes.*

human process. Benyus didn't invent the science of biomimicry. She coined the term and helped shed light on it. Years earlier, noted conservationist Norman Myers wrote a similar book entitled, *A Wealth of Wild Species*. In it, he demonstrates all kinds of human inventions inspired by nature. The steel I-beam, for instance, was patterned after support structures of the leaves of giant water lilies of South America.

The notion that human success hinges on learning lessons from nature has been an important theme for some time. Long before Thomas Paine penned his advice, the Roman satirist Juvenal wrote in *Satire XIV*, "Never does nature say one thing and wisdom another." Writer Alex Carrel wove this thinking into practical advice for all of humankind when he wrote, "To rebuild our civilization we must first rebuild ourselves according to the pattern laid down by life."

THE BONDS THAT TIE

Besides lifting our spirits, improving our health, and providing inspiration for design and guidance for creating a sustainable future, visits to natural areas provide valuable opportunities to create deep and lasting connections with the life-support system of the planet. The beauty of a grand vista, the gentle curve of the feather-soft petals of a columbine, and the eerie cry of the loon through the misty morning air — these are the things that inspire awe and open young hearts to the world outside cities and suburbs.

> *The human body is the most ingeniously contrived mechanism and most beautiful structure on earth. Every bone is a master-piece of architectural design. Every organ is a marvel of efficiency which no engineer can begin to equal. The smallest gland is a chemical plant that can outperform the greatest man-made laboratory in the world.*
> — Edmund Brasset

When our hearts open, our minds quickly follow. We become allies of nature, interested in voting the conservation ticket and living our lives consistently with the love we hold for the living world. As a parent, you can open your children's hearts and minds to nature, building compassion and love for the planet by introducing them to nature, and giving them opportunities to visit often.

KIDS WHO ARE MAKING A DIFFERENCE
SAVING NATURE ONE SIGNATURE AT A TIME!

One day, twelve-year-old Andrew Holleman discovered that a developer wanted to build 180 condominiums on private land next to his house in Massachusetts. This was no ordinary land. It was a place the boy knew well and loved dearly. He had fished for bass in the stream that ran through it and played hockey on it during the winter with his friends. Andrew had identified nearly all the plants and animals that lived on this piece of property, most of which qualified as wetlands. Wetlands, quite simply, are lands that are wet most of the time, like swamps. They often house many important plants and animals. They also serve many other functions. They help replenish groundwater and even filter pollutants from it. And they're critical wildlife habitats.

Like many children who live next to wild places, Andrew had a special place he called his own — a boulder by the stream on which he would sit whittling and thinking. While sitting quietly, he'd seen deer and foxes pass by and even observed red-tailed hawks landing in a nearby tree.

Because he knew and loved this land, the thought of losing it was unbearable. In four weeks, the developer was holding a meeting to describe his plan and seek approval from town officials. As Phillip Hoose documents in his book, *It's Our World, Too!*, which features many stories worth reading to your children, "Sitting at his kitchen table, Andrew went through a kind of metamorphosis. His initial shock melted into anger, and then the anger changed into a cold determination. Somehow Andrew Holleman was going to stop that development."

A pretty ambitious goal for a twelve-year-old.

Most adults would shy away from it, resigned to letting the developer do as he pleased. If he owned the land, they would reason, it was his to do with as he pleased.

Undaunted by the enormity of the task, Andrew went to work at the local library with help from his parents and the resource librarian. Andrew knew a little bit about Massachusetts law, though. He knew, for instance, that it prohibited development on wetlands. So Andrew began poring through legal books to find the details.

Andrew also located a master plan for the town that indicated which land could and could not be developed. Andrew discovered that the developer wanted to build on 16.3 acres (6.5 hectares), the entire site, but 8.5 acres (3.4 hectares) were classified as wetlands, and 5.6 acres (2.2 hectares) were considered to be poor soil, according to Hoose.

Technically, then, only a couple of acres could be developed. Technically, Andrew reasoned, the developer's plan was illegal.

But who knew?

Furthermore, who cared?

No one.

Undaunted, Andrew set out to inform the people in his town. He drafted a petition opposing the project and asked neighbors who would be adversely affected by it to sign the petition. "Every night for the next few weeks," writes Hoose, "Andrew raced home from school, did his homework, bolted down dinner, and then headed out to gather signatures."

Andrew talked to whomever he could for as long as it took to convince them, slowly gathering signatures. He also drew up a petition that he circulated at his school.

But his efforts did not end there. The resourceful young boy called the state Audubon Society and talked with a staff biologist, Dr. Dorothy Arvidson, who told him how to acquire a list of the state's endangered and threatened species. When the list arrived, he recognized three species that he had identified on the land.

Leaving no stone unturned, Andrew also wrote letters to the editor of the local newspaper, opposing the development. He sent his signed petitions to the town officials and state legislators. He even prepared a speech to give the night the developer was to present his plans to the citizens and town officials.

The day of the meeting, Andrew showed up with hundreds of concerned citizens. The developer and the town officials were amazed by the turnout. They scurried to find a larger meeting room to accommodate all the people, but that room quickly overflowed, and the group had to move to the girls' gymnasium to seat all 250 people.

As planned, the developer gave his speech and then asked for comments. Andrew stood up and delivered his well-prepared speech, which he'd practiced many times before his family. He outlined the problems with the site in meticulous detail.

But the battle was not over. Although many people opposed the plan, the developer continued to lobby the town officials who privately approved it. Andrew went to all of their meetings, determined not to let this project go through, even though he stayed up very late on many school nights.

He and his family recruited neighbors, who collectively raised $16,000 to hire a lawyer and a scientist to testify against the project.

Dr. Arvison, the Audubon biologist who had helped Andrew from the start, continued to offer advice. "Once, while she was giving him a long list of suggestions, Andrew interrupted. 'Hey, I'm only twelve years old,' he told her. 'That's no excuse,' she said, and went right on talking," reported Hoose.

In the end, the project failed because the site could not hold the sewage that would have been created by the condominiums, as Andrew had predicted early in the process. A simple test with a backhoe proved this beyond a doubt.

Two weeks later, the developer withdrew his application. He was hoping that he could resubmit a plan for a smaller number of condominium units. However, the board decided that the land was not suitable for development at all. The twelve-year-old boy with more drive and tenacity than most adults, had won! The land and the species that lived there are safe thanks to the determination and dedication of a twelve-year-old boy.

For a more detailed account, see Phillip Hoose. *It's Our World, Too!* Farrar, Straus and Giroux, 1993.

SACRED IN THE SMALL

As a boy, I was fortunate. My father saw to it that we lived in the country. So after a short stint in Niagara Falls, New York, our family moved to the "wilds" of Connecticut, and then to Hilton, New York, rural paradises for young lads with time on their hands and bountiful energy to burn. My friends and I spent our time wandering the woods, hiding in deep lush ferns, climbing to the tops of tall trees to sway in the gentle breezes, and swimming naked in cool streams. We hunted turtles and raided watermelon patches and apple orchards. We sat idly in the shade of trees, gazing up at the clouds. We sledded down steep hills, and ice skated in the dead of winter on wind swept creeks. We burrowed in deep snowdrifts and cooked over campfires.

Not only did my rural existence provide a joyful time, it also fostered a deep and abiding love for the natural world and a deep and abiding connection with it. Now when I read about suburban expansion swallowing up the countryside, I can see the forests that will fall to bulldozers. I can feel the quietness that will be disturbed by four-lane highways. I can imagine the killdeers, red-bellied dace, raccoons, skunks, and diamondback rattlers that will lose their homes as workers quickly assemble ours in their place. I feel a pain rooted in the soil.

> *We do not sufficiently cultivate in children, or, for that matter in ourselves either, the sense of beauty. Yet what pleasure is so pure, so costless, so accessible, indeed so ever present within us.*
> *— John Lubbock*

Interestingly, a number of people I interviewed while researching this book grew up in the country too. They noted that when their families visited or moved to cities the contrast often jarred their senses. When asked about the factors that influenced him in his quest for an environmentally sustainable lifestyle, Clarke Snell, who is author of *The Good House Book*, a book on building environmentally friendly homes, noted, "The main influence has been on my senses. Growing up in the country and then living in various cities, I have watched, heard, smelled, and felt environmental change all around me." He added, "I've read books and articles, joined organizations and so on, but I believe all of that has simply underscored what already seemed obvious to my senses."

If you are a parent cut off from nature, you'll have to make special efforts to get your kids out into the wildlands while they still remain so they can experience the difference between city and suburban ecosystems and the wilder ecosystems that exist outside these densely concentrated masses of humans. However, if Gary Nabhan and Stephen Trimble, authors of *The Geography of Childhood* are right, you won't need to go far and you won't need to climb to the top of Denali with your children to instill a love for nature. Kids, quite frankly, live their early lives on a different scale. They revel in the minute. Theirs is a world of close contact with what's at hand and in easy view. While we stroll along taking in the grand vistas, feeling uplifted, they're on their hands and knees exploring the microworld around them.

Speaking about a trip with his children, Stephen Trimble writes, "We [he and his children] would rendezvous with others now and then, and this was when I realized how much time adults spend scanning the land for picturesque panoramas and scenic overlooks. While the kids were on their hands and knees, engaged with what was immediately before them, we adults traveled by abstraction. We often had in mind finding one of those classic "photo opportunities," a vantage point over burnt orange and buff sandstone walls juxtaposed with cliff tops of massive shales." He goes on to say, "Whenever we arrived at such a promontory, Dustin and Laura Rose [his children] would approach with me, then abruptly release their hands from mine, to scour the ground for bones, pine cones, sparkly sandstone, feathers, or wild flowers."

Trimble adds, "Long after the trip, I was reminded again that Dustin's attention had hardly ever turned to the oversized scenes. When we opened up a packet of his snapshots from the trip, we were greeted with crisp close-ups of sagebrush lizards, yuccas, rock art, and his sister's funny faces. The few obligatory views of expansive canyons seemed, by contrast, blurred and poorly framed."

Save yourself a fortune. Don't book your kids on a flight to some distant land to view nature. Visit nearby places, even state parks, where your kids can explore off the trail.

I often took my kids on hikes when they were young. Wanting exercise myself, and hoping to expose them to the joys of hiking in our mountain home, I quickly realized that the complaints stopped and the smiles lit their faces when we (the adults) would stop for a rest. The kids, who'd been dragging their feet, were off and running, climbing over rocks, exploring streams, and catching insects.

If you are a parent cut off from nature, you'll have to make special efforts to get your kids out in the wildlands while they still remain.

So when you take your children out, be careful. Their views and yours are two different worlds. Don't be dismayed, as I have been, if your children aren't impressed with a sweeping view of a 14,000-foot (4,200-meter) peak covered with the first winter snow, but want to squat by a stream poking at a boatman or pulling out rocks to examine. Sit for a while, an hour or two, on a blanket and chat, while the kids wander around, exploring this fascinating world. Suspend your need to cover lots of miles when the kids are in tow, and get your exercise later. The task at hand is to let your children immerse themselves in nature.

Remember what Stephen Trimble says: "Over time, I've come to realize that a few intimate places mean more to my children, and to others, than all the glorious panoramas I could ever show them. Relax. You're doing your job. One day, they'll join you in the clouds, as my fourteen-year-old recently did on a horseback ride in the Flat Top Mountains of Colorado.

While camping at Sweet Springs Lake in Colorado, our family decided to join one of the local outfitters for a two-hour ride. In a long string of riders, about a dozen or so, my older son Skyler rode along without a word.

He seemed aloof through most of the ride. I presumed he was bored to tears, or upset with me for dragging him along on the ride, and wishing he were skateboarding. As we rode along, I would periodically ask him how he was doing, and he'd just mutter, "Okay." I was amazed when we got back home, though, and he came up to me and remarked how he loved the scenery. He'd spent most of his time gazing off at the mountains and the granitic walls of the canyon we were riding in. "Did you notice how beautiful it was?" he asked me.

Over time, I've come to realize that a few intimate places mean more to my children, and to others, than all the glorious panoramas I could ever show them.
— Stephen Trimble,
The Geography of Childhood.

Tears nearly came to my eyes. I was so bowled over. On earlier trips, I had pointed out beautiful vistas as we traveled the West. I'd tried hard to encourage the boys "to watch the scenery" instead of sleeping or playing GameBoy in the back seat, but to no avail. Little did I know that kids, as a rule, are not focused on the bigger picture.

To begin, you may want to take your children car camping. Pack up the car, and head to a nearby national forest or state park. Leave the modern distractions — TVs, radios, and other luxury items — at home, and let the kids run wild. After that, you may want to take your children canoeing or rafting. Give the kids ample time to explore. Remember, though, they may get more out of the trip if you spend a night or two camping by the river. If you're not up to organizing your own trip, contact a local outfitter.

There's no need to spend a week outdoors car camping or canoeing at first. In fact, a long trip might backfire on you and your plans to introduce your child to the glories of nature. If the weather is bad, your child might develop a distaste for nature. Start small. An overnighter might be just the ticket. I encourage people to try to make the first experience very enjoyable. You don't want your child to have a bad experience. That may mean waiting till the weather is absolutely perfect. It may take a while to find the ideal conditions, but it's well worth the effort! Linda, my partner, and I took her children and mine on a four-day canoe trip through southern Wyoming along the North Fork of the South Platte River. While it was a great river, the mosquitoes literally ate us alive. In this normally arid region, unseasonal rains put a serious damper on our fun. While the kids endured the rain with only a few tears and complaints, their reaction to mosquitoes was a different story. To this day, her kids are freaked out when a mosquito buzzes nearby.

Bird-watching is another activity that your kids might enjoy. But keep your ventures short. Remember, though, serious adult birders can tromp through the wilds looking for birds for days on end without eating. Kids' attention spans are shorter. To organize a trip, you may want to contact a local bird-watching group and join them on a Saturday outing. They may even have special trips for children.

When visiting state and national parks, check with the rangers to see if there are any short nature hikes or nature programs just for children. Entertaining and educational saunters through the woods can do a kid wonders!

Many people these days are partaking in ecoadventures — heading off to ecolodges for their ecovacations, and boosting the ecotourism industry. While I applaud ecotourism for many ecoreasons, bear in mind that you don't have to fly halfway around the world to introduce your child to nature. In fact, it may be better for them to know nature in their own vicinity, their own bioregion, than to be familiar with the wildlife of the Galapagos or the savannahs of Africa.

Local flora and fauna are what you, your children, and your community endanger most immediately — although with a global economy, our impacts stretch far and wide. An intimate knowledge of the plants and animals in your bioregion is more likely to spawn responsible behavior. Your advice on reducing impact will have a lot more impact on your child if the thing you are

Intimacy puts a face on the problem and makes a solution more compelling.

saving is known to them. Your children are more likely to respond to a statement such as, "It's better to use environmentally safe cleaning agents when cleaning the sink, because they will eventually get into the nearby rivers and poison the painted turtles we were watching last weekend," than, "We can't buy a gas guzzling car because it will pollute the atmosphere and destroy wildlife." Intimacy puts a face on the problem and makes a solution more compelling.

If you do decide to join the hordes of ecotourists flocking into wild places, be sure you select a low-impact opportunity. The closer to home, the better. Be sure that operations are truly environmentally friendly. You don't want to be driving around on the savannahs of Africa in four-wheel drive vehicles that are tearing up the land and spewing out noxious fumes just so you can catch a glimpse of a cheetah! Also, be certain that the facilities really were designed to have minimum impact, and that they're operated in a way that is truly sensitive to the environment. Don't be greenwashed — fooled by false advertising. Just because a vacation spot is labeled "green" doesn't mean it really is. So do your homework. Ask lots of questions before you book your trip.

Enrolling your child in Scouts can also help to introduce him or her to nature. However, my experience with Boy Scouts is that not all troops are created equal. If possible, try to find one that emphasizes outdoor activities. Scout camps offer nature and conservation classes, too, that can be helpful.

Even day camps can influence our children positively. However, unless teachers and camp counselors are really good and help your kids understand the need for conservation, and let kids have fun and enjoy and connect with nature, the experience may be abstract to them, as it was to me. Consider the experience of Claudia Browne, an environmental consultant from Golden, Colorado, who specializes in water resource management, conservation, and ecological restoration projects. She noted, "My love of the outdoors originated between the ages of eight and twelve at a wonderful day camp in Ohio."

What made it so special?

"What made it so fun was being outside and having fun in nature. When it rained, for instance, instead of going inside we'd put on our bathing suits and play in the mud! It was mud day … encouraged by a long-standing tradition."

VISITING SACRED PLACES

As your children get older, they will very likely open up to the bigger world around them, taking in scenery as adults do. This may be the time to head out to see nature's truly sacred places — like the old-growth forests I visited as a child while hiking along the Appalachian Trail. A few of my favorites that I strongly recommend taking your children to are: (1) the redwoods and sequoias of California, especially the very large old-growth trees of the Muir Woods National Monument just north of San Francisco; (2) the towering saguaro and organ pipe cacti of southern Arizona; (3) the old-growth forests of the Pacific Northwest; (4) the geysers and hot springs of Yellowstone (in September, if possible, after the tourists have left and the wildlife once again emerges in full force) and (5) the spectacular natural arches and scenery of Arches National Park and surrounding Canyonlands National Park.

Stop and get out of the car.

Don't view scenery from a moving vehicle. Don't settle for a few snapshots from scenic vantage points. Walk in and among these biologic and geologic features. Stop and sit and stare without talking. Touch them, gaze up at them, and take in their grandeur. These magnificent displays of nature could inspire a deeper awe and spark a more profound sense of love for nature.

As your children mature, they may find their own sacred places, areas that inspire an almost religious feeling. These may not even be the most splendid of nature's glories. Even small out-of-the-way places can be sacred.

I'm fond of taking my boys on river trips in the West and, because it is so dry most of the time, dispensing with our tent so we can sleep out under the stars at night. Sleeping sans tent allows us to stare up at the stars at night and look for satellites and shooting stars. In the morning, we can watch the sun strike the rocky cliffs as it peeks above

Don't view scenery from a moving vehicle. Don't settle for a few snapshots from scenic vantage points. Walk in and among these biologic and geologic features. Stop and sit and stare without talking. Touch them, gaze up at them, and take in their grandeur.

the horizon. It is these and other sacred places our children discover on their own that will speak to them in quiet whispers as they grow older and move into the working world with its everyday concerns. These hushed messages, in turn, may help them become grounded in their commitment to the environment, steady in their resolve in the everyday world where compromise is seen as a necessary way of life. It is these priceless moments that live in our memories, inspiring some to even greater heights, to become environmental professionals: teachers, writers, activists, lawyers, rehab specialists, and environmental scientists.

ECOWORK TRIPS

Developing a connection with nature can also come through yet another avenue: working in nature.

In Colorado, there's a nonprofit organization called Volunteers for Outdoor Colorado (VOC). Their mission is to make Colorado a better place by building hiking trails, restoring wildlife habitat, planting trees in public parks, and a host of other one- and two-day projects meant to restore nature and build infrastructure so that people can access lands safely and with little impact. Volunteers for Outdoor Colorado has its own youth program with projects just for youngsters or youth groups, as well as projects with adults and youth working side by side. Working with volunteer labor, VOC ultimately works on projects that many financially strapped county, state, and federal agencies simply can't afford.

According to Volunteers for Outdoor Colorado, "VOC's Youth Program provides youth with a rewarding stewardship experience allowing them to identify and connect with an environmental ethic." Their programs are designed to "empower young people to become active stewards of their public lands and provide them with opportunities to protect, enhance, and learn about the natural world." These experiences help children realize that they "are the future of their community."

With a dozen or several dozen volunteers — sometimes hundreds on really big projects — all chipping in to help, VOC is filling a valuable niche. Besides helping financially strapped organizations, it's providing adults and children an opportunity to invest their time and energy in the environment. Participants leave with a sense of accomplishment, pride, and connection. The trail I helped build in Roxborough State Park, southwest of Denver, in the late 1980s remains today an accomplishment I can look to with pride. It's a pride of ownership. That trail is mine. A piece of that park I helped make. We did it right, too, so the trail will withstand the test of time and won't erode away like poorly designed and built trails.

As an added benefit, now when I hike on a trail anywhere else in the world, I realize how much work went into making it, and I'm thankful for the paid and unpaid workers who made it possible. I am respectful of the trail, too, and unwilling to cut corners to shorten my route, because I know that the trail was placed where it was to avoid erosion. By staying on the beaten path, I help protect the land from erosion.

Volunteer opportunities that provide projects in which you and your children can participate are available through a number of state and national nonprofit organizations. Local chapters of the Sierra Club often offer such projects. Also check out Roots and Shoots, a project of the Jane Goodall Institute. Local groups plan and implement projects combining service and learning opportunities that promote care and concern for animals, the environment, and the human community. Another organization that you should contact is Earth Force. They offer programs for children that promote lasting solutions to environmental problems in local communities in a number of areas in the United States. You may also want to contact local conservation groups. If there aren't any nearby, you and your child might want to coordinate your own projects in conjunction with the local parks departments or state and federal agencies that manage forests or other lands for us. Be sure to find opportunities for kids to participate. The work can't be too difficult, though. If you haven't noticed by now, when it comes to work, most children seem to run out of energy very quickly.

You can also engage your children in eco-improvements around your own home. For example, many kids revel in the thought of creating wildlife habitat right in their own backyards. We're not talking about encouraging black bears and wolverines in our backyards, but rather creating habitat for butterflies, birds, and other friendly critters that have been displaced by suburban sprawl. A small garden with flowers, for instance, can attract butterflies and hummingbirds. For more information, contact National Wildlife's Backyard Habitat program, your state wildlife agency, or a local Natural Resource Conservation Service district office.

BIOPHILIA: TAPPING INTO OUR CHILDREN'S INNATE LOVE FOR ANIMALS

My children — like most others I've encountered — seem to have a natural love for and fascination with animals. They've been capturing grasshoppers, snakes, frogs, toads, turtles, and anything else they could get their hands on since I can remember, and then dragging most of these creatures into the house to show to papa! I'll never forget the time they brought a pregnant western garter snake into our house. A day or two later, momma escaped her temporary lodgings, an old fish tank with a wire mesh top. In the week after her escape, we found baby snakes writhing in the hallways and the living room on their way toward freedom. One morning, I nearly stepped on two babies on the stairs as I was trudging half asleep to the kitchen to prepare breakfast.

A child's innate love for animals is a great ally. We can use it to help children develop an even stronger bond with nature. Although you may have misgivings about your children wandering neighboring fields and woodlots, letting kids explore the natural world and letting them catch snakes, toads, and tadpoles helps children learn that the great out-of-doors is not just vacant land, as real estate agents and developers are fond of saying. "Vacant land" is actually teeming with life. You'll help them look at land in a new light, and hopefully avoid the same mistake most adults make when they refer to an "undeveloped" piece of property as "vacant land."

They'll learn that land without shopping malls or houses is highly developed. There's a whole network of organisms that have "developed" the land. Here they find food, breed, raise young, and sleep. This is their home! This is a complex biological development.

A child's innate love for animals is a great ally. We can use it to help children develop an even stronger bond with nature.

Fortunately for us, children have a natural empathy for living things, and when they learn how our actions affect the things they love, they become incensed. Why? Because their experience with the wild things around them puts a face on human development ... or thousands of faces on it. When a bulldozer blade turns up sod, it is more than grasses that are being uprooted (which are important, too!). It is an entire living world full of interesting and often lovable creatures.

Pulitzer Prize-winning author and biologist Edward O. Wilson wrote a book outlining evidence that adults also have an innate sensitivity and need to be around other living things. He called the book, and this phenomenon, *Biophilia*. In it, Wilson argued that humans subconsciously seek connections with the rest of life. These connections, he conjectures, are determined by a deep biological need, which stems from the fact that we have co-existed in close relationship with the natural world for so much of our evolutionary history.

I see biophilia in action in children and adults alike whenever I visit local pet shops. People swarm to the shops and many soon walk out with guinea pigs, hamsters, gerbils, kittens, birds, fish, and even horny toads that will soon join their families. Americans may be the ultimate biophilians with 60 million cats and 55 million dogs for about 300 million of us.

We love animals!

We love being around them, looking at them, playing with them, cuddling them, and taking care of them.

Biophilia may extend beyond cute, cuddly creatures that we can snuggle with on the couch. It may also extend to nature in general.

As Drs. Patrick and Gael Flanagan write in an Internet piece, *Biophilia and Emotional Well-Being,* "We need nature to feel alive and whole because it is in our genetic makeup." Nature has a healing power, as noted earlier in the chapter, and people are drawn to nature. In fact, when given a choice, write the Flanagans, "People will choose a (picture of a) natural landscape over a city skyline even when the skyline photo is quite spectacular and the nature scene is quite ordinary." They say natural landscapes give them a "better feeling."

Despite our innate love for nature, and what may be a genetic need to experience nature, as a society we often act in near total disregard for it. Something happens to us along the path from childhood to adulthood. Other concerns crowd out idealistic notions. We become willing to compromise our love of nature for profit and jobs. It becomes nature versus us. We permit bulldozers into a prairie dog village if the new subdivision promises a better economy. And we're willing to allow oil and natural gas development on pristine wilderness if it means keeping our cars running.

We become pragmatic and self-centered. Ideology is bulldozed in the name of personal gain. Our love for nature withers.

Henry David Thoreau once wrote, "Measure your health by your sympathy with morning and spring." Not only is our sympathy for nature a sign of good personal health, it is a prerequisite to building a sustainable future. By holding on to our love of nature, we retain an interest in the natural world and

Holding on to our love of nature is an important prerequisite to building a sustainable future.

strive for ways to seek cooperative solutions, discussed in Chapter 4. Cooperating with nature means meeting our needs without plowing under prairie dog colonies or clearing woodlands. It means fitting in with nature's cycles, taking a softer path to human success. More on this in Chapter 4.

AGE-APPROPRIATE EDUCATION

As a parent, you can spark your child's love of nature by exposing him or her to wild places. Remember, as Randy White of White Hutchinson Leisure and Learning Group, a company that designs family- and children-oriented leisure, entertainment, and recreation projects, notes: "Children experience the natural environment differently than adults. Adults view nature as background for what they are doing, as a visual experience. Children experience nature not as background for events, but rather as a stimulating experiential component of their activities. The total sensory experience of touch, sight, smell, hearing needs to be present so it can become part of the world of imagination and wonder." Books and stories and nature programs are good, but they're no substitute for letting your kids get dirty.

Avoid the tendency to try to teach young children abstract concepts like I did with my children. Being an environmental scientist, writer, and educator, I found myself lecturing about air pollution long before my boys could understand what I was talking about. (Sorry guys.) Rather, let your prized possessions muck around in the mud puddles and streams and forests, learn who lives there, and spark their love for all this novelty and beauty.

"From nine months of age til age seven," says White, "the main objective of environmental education should be the development of empathy. ... One of the best ways to foster empathy with young children is to cultivate relationships with animals. This includes exposure to indigenous animals, both real and imagined."

White goes on to say that young children are drawn to animals, especially baby animals. (Which explains the popularity of petting zoos!) "Animals are an endless source of wonder for children, fostering a caring attitude and a sense of responsibility towards living things. Children interact instinctively and naturally with animals, talk to them, and invest in them emotionally."

What animals?

"The common animals, everyday species that fill children's yards, neighborhoods and communities are the developmentally appropriate choice."

Contact with live animals, stories, songs, and other experiences can help develop an "emotional connectiveness — empathy — with the natural world that is an essential foundation for later stages of environmental education," observes White.

From age 8 to 11, White asserts that kids should still engage in bonding, primarily through exploration of the nearby world. Children, says White, should be given opportunities to explore and experience the surrounding wild and semi-wild natural world found in our neighborhoods and our communities. Even empty lots or stream banks of nearby creeks can give kids an opportunity to explore.

In early adolescence, from around age 12 to beyond 15, children start to discover the self. They begin to feel a connection to a larger community, and are "naturally inclined toward wanting to save the world, assuming of course that they had the opportunities in their earlier years to develop empathy for and to explore the natural world." It is now, as their abilities to engage in abstract thinking emerge, that they best understand environmental problems.

While White seemingly believes that we should shelter our children from the bad news, not all others agree. I, for one, believe that we should start talking about issues much earlier. It is my opinion that children in the 8 to 11 age group can easily grasp the threat some human activities pose to the environment. Although they may not understand global warming and its vast impacts, or the chemistry of ozone depletion, they can easily understand how pesticides and habitat loss impact wildlife. They can also understand other issues on a more general level.

Because of this, I strongly believe that these issues can — and should — be explained to children at this age. Explain the problems in language appropriate to their age, of course. They can develop a deeper understanding of the issues as they grow older. And, whatever you do, be sure to give ideas on ways that these problems can be solved by governments, businesses, and families like yours.

White suggests that at this age opportunities to protect the environment should be locally based. At this level they can relate to the threat and the outcomes of taking action. Global environmental protection will come later in life, as children mature and form a more solid understanding of the human and biological world beyond their front doors.

As your children grow older, you can take them on tours of power plants, sewage treatment plants, landfills, clearcuts, open pit mines, and eroded farmland in the vicinity to get a real glimpse of human impact. I frequently take my college students on field trips to ranches and power plants. They're often amazed by the experience.

"If you live in the country or even a cozy suburb," says green builder and author Clarke Snell, mentioned earlier in this chapter, "visiting a large city like Los Angeles is a great way to cultivate an environmental consciousness." Such experiences show just how far human development can progress and how much nature can be lost. They also demonstrate that dense aggregations can lead to a wide range of environmental problems such as air pollution. Ianto Evans, a natural builder, writer, educator, and splendid orator, who grew up in Wales, names "a country kid visiting cities" as one of the factors that most influenced his path toward a lifetime of environmental responsibility.

Be sure, as I do, to balance these experiences with positive examples: tours of homes or buildings powered by solar electricity, biological waste treatment facilities, composting facilities, sustainably harvested forests, recycling facilities, and organic farms. In other words, let children glimpse the solutions as well as the problems.

You may suggest that your children enroll in environmental science courses in high school and college. Here, they may expand their horizons even further. A good teacher can transfer his or her insights and enthusiasm. You may even suggest that they go to a college known for its environmental programs, such as Prescott College in Arizona, Oberlin College in Ohio, Evergreen College in Tacoma, Washington, or Colorado College in Colorado Springs, Colorado.

DESTROYING IGNORANCE

In the summer of 2003, a colleague and I took a group of students enrolled in our sustainable systems course at Colorado College, where I am a visiting professor, on a tour of an organic cattle ranch, located in a dry, dusty, drought-plagued part of southern Colorado. We toured the ramshackle barns and outbuildings, heard stories about how difficult it was to grow beef organically, visited the cattle, and bucked hay bales.

I was surprised after the tour to hear a couple of students say they'd never eat beef again. It was not our goal to turn them off beef, but rather to show them that food could be grown with minimal impact on the land. As it turns out, however, being close to the source changed some minds about food. Those lovable eyes of the gentle cattle raised on the ranch pulled too hard on their heart strings. That's what connection to the world around us does for us. It destroys ignorance and opens us up to the reality of our lives, which can be a bit shocking at times. It changes our attitudes and our actions.

In another class I taught at Colorado College, I took my students to visit a coal-fired power plant in the Denver Metro Area. We then climbed in the vans and drove north to the windswept plains of southeastern Wyoming to tour a small wind farm where huge wind machines cranked out electricity quietly and efficiently without pollution. Buffalo grazed around the wind generators. It was quite a contrast to the dirty, hot, noisy, mechanically complex coal plant. Students were amazed at the differences and changed forever. They would no longer take electrical energy for granted and would forever understand the options available to us as a society.

MODELS OF SUSTAINABILITY
WOLF COUNTRY BEEF AND PREDATOR
FRIENDLY WOOL?

Imagine going to the store at the mall to buy a new sweater. One particular brand catches your eye. It's made from Predator Friendly Wool. After you pay for your purchase, you stop in at the restaurant next door to buy a salad made from Salmon Safe vegetables, while the gentleman at the next table munches on a hamburger made from Wolf Country Beef.

Thanks to the efforts of environmentalists, farmers, and ranchers, all of these ideas are real. In Oregon, for example, the Pacific Rivers Council is spearheading a program that encourages farmers to grow crops in ways that help protect salmon and the streams they live in. Farmers who join the program are seeking to find ways to reduce the amount of water that drains from their fields into streams. This water, called surface runoff, often carries sediment and pollutants that destroy salmon habitat. Surface runoff can be reduced by planting vegetation between crops and streams. The vegetation traps sediment running off from crops, saving lakes, rivers, and streams. Cover crops, such as clover or rye, may be planted between growing seasons, or in fallow fields to protect the fish. Crops such as these absorb water, and reduce surface runoff and soil erosion.

Although the Salmon Safe program doesn't require farms to avoid potentially toxic pesticides, organizers do recognize the importance of doing so for protecting fish and wildlife. Their goal is to complement organic certification programs that focus on chemical use. Combined, the two programs provide optimal levels of protection for the salmon and other animals that live in salmon streams.

In Montana and Idaho, sheep ranchers are trying their own brand of animal protection, thanks to the efforts of a group called the Growers' Wool Cooperative. Its Predator Friendly Wool Certification program is trying to promote peaceful coexistence of sheep and native predators, the wolves and coyotes. Ranchers use natural methods to keep wolves and coyotes away from their sheep, including llamas and guard dogs, both of which, when raised from early age with sheep, become quite protective of "their" flocks. These measures make Predator Friendly Wool popular with some buyers.

In Arizona and New Mexico, the Defenders of Wildlife, a national organization, is working with cattle ranchers to help reintroduce the Mexican wolf. The Mexican wolf or *El Lobo* is a subspecies of the gray wolf. It once roamed freely through many parts of these states. Ranchers and government agents took a dim view of this predator, along with many others, shooting them, poisoning them, and catching them in traps. By 1950, the Mexican wolf population was nearly gone. The last remaining wild wolf was shot in 1970.

Defenders of Wildlife, already has actively helped to reintroduce the gray wolf in Montana, Idaho, and Wyoming, using animals bred in captivity. In 1997, the first wolves were introduced into the wild in Arizona. Released by the US Fish and Wildlife Service in the Apache National Forest straddling New Mexico and Arizona, the wolves are having a rough go of it. Although breeding pairs have stayed together and animals are feeding on natural prey species, a number of wolves have been shot and two have disappeared but are presumed to be dead, killed by people who don't agree with the program. Wolves have left the National Forest and preyed on some livestock as well.

Because wolves cannot be expected to remain in the National Forest, Defenders initiated a fund, known as the Wolf Compensation Trust, to reimburse ranchers in nearby areas for any losses incurred by wolves. The Fund pays ranchers in Montana, Wyoming, and Idaho, and has so far paid over 100 ranchers for loss of sheep, cattle (mostly calves), colts, and guard dogs killed or presumed killed by gray wolves released in Yellowstone and the northern Rockies. It also covers losses from wolves that have naturally migrated from Canada into Northwestern Montana. The Fund will be used to reimburse livestock losses in Maine, New York, and the Olympic Peninsula of Washington, should the proposed wolf reintroductions occur there. According to their website, the goal of Defenders of Wildlife is "to shift economic responsibility for wolf recovery away from the individual rancher and toward the millions of people who want to see wolf populations restored." Money for the fund comes from private donations. "When ranchers alone are forced to bear the cost of wolf recovery, it creates animosity and ill will toward the wolf."

But Defenders has taken the idea one step further, thanks to their southwest representative, Craig Miller. Miller proposed that Defenders create a Wolf Country Beef certification program to provide further incentives to ranchers. For ranchers neighboring the National Forest who agree to allow wolves to roam freely on their land, Defenders provides special stickers for their meat products sold in grocery stores. The Wolf Country Beef stickers "brand" their beef in the market as coming from ranches that support wolf recovery. To date, the Wolf Country Beef certification program includes 70,000 acres (28,300 hectares) of private ranch land in Arizona and New Mexico. Wolf Country Beef is now available in grocery stores in Arizona.

Ranchers in the program agree to use nonlethal means, such as guard dogs, to keep wolves away from livestock. They also agree not to set out traps, poisons, or explosive devices that not only kill wolves, but lots of other predators as well. This program, therefore, also protects many other species such as foxes, coyotes, mountain lions, raccoons, and eagles that might be tempted by a baited trap or poisoned bait. It also protects scavengers who might feed on carcasses of animals poisoned by ranchers.

Wolf Country Beef is a program that demonstrates that endangered species can be an economic asset to communities. It fosters a sense of ownership and pride in wolf recovery. Ranchers become an active part of the process, becoming allies and benefiting economically. Given the choice of a steak from a Wolf Country Beef producer or a rancher less sympathetic to these wonderful animals, with both products priced the same, which would you choose?

Adapted from Daniel D. Chiras, *Environmental Science: Creating a Sustainable Future, 6th ed.*, Jones and Bartlett Publishers, 2001.

FAMILY ACTIVITIES

Below is a list of activities for children of various ages. I have tried to gear most of these to specific age groups. You may still need to tailor some of these activities to your own children, simplifying them for younger ones, for instance.

1. For children from nine months of age till age seven: (a) Get a pet or (b) visit a petting zoo or farm where you can view *and* pet animals. (c) Or, you may want to visit the local zoo, especially if your zoo humanely houses its animals, which most do these days. (d) Visit a local butterfly pavilion, if there is one in your area or while you are traveling with your children. (e) Read animal stories. Repeat these experiences many times.

2. For children aged 8–11: (a) Take your child to a local park (preferably a State Park with some wild land) or visit a local forest, field, lake, pond, or ocean. Sit with your children, while they play. Share their fascination if they are eager to show you what they're finding. Don't worry about them getting dirty. In fact, expect them to get dirty and don't punish them if they come back muddy. Go back often. (b) You may want to take your children camping, fishing, hiking, canoeing, rafting, or birdwatching. Take a camera along and encourage your children to photograph what they find interesting. Keep trips short at first and leave the distractions (portable TVs and the like) at home.

3. For children from age 12 to beyond 15: (a) Take your children camping, fishing, canoeing, hiking, rafting, or birdwatching, or encourage them to engage in these activities through camps, Scout troops, outfitters, clubs, or schools. (b) Now is a good time to start talking about issues. Show videos of environmental problems such as global warming, overpopulation, acid rain, and species extinction. Talk with your child about problems and solutions. Visit examples of activities that both create problems that solve them.

4. Go on a nature hunt in your backyard, photographing or videoing local plants and animals, and then go to a wilder area such as a local park, field, forest, lake, or seashore. See how many plants and animals you can identify in 30 minutes at each site. Compare the two sites. Ask your children what they think were the most unusual species or the most beautiful species. You might ask them what these species need to survive and how they are similar to and different from humans. What lessons can we learn from nature? You might ask them why a developer would call the field or forest "vacant land."

5. Camp out under the stars and look for satellites and shooting stars. Identify constellations. Set up a blanket with your child in an open field and watch the clouds. Take time to listen for all the different bird calls.

6. Sign your child up for a work trip with a local conservation group to build or repair trails or plant trees. Go along with your child, if possible, to share in the work and the fun. Talk about why you are doing it, especially the benefits your work will create.

The great end of living is to harmonize man
with the order of things.
— Oliver Wendell Holmes

3 ECOLOGICAL LITERACY: TEACH YOUR CHILDREN WELL

In the 1980s, I taught ecology as part of my general biology course at the University of Colorado at Denver. Like most other professors, I mostly lectured to my students with an occasional chalkboard drawing to illustrate some key point. During what I have come to call my "chalkboard ecology years," I described ecosystems and how they function. I talked about food chains, food webs, consumers and producers and all of the other details I thought students needed to know to understand ecology.

One day, though, it struck me that I was going about this all wrong. Sure, students seemed to be getting the information. For the most part, they did fairly well on exams, spitting back the information I'd crammed into their heads. But did they really understand what I was talking about, or was this just more abstract knowledge they were stuffing into their memories, quickly to be forgotten after the test?

I suspected the latter, and set out to change my ways.

The next summer I taught the course, I canceled class for the ecology week, and asked students to reserve the following weekend for a camping trip. I announced, "We are going to venture into nature to learn about nature."

However, I wasn't about to take the naturalist approach, assiduously flitting around naming and numbering things and spewing out interesting but largely useless facts. Rather, it occurred to me that what my students really needed to know was how nature worked, what role we humans played in nature, including how we were affecting it, and how we could change our ways to better fit within nature's grand scheme.

So we headed out of Denver into the mountains of Colorado. We met on Friday evening at a National Forest campsite and sang songs around the campfire, with my amateur guitar playing helping to hold the group together.

The next morning after breakfast, we hiked off into the woods and fields and immersed ourselves in nature. The first stop along the trail was at a majestic ponderosa pine tree. With the class gathering around, I asked, "What is this?"

One bright student chimed in, "It's a ponderosa pine."

I shook my head, and chided in a good-natured tone, "Oh, come on ... what is this?"

"A Douglas fir?" another student offered.

I laughed.

"You're going in the wrong direction."

"Well, it's not an aspen," another student joked.

We all laughed.

"And it is not a grizzly bear," I said. "So what is it?"

The students looked puzzled.

"Come on," I laughed. "What is this? Let me give you a hint: be more general."

Still more puzzled looks.

"A tree," one student offered nervously.

"Yes," I said, "a tree. But isn't that just a name? Do you think this tree cares what its name is? What is this?"

By now I'm sure some of the students were beginning to worry about spending the weekend in the mountains with their crazy professor. I wasn't carrying any sharp implements, so they must have figured I was okay for a while.

Still, however, there were no answers.

I waited.

After a while I said, "Let me tell you. It's an oxygen producer. It cranks out tons of oxygen that the cells of your body need to break down glucose to make energy. Without it, you could not survive."

Some nods of appreciation. We'd already studied cellular energy production.

"See those tiny needles? They contain chlorophyll, which you learned about in class. They are nature's solar collectors. They capture the sun's energy and use it to make plant matter: roots, branches, and limbs. Interestingly, one of the byproducts is oxygen. It's a waste product, really, but this waste is gold."

I pointed to the neighboring hillside, covered with trees. "This is what keeps all animal life going. Without it, none of you, and not one other living animal on the planet could survive. We'd all perish."

Some nods of appreciation.

"So to call it a tree really misses the point, don't you see?"

Some more nods.

"But you keep it alive, too," I announced. "The carbon dioxide you're exhaling right now, which comes from the breakdown of sugar molecules in the cells of your body to make energy, feeds this plant. The trees and all other plants on Earth and in its oceans, lakes, rivers, and streams use carbon dioxide to make plant matter. Without you, the plant kingdom could not survive."

> *How much better it is to get wisdom than gold; and to get understanding than silver.*
> — *Solomon*

Some smiles emerged on their faces. Some of them had never really ever thought of a tree, or themselves, in this light — as partners in (excuse the reference to the movie *Lion King*) the circle of life.

I smiled too. I'd given the lecture a dozen times before on a chalkboard. Students had dutifully written notes as I blabbered on. But I'm not sure anyone really ever got it like this group. Not a word was spoken.

"So when we cut down trees in the rainforest or in the deciduous forests of the eastern United States or destroy any living plant matter for that matter ..." I stopped.

They all knew where I was going.

"You get the point," I said.

More head nodding.

We left, patting the tree, a little sign of our gratitude.

You might want to try this with your children.

THE DIFFERENCE BETWEEN LIFE AND DEATH

Later on, we stopped by the side of a trail cut deep into a hillside. My students all huddled around in the warm sunshine. When they'd settled down, I said, "Look here. What do you see?"

"Just dirt," one of them said a bit warily.

"Just dirt?" I responded, a bit dramatically.

"It's dark dirt on the top, and light dirt on the bottom," one said.

"Good," I smiled. "You're on the right track."

"Topsoil and subsoil," another offered, hesitantly.

"What you really see here is the difference between life and death on the planet."

A few perplexed looks shot my way.

"The difference between life and death," I repeated.

"What do you mean?" one of the braver students asked.

"I mean the topsoil is what supports life. Without it, without this thin layer of rich organic soil on planet Earth, there would be no life."

I paused a moment to let this thought sink in, and then went on, shifting gears a little. "The Bible says, 'All flesh is grass,' which is true."

A few more puzzled looks.

"All animal matter is made from plant matter. All terrestrial plant matter grows in topsoil."

I repeated this little triumvirate of ecological sustainability a few times.

Then, I paused to let the idea sink deeply into their psyches.

"Scrape it away," I said, "and you've got a lifeless planet. Nothing can persist. Nothing. Not this tree or this blade of grass or even you. With all of our technological know-how, not a single human being can survive on Earth without the topsoil. It's that important."

A few students nodded. I hesitated once again.

"And yet, we treat the soil like dirt."

I then launched into a lecture — albeit a short one — on how much topsoil we lose every year to wind and water erosion, largely as a result of poor agricultural practices. I then talked about how much topsoil is covered each year by development, notably new runways, roads, shopping malls, parking lots, tennis courts, subdivisions, cities, towns ... and so on.

"We need to take care of our topsoil. You know, planet care isn't about protecting pretty places for birdwatchers and backpackers and day hikers, as critics might contend."

Doubling around the idea I was getting to, I added, "What we do to the planet, we do to ourselves. When we pollute the water, we pollute our drinking water. When we pollute the air, we pollute our lungs. When we let the topsoil wash away, we destroy our food source. It's that simple. Planet care is the ultimate form of self-care," I said, and got up to continue our walk through the woods. All the chalk in China couldn't have helped me make this point any more strongly in a classroom.

Later on, I talked about the economy of nature, and how all energy in the natural world, and most energy in our world, too, comes from the sun. We learned about nutrient cycles and the importance of food chains and solar energy in recycling nutrients. We talked about population control and a host of other vital ideas. At the end of the day we had dinner, pointing out where everything we ate came from, and recognizing that the nutrients we were about to ingest came from the soil, the air, and the water and that the energy that would soon power our bodies ultimately came from the sun. We drank a few beers, which was legal in Colorado back then, and sang more songs around the campfire, comforted by our new understanding of Mother Earth.

LEARNING ABOUT ECOLOGY AND ENVIRONMENTAL PROBLEMS

I tell this tale not to give you the impression that I'm the world's best ecology and environmental science teacher. I've done a lot of things wrong. For years, I was a "namer" and "numberer," passing on bucketloads of largely useless information that I'm certain most of my students have long since forgotten. (Sorry, guys.)

I just came to my senses in time.

Unfortunately, many teachers still remain stuck in the old way of teaching ecology and environmental science.

My colleagues will burn me at the stake for this heresy, but frankly, there's very little that children really need to know to acquire a useful, working knowledge of ecology. Sure, there are books packed with fascinating information but, bottom line, there's not that much they really must know to become good environmental stewards.

One thing we need to know for sure is that the planet's ecosystems are its life-support system. The plants produce oxygen that keeps us — and a host of other living species — alive. The plants produce food and hold the soil in place, even helping to build soil, which they need to grow in. And some plants remove pollutants. All of these functions are vital to life on Earth.

We also need to know about nutrient cycles. Most notably, that all the nutrients required by living things are recycled over and over again through food chains. Plants tend to incorporate these nutrients into their bodies, which we and virtually all other living things consume. Even a juicy steak is plant matter reprocessed by a beef cow. The Bible said it best, as I mentioned earlier: "All flesh is grass."

> *Ecosystems constitute the life-support system of the planet.*

Nutrients passed from plants to animals re-enter the nutrient cycles through waste and decay. These processes have ensured the continuation of life since the first living organisms emerged about 3.5 billion years ago; each generation that's been produced has been built on the remains of past generations. Without these cycles, life would come to a halt. Let's not forget: We mess with the cycles at our own peril!

There's another point that a renowned ecologist, Professor Gordon Orions, made to me while I was a visiting professor at the University of Washington in 1989: Not all that's important is visible to the naked eye. Be aware of hidden connections. Translated: Much of what occurs in nature's giant cycles of life is hidden from us. We don't observe carbon dioxide being absorbed by plants; we don't see microbes processing wastes. A large amount of what's important to us in nature is entirely invisible to us. It occurs at the molecular, even the atomic, level.

Invisible?

Yes.

Unimportant?

Absolutely not!

> *A large amount of what's important to us in nature is entirely invisible to us. It occurs at the molecular, even the atomic, level. Invisible? Yes. Unimportant? Absolutely not!*

I can't say it strongly enough: Just because you can't see the hidden connections between human life and nature does not mean they're unimportant.

As we'll see in Chapter 4, we must never lose sight of the fact that humans are a part of nature, not apart from it. We participate in nature's grand cycles through food chains and food webs — and a host of other areas. And we should never lose track of the fact that the Earth and its ecosystems are the source of all our resources and the sink for all of our wastes.

To create a sustainable society, we need generations of ecologically literate adults, people who understand the basics I've just presented. Parents — and teachers reading this material — must not fall prey to the false notion that a mind full of facts about nature is what's needed. A mind full of useless trivia is no substitute for a few good solid pieces of working knowledge — a few good concepts.

If your child is enrolled in an ecology or environmental science class in high school or college or if you tour a nature center together, you can help him or her discern the big picture from the splendid but often useless facts he or she learns, by asking the right questions. For example, you might ask, "So how does all this work? Tell me about nutrient cycles. How do we depend on nutrient cycles. How do we affect nutrient cycles? How can we behave differently?" (You might need to do a little studying on your own to help your child see the light. At the risk of sounding like a commercial advertiser, you might want to get a copy of my environmental science book, *Environmental Science: Creating a Sustainable Future*, and read the chapters on ecology. They're simple, straightforward, and focus on the big picture.)

If you're really daring, you can even talk with the teachers about the big picture if they are not big picture teachers. Give them a copy of this book, and suggest diplomatically that they might enjoy hearing what I have to say. Or, you might volunteer to lead field trips for your school or give talks that help draw all this information into a meaningful whole.

TEACHING KIDS ECOLOGY THAT MATTERS

As a parent, you shouldn't have to teach ecology. That's not in your job description, although maybe it should be. Without you and your teachings, your child may never receive any meaningful education in this vital subject. Sure, grade school and middle school teachers will tell your child about ecosystems and such, but at the risk of offending many teachers, for the most part this instruction is just gobbledygook with very little, if any, direct bearing on your kid's life. Nature centers and outdoor education programs often don't do much better, though I've seen notable exceptions.

For instruction on the matter of ecology that really matters, I recommend Steve Van Matre's work, *Earth Education: A New Beginning*. Van Matre aptly points out the need for three basic understandings. First, he says, students need to understand how life functions. Most importantly, we need a big picture understanding of how the ecosystems of the Earth work.

Second, we need to understand how our own lives are "directly connected to and supported by" ecosystems.

Third, we need to learn how we need to change — individually and collectively — to live more in harmony with these systems. You might want to get a

Steve Van Matre, author of Earth Education, *points out the need for three basic understandings. First, he says, students need to understand how life functions. Most important, we need a big picture understanding of how the ecosystems of the Earth work. Second, we need to understand how our own lives are "directly connected to and supported by" ecosystems. Third, we need to learn how we need to change — individually and collectively — to live more in harmony with the systems.*

copy of his book and read the sections that teach the fundamental elements of solid Earth education.

Environmental education is probably the most important aspect of our child's learning, yet it is relegated to a minor place in the curricula of public schools, taught as a brief module here or there, then quickly forgotten. Although an increasing number of high schools offer environmental science courses, only a small subset of the student population actually enrolls in these courses. It's a national tragedy.

In most colleges, environmental science is an elective in which, once again, only a small minority of students enrolls. Although there are notable exceptions, much of the teaching that occurs in college classrooms is "chalkboard ecology." Students learn about the living world through diagrams and lectures and by reading textbooks or watching videos. Moreover, students tend to learn about environmental problems and how they can be solved as if each problem were isolated from the next, when in fact they're all connected to a common set of root causes. Very little thought is given to common root causes. And very little effort is made to teach students what they can do individually. Most classroom lectures and readings focus on what business and government can do. When the class is over, many students ramp up for their next courses, although some students do report this to be a life-altering experience and go on to environmental careers.

By relegating environmental education to a footnote in our children's academic life, we do a disservice to our offspring and our society. Each ecologically illiterate child produced by the educational system becomes a detriment to our future, a liability, rather than an asset to the task of building a sustainable society.

Imagine if more children were raised to understand the benefits of nature and the importance of protecting natural systems, like Jared Duval, whose story is told in the accompanying piece on "Kids Who Are Making a Difference."

> *Each ecologically illiterate child produced by the educational system becomes a detriment to our future, a liability, rather than an asset to the task of building a sustainable society. Imagine if more children were raised to understand the benefits of nature and the importance of protecting natural systems, like Jared Duval, whose story is told in the accompanying piece on "Kids Who Are Making a Difference."*

You can bridge this gap by becoming a mini-expert in ecology and environmental issues. Read case studies in this book to your students, read textbooks on the subject or parts of textbooks to learn more about global warming and other pressing issues, then teach them to your children.

KIDS WHO ARE MAKING A DIFFERENCE
HOW DOES SENATOR JARED DUVAL SOUND?

Jared Duval, like Andrew Holleman, whom I introduced you to in the last chapter, led a successful effort to save a 12-acre (4.8 hectare) wetland and forest in his home town of Lebanon, New Hampshire while still a high school student. Like Andrew's beloved wetlands, the Great Hollow Wetlands was slated for development — construction of a 56,000 square-foot (5,202 square-meter) supermarket. The development would have necessitated draining and filling of the wetland. These activities, in turn, would have led to the death or displacement of virtually every living thing that depended on this unique natural habitat. In addition, says Jared, "Such a project would have opened the door to further sprawling development in one of the city's last remaining natural areas."

Jared Duval, like Andrew, knew the land and understood its true value. He understood it was a "vital part of a larger ecosystem," the biosphere. He had seen deer and many birds on the property and had discovered black bear and red fox tracks. He knew the land was alive. It was not just some vacant piece of property ripe for development. He also understood what many adults fail to grasp: Land should be preserved not just for its scenic beauty, but also for its intrinsic value as wildlife habitat.

Jared rallied fellow students and formed a group called Students for a Sustainable Future. Together, they gathered public support to halt development of the wetlands adjacent to his school.

Saving the wetland took nearly a year and a half. During this time, Jared and his friends attended zoning meetings, then planning board meetings. They sought public comments and drafted and circulated a petition in their school, which was presented to the school board. Later, the school board sent a letter to the zoning and planning boards, opposing the proposed development. "At every zoning and planning board meeting, we had between 15–50 students in attendance," notes Jared. "That's quite a feat," he adds, "considering the attention span of many students and the ongoing, seemingly never-ending nature of city decision making."

Their efforts did not end there, however. "We wrote letters to the editor of the local newspaper, made buttons and signs. I wrote articles about the campaign in every issue of the high school newspaper, *The Lebanon High School Times.*"

In May of 2001, the Lebanon Planning Board voted 4–3 to deny the request of Hanford Supermarket for site plan approval. Later that year, Jared was given the Brower Youth Award from the Earth Island Institute in recognition of his work to save this piece of land from development. In his acceptance speech, Jared noted, "'The world is run by those who show up.' This quote is even more accurate when applied to students. So many people in our society expect us to be passive and apathetic. Yet when we refuse to have our future compromised, when we speak up for our beliefs, people and society take notice. Why? Because student involvement is a rare occurrence that makes people think, 'Something must really be wrong if students are concerned.'"

Fortunately, Jared's story does not end here. As it turns out, this was really only the beginning. After high school, Jared went on to Wheaton College in Norton, Massachusetts, where he is studying political science and economics. Here, too, he continues his political activism. In 2003, he was awarded the Morris K. Udall Scholarship.

This national scholarship is awarded annually to 80 sophomores and juniors in environmental studies and related fields for excellence in academic performance. Jared was also cited for his work with the Sierra Student Coalition and with Students for Economic Justice, a group he founded at Wheaton College. The scholarship comes with a $5,000 cash award. He won the award the next year, too.

Jared Duval is aiming his sights on a public policy career that focuses on renewable energy and other environmental issues. He has served on the executive committee of the Sierra Student Coalition, the largest student environmental organization in the country. It is the student arm of the national nonprofit group, the Sierra Club. Jared has also directed high school environmental leadership trainings over the past three summers through the Sierra Student Coalition. These workshops are designed for budding high school environmental activists.

At Wheaton, Duval also received the Emily Susan Hartwell Leadership Award, which is given each year to a student who has motivated others to action in the areas of social, political, or global responsibility. Jared had worked on a World Bank bonds boycott campaign with Students for Economic Justice. Jared is also an advisor to Wheaton's Sustainable Environment Club.

By now you're asking, "When does this kid rest?"

I'm guessing not often.

During the summer of 2003, Jared worked full time as Howard Dean's energy and environmental policy intern at the Burlington, Vermont, headquarters of the former Vermont governor's campaign for the Democratic nomination for president in 2004. Jared bunked with eight other young volunteers in an apartment he described as "wall-to-wall mattresses." While the campaign paid the rent, they were on their own when it came to food, so the group often subsisted on ramen noodles and an assortment of canned foods that Jared's aunt donated from her pantry.

Often working 10 to 12 hours a day, he and others toiled on the campaign. Jared performed in-depth research on many important environmental issues, such as global warming, pollution of the ocean, and land protection. You can imagine the young man's glee when facts and figures from his research and analysis appeared in Howard Dean's speeches!

In the summer of 2004, Jared was back at it, this time in Tanzania. Jared received a Wheaton College fellowship to volunteer with the Foundation for Sustainable Development. In Tanzania, he taught high school economics at an international school in Dar Es Salaam. While there, he organized funding to obtain sports equipment for the school and coached the basketball team. He also formed a student-run AIDS awareness and sex education group called Straight Talk St. Mary's. The group hosted an AIDS awareness day on July 24, 2004. Attended by over 500 students, the event featured drama, songs, poetry, and speakers and was a smashing success that fostered many discussions. "The students at St. Mary's are confronting issues of sex and AIDS head on," says Jared, "trying to overcome cultural aversions to talk of these subjects." After the event, he began work on a day focusing specifically on STDs. Jared also noticed the abysmal lack of books in a school library. In typical fashion, he set out to do something about it. He sent an e-mail request to a list of friends and family. His mother sent the request on to others like me, asking for old college textbooks to help stock a school library.

Mother Earth News sent five boxes; two boxes were sent by his father and mother who had collected books that people sent in. (I sent his mother a full box of textbooks, including some I'd written.) In addition, nearly $750 was raised to buy additional books.

After graduating from Wheaton, Duval plans to pursue a graduate degree in public policy or political theory. And after that he hopes to pursue a life of public service — or shall we say, additional public service. His graduate work will be supported by the Truman Scholarship that he won in 2004, a graduate scholarship awarded annually by the Harry S. Truman Foundation to 80 college juniors from across the country who have demonstrated a commitment to public service.

Someday Jared hopes to serve as a US congressman or senator for his home state of Vermont. His goal, in his own words, is to "serve as a conscientious, unwavering agent for positive social and environmental change" locally and globally.

I have a feeling he will do just that.

In fact, I have no doubt that someday we'll be hearing about the successful campaign of Senator Jared Duval.

Who knows? One day it may be President Jared Duval who helps lead us toward a sustainable future.

HELPING YOUR CHILDREN BECOME MORE CRITICAL THINKERS

Another part of the challenge of raising environmentally responsible children is to help them become more critical thinkers. Critical thinking isn't about being critical or judgmental. It is about discerning fact from fallacy. It's about critically analyzing arguments and assertions, looking at research, and discerning the validity of the conclusions. "Becoming a critical thinker means bringing both curiosity and a healthy dose of skepticism to all information, listening to many points of view, asking questions, and believing nothing until it has become true for us," says Zoe Weil in her book about raising children, *Above All, Be Kind*. We'd be a much better society if more people had honed this skill.

I've spent a good deal of my academic career helping to promote critical thinking. In fact, it is a central feature of all my college textbooks and, not to brag, I was one of the first — if not the first — textbook writers to make it a central theme. (And if you want to learn more about it, you might snag a copy of my text, *Environmental Science: Creating a Sustainable Future*.)

How does a parent help a child become a more critical thinker?

You can begin by talking about bias, describing what it is and discussing how it affects the way we view the world around us. You can talk about your own biases, in fact, and how most people interpret information in light of their biases. When listening to the evening news, political debates, political ads, or commentaries in various media, you can ask your children, "Do you suppose this person's argument is biased?"

You can also help your children become more critical thinkers by helping them understand their biases, and how their biases taint their thinking. You might ask questions such as: "What facts support that conclusion? Do you suppose there are other explanations?"

I also recommend that critical thinkers begin by gathering as much information as possible *before* formulating an opinion. Gathering all information also means looking at facts the "other side" uses to support their viewpoints. If you don't, you take the risk of oversimplifying. The result is often simple solutions. As H.L. Mencken once noted, "There's always an easy solution to every human problem — neat, plausible and wrong."

To know much is often the cause of doubting more.
— Michel Montaigne

Critical thinking requires that we and our children question how facts are derived. When listening to the latest study on the environment — or any other issue — it is important to see how the study was conducted. Unfortunately, the news media rarely provide enough information about the scientific studies they report on for us to discern whether the experiments were conducted properly — for example, if the sample size was adequate.

Critical thinking skills also mature when students learn to examine the big picture. In modern society, we often get bogged down in arguments over minor details while completely ignoring the big picture. We might argue over the exact amount that humans contribute to global warming while the Earth burns. We argue over acid rain and a host of other environmental issues while we plod unwittingly along an unsustainable path.

By teaching your child critical thinking skills, you can help root out the lazy thinking that plagues both sides of most, if not all, environmental debate. Critical thinking skills will also help children view advertisements and political rhetoric skeptically. It will help them break out of the social mold perpetrated by such propaganda, an ideology that would have all of us subscribe to the megaconsumer mentality — shopping till we drop, or dying with the most toys to win some elusive game that is undermining society's long-term chances of creating an enduring human presence. So when your children ask a question, be sure not to give pat answers. Instead, you may want to invite your children to explore this issue with you using the advice given above.

UNCOVERING THE MYTHS OF MODERN SOCIETY

Another essential attribute of a critical thinker is a wariness toward thought-stoppers — seemingly logical statements that literally halt thought. In many cases, thought-stoppers are expressions of widely held myths of modern society that are, in part, responsible for steering our society off a sustainable course.

Most of us have been assailed by a thought-stopper in a debate with a friend or colleague. For example, I have a dear friend who once countered my arguments for environmental change by saying, "That's all well and good, but people won't do it unless they can be shown how they can profit from the changes you are proposing." In other words, all people care about is money.

For some time, his economic cynicism terminated nearly all of our amicable debates. And it was probably meant to. In fact, this argument has been used to slam many a door shut on many good ideas over the past few decades.

Frustrated, I began to think about the statement a bit more deeply. It didn't take too long to realize that while his argument may be true for some people, many others respond to different stimuli or "buttons." That is to say, many people may require an economic rationale to make changes in their lives that also benefit the environment. That's their button. However, I know a great many people who are compelled by altruism — for example, leaving behind a better world or helping others in need. Some people are simply compelled to action because something is morally correct.

From that point on, when my friend delivered his final economic thought-stopper, I just smiled at him and said, "Not always," and I pointed out the things he did for the good of the world that didn't net personal economic prof-its. He got the point.

President Ronald Reagan posed a classic thought-stopper one day when he announced that "conservation means freezing in the dark." Put in other words, conservation means sacrifice. In order to steward our natural resources and use them judiciously, we're going to have to sacrifice brutally, giving up on comfort and convenience.

> *Those who are of the opinion that money will do everything, may very well be suspected to do everything for money.*
> *— Lord Halifax*

Surely, this is not the case. If we're smart, we can have cold drinks, hot show-ers, and many of the amenities we desire, and have a clean environment! According to energy expert Amory Lovins of the Rocky Mountain Institute, Americans could cut energy consumption by 75 percent without sacrificing one iota of comfort or convenience.

Why?

Because we have the energy-saving technologies that allow us to achieve this goal.

Although other experts quibble over the exact percentage, arguing that it is not so high as Lovins contends, they don't argue with the basic premise: We waste a lot of resources and have the wherewithal to live well without freez-ing in the dark. Conservation doesn't mean living in a cave and drinking goat milk.

> *Conservatism is humanity caring for the future.*
> *— Nancy Newhall*

"Growth is good, indeed essential" is another thought-stopper that drives us (mad?) as a society. "Happiness stems from material possession," is yet another.

You may want to take a look at the accompanying list of thought-stoppers from the late Donella Meadows and me, and work with your children on them over time. You can discuss them with your children. Make them aware of thought-stoppers and help them develop intelligent responses to them. Help your children understand the myths of modern society and how they can detract from the task of building a sustainable society.

EIGHTEEN MYTHS AND ASSUMPTIONS
OF MODERN SOCIETY

1.   People do not shape their future; it happens to them.
2.   Individual actions don't count.
3.   People care only about themselves and money; they can't be counted on to take action on the part of a good cause unless they'll gain.
4.   Conservation is sacrifice.
5.   For every problem there is only one solution; find it, correct the problem, and all will be well.
6.   For every cause, there is one effect.
7.   Technology can solve all problems.
8.   Environmental protection is bad for the economy.
9.   People are apart from nature.
10.   The key to success is through the domination and control of nature.
11.   The natural world is here to serve our needs.
12.   All growth is unqualifiedly good.
13.   We have no obligation to future generations.
14.   Favorable economics justify all actions; if it's economical, it's all right.
15.   The systems in place today were always here and will always remain.
16.   Happiness stems from material possession.
17.   Results can be measured by the amount of money spent on a problem.
18.   Slowing the rate of environmental destruction and pollution solves the problems.

Adapted from Donella Meadows, *The Global Citizen,* 1991, Island Press; and Daniel D. Chiras, *Beyond the Fray: Reshaping America's Environmental Response,* Johnson Books, 1990.

MYTHS AND PARADIGMS

The myths we embrace are part of a big picture view of the world. Some like to call it our paradigm. You may want to warn your children that when they venture into the outside world, they'll very likely encounter people who embrace an entirely different paradigm. They believe strongly in this view and can argue convincingly in favor of it.

Furthermore, when two people with conflicting paradigms engage in discussion, they often can't even begin to understand each other. It's as if they are speaking entirely different languages.

The reason for this total disconnect has a lot to do with deeply held values and beliefs. We look at their beliefs and call them myths; they'd probably do the same with ours. Ecological literacy requires that our children understand that values and beliefs affect people profoundly. If nothing else, they'll be a lot less frustrated and perhaps a lot less judgmental of "the other side."

UNDERSTANDING ROOT CAUSES AND ROOT-LEVEL SOLUTIONS

Thought-stoppers kill debate and thwart creative solutions. But the way we look at cause-and-effect can be just as crippling to our quest for viable solutions.

For many people, the search for causation is like peeling the skin off an apple. Tease off this layer, and presto, you're there! Unfortunately, there are many other deeper layers. Henry David Thoreau used a different metaphor to make the same point: "There are a thousand hacking at the branches of evil to one who is striking at the root."

Fact is, most problems have more than one deeply rooted cause. Over the years, my experience in environmental issues has made it clear to me that understanding ALL of the root causes, and addressing them, is very likely the only way we're going to formulate lasting solutions.

Unfortunately, our tendency to look only at superficial causes results in equally superficial responses. The typical solution often tends to be nothing more than a Band-Aid. Although a stop-gap measure may work for a while, and certainly gives the impression to onlookers that something is being done, in the long run Band-Aids peel off and the problems re-emerge. When they reappear, they are often larger, more intractable, and more costly to solve.

Take air pollution, for example. For many years, we Americans have been solving air pollution by slapping pollution controls on power plants, factories, and automobiles. While these stop-gap measures have successfully reduced emissions of many pollutants, they create waste products that must be disposed of elsewhere, typically in landfills. Pollution control devices on power plants, for instance, reduce atmospheric concentrations of particulates and sulfur dioxide, but the toxic chemicals that would have ended up in the atmosphere end up in landfills where they have the potential to leach into groundwater. We're creating a toxic shell game.

Even more importantly, gains afforded by pollution control devices can often be overwhelmed by growth. For example, many cities are finding that after years of gradually improving air quality, their gains — largely due to more efficient cars and the installation of pollution control devices on various sources such as automobiles and trucks, are being offset by growth. In many cases, the brown clouds of toxic pollutants that hover over our cities are reappearing.

Why?

Because cities are sprawling outward and to get to work and to run errands citizens must travel greater distances by car. Population growth within metropolitan areas is also resulting in a dramatic increase in the number of cars on the road. And people are driving more to do this and that. With vehicle miles traveled each day climbing, prior reductions from pollution control devices are negated.

Nowadays, more and more pollution experts are recognizing that a pollutant once produced is a social, economic, and environmental liability. I also assert that pollution is a sign of an improperly designed system. To address air pollution, we need to "attack" pollution at its source. We do so by preventing pollution from being created in the first place. This may require a complete redesign of the systems we rely on to meet our needs: energy, agriculture, industry, transportation, and so on. Environmentally friendly fuels, like hydrogen, are a good way of avoiding many of the current problems facing polluted urban areas. When used to power efficient mass transit, the effect is even greater!

This discussion may give the impression that faulty systems are the root cause of many of our problems. This is true. Most systems we rely on were designed in times when our understanding of environmental problems was nonexistent, our numbers were small, and our impact was negligible. In truth, then, the root causes have to do with the minds of the designers and the society in which they lived. But the roots of the problem also lie in our continuing inability to adapt mentally to changing realities. We continue to design and operate systems with a frontier ethic, a topic discussed in Chapter 4. To solve problems, we're going to need to rethink and restructure systems. We need new thinking and new ethics to produce new systems.

As your child matures and becomes an abstract thinker — sometime around ninth grade, according to psychologists — you can broach such issues.

> *To solve problems we're going to need to rethink and restructure systems. We need new thinking and new ethics to produce new systems.*

That is, you can help them understand root causes. Teach them to search for root causes and to discern ways to address the roots of the many problems we face. If you are an educator, you may want to incorporate root-level thinking in your classroom lectures and discussions. Using urban automobile pollution as an example helps. Kids can see how changing the type of fuel and changing the make-up of the transportation system — for example, by promoting energy-efficient mass transit — would address one of the roots of the problem. Creating more compact settlement patterns would also help, as it reduces the need for transit and makes mass transit even more feasible.

Strike while the iron's hot. The window of opportunity closes as students get older. For example, I've always found firstyear college students better able to grasp this idea — the need for root-level solutions and system change — than master's degree students, especially those who have already ventured into the business world.

TEACHING CHILDREN ABOUT SUSTAINABILITY

In Chapter 2, I mentioned the importance of letting nature be our teacher. Nature has a great deal to "say" about living sustainably on the Earth — if we're smart enough to turn down the TV for a while and look and listen. I have spent a good part of my life, as have others, trying to discern nature's secrets: biological principles of sustainability.

Here they are in simple form: (1) Use what you need and use it efficiently. (2) Recycle everything — don't waste a thing. (3) Hitch your wagon to renewable resources — it's the only way life can persist on a finite planet. (4) Restore the damage you create — you can't afford to wreck your only home. (5) Control population so that all organisms live within the limits of resource supply; those that violate the rule will pay the penalty. (6) Be adaptable — organisms must change or perish if conditions shift.

We too can benefit from the wisdom of nature. If we apply these simple yet powerful ideas to our lives, to our businesses, indeed to all human systems, we can begin to steer human society back onto a sustainable course.

Interestingly, the reason we're not on a sustainable trajectory is that we (1) are terribly inefficient in our use of resources; (2) recycle only a fraction of the materials we use; (3) rely almost exclusively on non-renewable resources, especially non-renewable energy; (4) fail to restore much of the damage we create; (5) have let our population run wild, increasing in number and spreading over the landscape like wildfire; and (6) remain married to outdated ideas, technologies, and laws that contribute to our undoing.

> *Short of nuclear war itself, population growth is the gravest issue the world faces over the decades ahead. If we do not act, the problem will be solved by famine, riot, insurrection, war.*
> *— Robert McNamara*

Sure, nature also relies on other ideas, like diversity and redundancy, to achieve sustainability. But to me, the above points are the main operating principles. They've been derived over millions of years of evolution, and they work. They ensure that natural systems persist in the absence of human activity or major natural geologic or climatic change. And it is hard arguing with success.

Whether we're building a new house or designing a new car or pondering a new energy system, nature's plan should be the foundation. Never does nature say one thing and wisdom another.

We're foolish to ignore these guidelines, because not only is nature the master teacher, she's also the judge and jury. She'll let us know if we fail, sometimes brutally. And don't forget: nature bats last in the game of life.

An engineer wouldn't think about designing an airplane that violated the laws of aerodynamics. We shouldn't design a society that violates ecological principles. It's bound to crash.

You can teach your children about sustainability on camping trips or while hiking. I like to ask my kids, "Why do you suppose this ecosystem would remain more or less unchanged over thousands of years if we didn't intrude?" and then let them struggle with ideas. You can even incorporate the principles of ecological sustainability into your family's plan to create a more environmentally sound lifestyle. You might want to read aloud the "Models of Sustainability" piece in this chapter, showing how I used the principles of ecological sustainability to design and build my home.

> *An engineer wouldn't think about designing an airplane that violated the laws of aerodynamics. We shouldn't design a society that violates ecological principles. It's bound to crash.*

MODELS OF SUSTAINABILITY
LIVING LIGHTLY/LIVING WELL

If the idea of using biological principles of sustainability to fashion human society strikes you as peculiar, you might want to read this piece, which I published in Solar Today *magazine. This shortened version is about the construction of my house, a project guided by nature's design principles. Be sure to check out the list of features that show specific examples of building materials and design ideas inspired by principles of biological sustainability.*

Although few of us know it, homes and home building have a huge impact on the environment. American homes, for instance, consume about one-fifth of the nation's energy, and are responsible for about one-fifth of our nation's annual emissions of greenhouse gases. Home construction and remodeling are responsible for about 60 percent of all trees harvested each year, many of which are removed in huge clear-cuts. Building the average new home in America, covering about 2,250 square feet (209 square meters), will create a one acre (0.4 hectare) clear-cut. Mining operations to produce the minerals required to make cement and a host of metals used to build and supply the average new home will create a hole in the ground about the size of the house. Construction also produces huge amounts of waste. Nationwide, construction and demolition waste is responsible for about one-fourth of the solid waste that goes to landfills each year. Our homes also produce billions of gallons of waste water from showers, sinks, and toilets.

In 1995, I decided to build a house from scratch. I wanted to minimize both the construction impacts and the occupation impacts — the impacts of living in the house once it was finished. As an advocate of solar energy, having passive solar heating and passive cooling were my first criteria. They're just too economical to pass up, and they can create unrivaled comfort — if carefully designed and constructed.

Solar electricity was high on my priority list, too. Even though I would be building near electrical power lines, I wanted to go off grid — as a hedge against rising electrical rates and as a means of avoiding environmental problems that result from grid power.

Important as it is, I knew that solar power wouldn't be enough to create a sustainable home. In order to create truly sustainable shelter, we need to do a lot more.

Committed to creating a home that had as little impact on the environment — in both construction and long-term performance — I worked with my builders to design a state-of-the-art environmental home (Figure 1).

DESIGN WITH NATURE

For years, I'd been telling my readers and the students the importance of principle-based sustainable development. To create a truly sustainable society, I'd lectured, we need to tap into the wisdom of nature. Nature's hard-earned strategies for sustainability could prove to be a valuable tool for reshaping human systems.

Figure 1. The author's 2,400-square-foot (223-square-meter) passive solar, solar electric home. The house was built long and narrow so that each room serves as a passive solar heat collector.

The secrets of sustainability in natural systems are deceptively simple: To sustain life we must recycle all we can, use recycled resources, rely on renewable resources, harvest sustainably, and restore damage. We must also practice conservation — that is, use only what we need and use it efficiently. And, of course, we must also control our numbers so as not to overrun the life-support system of our precious planet.

These elegantly simple, yet effective principles, have ensured the success of many a species over the long course of time. It seems to me that human society could benefit as well and, in my case, that they would prove to be effective guiding principles as I built my home (see table).

DESIGNING WITH NATURE

In designing and building this house, I tried to abide by the biological principles of sustainability. Below are some examples of features that comply with nature's guidelines.

GOING GREEN

As the builders and I pondered designs, materials, and building techniques, we passed every decision through a sustainability filter. It was surprisingly simple. Did a material, for instance, contribute substantially

Conservation/Efficiency

- Highly insulated walls, ceilings, and foundation
- Insulation around foundation
- Earth-sheltered design
- Energy-efficient windows
- Energy-efficient refrigerator, washing machine, and other appliances
- Energy-efficient electronic equipment
- Compact fluorescent light bulbs
- Outdoor clothes line
- Insulated slider panels for skylights
- Insulated shades for windows
- Water-efficient showerhead and toilets
- Water-efficient irrigation system for garden
- Air locks
- Wooden I-beam roof rafters

Recycling

- Packed tire walls (used automobile tires)
- Recycled carpet, carpet pad, and tile
- Recycled cellulose insulation
- Salvaged doors
- Salvaged wood for cabinets and vanities
- Reclaimed paint
- Recycled asphalt driveway
- Built-in recycling center
- Recycled concrete block for planters
- Recycled all aluminum, glass, wood, cardboard, and other waste from the job site
- Front door mat made from recycled tires

Renewable Resource Use

- Passive solar heating and cooling
- Solar panels and wind generator for electricity
- Straw bale walls
- Light straw-clay generator shed
- Natural linoleum made from jute, sawdust, and other natural materials
- Earthen plasters

Restoration

- Living roof
- Native grasses, wildflowers, and trees planted on the site

to manifesting a principle of biological sustainability? Did it promote recycling, renewable resource use, efficiency, and restoration? If something didn't fit, it was usually rejected.

As in any building project, costs played an important role in decision making. In this project, we were pleasantly surprised to find that very few things we wanted to do cost more than non-environmental choices, although there were some notable exceptions. Many decisions, such as superinsulating the home, would not only enhance environmental performance, they would save enormous amounts of money over the long run.

Ten months after the construction began, I moved into my 2,400-square-foot (223-square-meter) home and office, which cost $95 per square foot in a region where most custom-built homes cost $100 to $150 per square foot. Sweetening the deal, my home came with a life-time supply of free heat and electricity from wind and sunlight, two renewable sources!

As you head up the driveway, the first thing you'll notice is your tires crackling over the 100 percent recycled asphalt. The front walkway is lighted by a solar-powered garden light. The roof houses 22 50-watt solar electric panels. Rising high above the roof on the west end of the house is a small wind generator. In back of the garage is a small shed, built on a rubble trench and earthbag foundation, with walls made from straw-clay. It houses the back-up generator, in case we run out of power.

Walking in the front door, you find yourself in the front entry way. It is one of two air locks, which prevent cold winter air from streaming into the house when the front door opens — a feature vital in all cold climates.

The tile you walk on is recycled feldspar, a mine waste. The carpet is made from recycled plastic pop bottles and the carpet pad is made from waste from a clothing factory. All three products were cost competitive with conventional materials.

Next on the tour is the living room. It's made from straw bales finished with an earthen plaster, made from dirt on the site. The straw bales are protected by a generous overhang and a foundation design which prevent the walls from absorbing moisture so the bales — like any form of insulation — stay dry. The bales produce a 24-inch (61-centimeter) thick fireproof wall with an R-value of about 40. (R-value is a measure of the resistance of a substance to heat flow. In most homes, walls have an R-value of 13 to 20.)

The design we used required very little lumber. Further reducing lumber use, the ceilings of this house were framed with wooden I-beams (Figure 2). Wooden I-beams require about 40 to 60 percent less lumber than similarly sized dimensional lumber, while providing all of the structural strength. This option meant no old-growth trees were cut down to build my house.

The roof trusses also created a 12-inch (30.5 centimeter) cavity that we filled with 100 percent recycled wet-blown cellulose insulation — ground-up newspaper treated with a non-toxic flame retardant. The

Figure 2. Wooden I-beams like these use about half the lumber of a similar piece of solid dimensional lumber. Courtesy of Truss Joist Macmillan.

cellulose insulation provides a R-38 barrier to heat loss, but it's supplemented by rigid foam insulation applied to the inside and outside, bringing the ceiling insulation to R-65 in most of the house — a great asset on those frigid winter nights! To protect the insulation in walls and ceilings and to reduce air infiltration, a polyethylene vapor barrier was stapled to the framing lumber. The house was also weather stripped and caulked to reduce air infiltration, one of the biggest sources of heat loss in a house.

The walls and ceilings of my home are painted with reclaimed paint. It consists of 50 percent salvaged white latex paint mixed with virgin latex paint. It cost $8 per gallon in 5-gallon (22.5-liter) buckets.

Next on the tour is the dining room. Here curved walls made from used automobile tires arch into the hillside, providing earth-sheltering for summer cooling and winter heating (Figure 3). The tire walls were made by laying used automobile tires on compacted subsoil. The tires were then packed with dirt from the site using a pneumatic tamper. Each tire holds approximately 350 pounds (157.5 kilograms) of tightly compacted soil. The tires are laid down in an overlapping pattern, like bricks, and then finished with cement stucco or earthen plaster to create sensuous, curving walls. All told, the house reclaimed 800 tires, many of

Figure 3. Tires are laid on well-compacted subsoil, packed with dirt, then tamped. When the walls are completed, they're covered with an earthen plaster or cement stucco, producing delightfully curved walls in an otherwise linear world.

them acquired from local tire shops. Packed tire walls coated with cement stucco provide a huge amount of thermal mass — vital in a passive solar design. During the winter, thermal mass absorbs heat from sunlight streaming in through south-facing windows during the day.

As you tour the house, you'll notice that almost all of the light fixtures are fitted with compact fluorescent light bulbs. These remarkable inventions use about one-fourth of the power of a standard incandescent bulb, while producing the same amount of light. The bulbs are color adjusted, too, so the light is warm and inviting, not cold like conventional fluorescent lamps. Over its lifetime, a bulb that costs $8 to $12 can save you $40 to $50 in electricity, and even more. In my case, it also allowed me to install a smaller array of solar electric panels, saving a considerable amount of money.

In keeping with the recycling principle, the cabinets in the kitchen and the bathroom vanities are made from salvaged wood. In fact, they're made from the siding of a 150-year-old barn torn down a few miles away. The wood was removed, remilled, and then fashioned into

Figure 4. Strolling to the bedrooms and the author's office, you pass through the growing area, which houses bananas, bougainvillea, hibiscus, orange trees, cacti, and other plants. This area gathers sunlight and serves as a buffer against incoming sunlight so there are some sun-free zones in the house.

cabinets. They were finished with a non-toxic, water-soluble sealant. Their life is easier now. Nestled inside my home out of the elements, they could last another 150 years or more.

As you step into the kitchen, you'll notice virtually all of the amenities of modern life, except an automatic dishwasher and some of the sillier electronic devices. The kitchen contains a built-in recycling center to make this task easier — a feature all modern builders should consider.

The refrigerator is a super-efficient model from SunFrost. It is quiet and an energy-miser, using much less electricity than a standard unit. It did cost a lot more than a normal refrigerator — about $2,600 — but the extra cost was well worth it. With 4-inch-thick (10-centimeter) foam walls and other energy-saving features, SunFrost refrigerators require three to eight 50-watt solar electric panels, depending on the size of the unit, indoor air temperature, and use patterns. A conventional refrigerator would require at least four times as many — 12 to 21 modules. The savings in panels easily paid the additional cost of the fridge.

Like energy, we use water efficiently. Water-efficient showerheads, low-flush toilets, and a super-efficient Frigidaire front-loading washer help us live on surprisingly little water. My two boys and I use only about 50 gallons (225 liters) per day.

Strolling from the kitchen to the bedrooms, you travel through a large growing area (Figure 4). It provides a little food, including chard and tomatoes, and helps humidify the home and gather heat to warm my office and the bedrooms. One 40-foot-long (12-meter) planter along the south wall was built from salvaged concrete blocks. We use rinse water from washing dishes in the sink to water the plants.

Skylights in the ceiling of the growing area provide sunlight year-round for growing plants. And because this house is earth-sheltered (built into the hillside) and highly massed, overheating isn't a problem. In fact, we welcome a little heat in the summer! My younger son Forrest and I invented an insulated slider panel to cover the skylights on cold winter nights to cut down on heat loss.

The bedrooms and my office are also built out of packed tires, and the roof over these rooms is completely underground — that is, it is covered with dirt and has been revegetated using topsoil and sod from the excavation. Elk occasionally graze on the lush grass and wild-flowers of my living roof. The soil cover helps insulate the ceilings, which reach about R-72, in this part of the house. Earth-sheltering and natural ventilation keep the house cool as a cucumber in the summer.

Outside are several gardens that supply some of our food. They are heavily mulched and watered by soaker hoses, greatly reducing water demand. The lawn has been seeded in native meadow grasses, creating a small island of native vegetation in a sea of imported brome grass. It isn't much more than a symbolically defiant act. Recently, we've begun to convert the lawn to an edible landscape by planting raspberries, asparagus, and an assortment of berries that birds can eat.

This house is heated by the sun, thanks to energy-efficient south-facing windows and thermal storage mass that's in the floors and walls and widely distributed throughout the structure. High levels of insulation in the ceiling and walls and around the perimeter of the foundation help reduce heat loss, as do the (nearly) R-4 window shades and R-7 slider panels over the skylights.

LIVING LIGHTLY/LIVING WELL

When I built this house, it wasn't my intention to prove that you could live lightly, and still live well. I just wanted to build a home and office that met the needs of my family as benignly as possible. Along the way, I've learned that you can build a home using the biological principles of sustainability as your guide.

This piece was adapted from Dan Chiras, "Living Lightly, Living Well," published in *Solar Today*, Vol. 15 (September/October), 2001, pp. 34–37.

TEACHING YOUR KIDS ECOLOGY

I've given you a lot to think about in this chapter. It's my recommendation that you discuss these ideas with your child. Go for a walk and talk about the trees as I did with my general biology students. Show them the topsoil and explain that it represents the difference between life and death. Talk about nutrient cycles and how we're part of them. Discuss ways that we alter nutrient cycles and how such changes accrue to our own detriment — for example, overloading farm fields with nitrogen fertilizer pollutes our drinking water. Talk about principles of sustainability, and how they've helped the living world for so many years. Talk about how we violate them, as a society, and how you and your family can try to comply with nature's laws. And then try to incorporate them into your life.

Although I said "talk about" a lot in the previous paragraph, it's prudent to let your kids do as much thinking and talking as possible. "Talk with" might be better advice. How can you do this? By asking questions about what they're learning in school to open up the subject. I ask my kids what they know about ecosystems, and they tell me. My role is to amend their knowledge, saying, "Did you also know ...?" I probe deeper, asking them what they think about this idea and that. "So how important is the carbon cycle? How do you think we're affecting it? What can we do differently?"

Like many other parents, I've found my children fairly resistant to lectures, but more than happy to join in a mutual exploration. Jot some of the ideas outlined in this chapter on a note pad and take them along next time you take your kids for a hike or a camping trip.

TEACHING THE IMPORTANCE OF ACTION

The late, sometimes great Edward Abbey, author of *Desert Solitare* and other influential books like *The Monkey Wrench Gang*, once said that, "Sentiment without action is the ruin of the soul."

It's great to hold environmental values, to talk the talk, but if you don't walk the talk, you're not going to make much of an impression. I've said it before in this book, and I've devoted an entire chapter to the subject: Show your kids "the way" by example — by the way you treat the Earth. Use only what you need and use it efficiently. Make it a point to live a life that seeks every opportunity to conserve our world's precious resources. Recycle, compost, and reuse everything you can. Buy products that are made from recycled materials or are previously owned. Tap into renewable resources and support government policies and organizations, like the American Solar Energy Society and the American Wind Energy Association, that encourage rapid deployment of currently available renewable energy technologies. Encourage restoration of the Earth's ecosystems.

Establish wildlife habitat in your backyard or the lower forty. Support policies and organizations that help restore the Earth and wild populations of commercial as well as noncommercial species. Support population control — that is, family planning, birth control, and growth management in and around cities and towns — to prevent the continual loss of valuable farmland, wetlands, forests, and other wildlife habitat. Support policies, political leaders, and nonprofit groups that recognize and work on ways to adapt to the changing realities of our world — a world in which economic growth, consumption, and sheer numbers threaten our future. I'll have more to say on the subject in Chapter 6.

To know the answer is not always to live the answer.
— R.J. Sneed

Whenever possible, expose your children to positive examples. Visit friends who live well while living lightly on the planet. Tour organic farms and renewable energy facilities. Take your kids to recycling centers and solar and green-built homes. The American Solar Energy Society sponsors an annual tour of solar homes in nearly every major city in the United States in early October. For a small fee you can tour a dozen or more interesting homes or commercial buildings powered, at least in part, by the sun.

EcoFairs are a great way to expose kids to new ideas and folks of similar viewpoints. Each August, the Solar Living Institute sponsors SolFest in Hopland, California, two hours north of San Francisco. It's a gala event with inspiring speakers, workshops on a wide range of topics from solar living to natural building, to the use of healthy products for cleaning your house. You might take your family there, or to similar events elsewhere, such as the Iowa Renewable Energy Expo, Midwest Renewable Energy Expo, or one of the newest; the Sun Festival Southwest in Phoenix, Arizona.

Don't forget to have fun with your children as you explore ways to adopt a more sustainable lifestyle.

FAMILY ACTIVITIES

Below is a list of activities for children of all ages. You will very likely need to tailor them to your children, simplifying them for younger children, for instance.

1. Take a hike or a stroll through a park with your children. Talk to them about trees as I did with my class, as described earlier in this chapter. Ask them what a tree does. Why are trees so important to life on Earth? You may need to help fill in their knowledge, telling them that trees produce oxygen and

consume carbon dioxide and provide food and shelter for various animals. You can tell them how trees help to hold the soil in place and how they provide shade to cool our homes naturally. You can tell them how trees nourish soil through annual leaf fall.

2. While on a walk or hike, find a place where topsoil is showing. Sit down with your kids and show them the difference between topsoil and subsoil. Explain to them how important topsoil is to humanity; it supports all plants and plants are important to us. Explain to them that topsoil is the difference between life and death on the planet.

3. Ask your children what the statement "Ecosystems are the life-support system of the planet" means. You might need to help them understand this by explaining the functions performed by natural systems to benefit humankind, as explained in this chapter.

4. After the previous discussion (activity 3), ask your children what is meant by the following statement: "Planet care is the ultimate form of self-care." Help them understand it, if they don't get it.

5. Talk with your children about nutrient cycles. Take the water or carbon cycle and trace it for them — preferably outside. Make sure you help them see how they affect these cycles.

6. With older children, talk about ways human society, even your own family, alters nutrient cycles such as the carbon cycle. You may want to study these topics in a bit more detail in an environmental science or basic ecology book in advance. Then make a list of things you and your child are willing to do to reduce your family's impact on these cycles.

7. Read the case studies in this chapter ("Kids Who Care" and "Models of Sustainability"), and talk about them with your family after dinner or while on a family picnic or vacation. They'd make great reading in the car.

8. Talk with your children about critical thinking. You might introduce one critical thinking rule each night at dinner and discuss what it means. Ask your children to give examples of times they have seen that rule being violated. You can then begin applying the rules to evening news reports, commentaries on TV and commentaries you read in various publications.

9. Read the list of myths of modern society to your children, introducing them one at a time over dinner.

10. Introduce your children to the idea that many problems have deeper roots. Choose an example such as urban air pollution. What are the roots of the problem? Too many cars on the road might be their answer. But you could also suggest that suburban sprawl might be a deeper root. So is our dependence on fossil fuels. What if we used hydrogen fuel or ethanol made from

corn instead of fossil fuels?

11. Introduce your children to the biological principles of sustainability described in this chapter. You might do this while sitting in the woods or in a field. You can use these principles to explain why natural systems sustain themselves. You might note that life has "worked out" these principles over millions of years, and then ask your children how they can be used to create a sustainable human society. How can they be used in your family life to create a more sustainable way of living?

12. Read the two case studies in this chapter to your children; the case study about my house and the one about Jared Duval's amazing accomplishments.

*All that a man achieves and all that he fails to achieve is
the direct result of his own thoughts.*
— James Allen

4 PROMOTING ENVIRONMENTAL VALUES

Ask most Americans if they're "for" clean air and clean water and the answer is almost overwhelmingly "yes". Ask them if they would buy environmentally friendly products, and you elicit the same response. Ask them if they are opposed to hazardous waste being dumped illegally and … well you get the point.

Over the past two or three decades, numerous polls have shown that Americans are almost unanimously in favor of clean air and a host of other desirable environmental goals. America is pretty green, according to the pollsters. In fact, most Americans who are polled even express a willingness to pay more for "green" products.

So why is it then that so many supporters of a clean environment drive energy-inefficient gas-guzzling cars and live in energy-guzzling homes? Why is it that so many people consume in excess? Why is it that so many people pass up the environmentally friendly paper towels and toilet paper, choosing the cheaper mainstream alternatives instead? What is that when the economy falters, environmental laws and regulations topple like dominos at the hands of the very people who just raised them in favor of a clean environment in the latest poll?

"Between saying and doing there is a great distance," wrote F.W. Roberston, a 19th century English clergyman. Part of the reason for this gap is that while many people seemingly value the environment, they still see it as merely a "pretty thing for birdwatchers;" that is, something of a luxury item. Because of this widely held but false notion, the environment often plays second fiddle to economics. When the economy is threatened our environmental commitment goes out the window.

For a great many people among us, the environment and the economy are opposing interests. We pit spotted owl protection against the loss of jobs, clean air against corporate profits and jobs, fuel efficiency against the American way of life. It's always an either-or, never owls *and* jobs, clean air *and* corporate profits, or fuel efficiency *and* a good life — as it should be.

Another part of the explanation for our lack of follow-through on our proclaimed environmental commitment is that many people see no connection between their actions and environmental problems. Houses are not viewed as a major source of environmental damage. Consumption is just consumption. The long trail of environmental problems is invisible to most of us. By and large, personal actions are without consequence — or so we think.

Yet another problem is the phenomenon called the paradox of inconsequence, discussed in Chapter 1. As you may recall, that's a phenomenon in which most of us view our part in the environmental problems we face as being so small that our actions simply could not matter. It's a logic that creates many of our problems and simultaneously freezes us from taking the actions required to solve them.

But there's another very powerful influence that deserves attention: a lack of solid environmental values. We care for the environment, enough to respond affirmatively on poll after poll, but if the truth be known, there's a huge gap between a positive response to a poll and a life of environmental commitment. Frankly, and I don't mean to be critical, by and large most of us are more concerned about our own well-being than the well-being of the environment. Personal convenience and comfort trump environmental protection in the card game of life. It's a very natural trait.

What all this means is that we abide by a fairly superficial environmental value system. This, in turn, causes us to live less than conscientious lives and forces us to turn our backs on the environment when times are a little rough.

Inspiring a deep, abiding love for the environment (Chapter 2) and fostering a solid understanding of the importance of the environment to our lives — and our economy — (Chapters 1 and 4) are vital to the task of creating children who live their lives responsibly — as youngsters and later as adults. Love and knowledge help foster deeply rooted convictions; in other words, they help shape profoundly powerful environmental values. As Albert Einstein once wrote, "It is essential that the student acquire an understanding of and a lively feeling for values. He must have a vivid sense of the beautiful and of the morally good.

Otherwise, with his specialized knowledge, he more closely resembles a well-trained dog than a harmoniously developed person."

Deeply held environmental values that resist the ups and downs of our everyday lives — or downturns in the national economy — are the foundation of a sustainable society. Our society cannot steer back onto a sustainable course solely by enacting new laws and regulations and developing new, environmentally friendly technologies. They'll fall in the face of adversity. To create a sustainable society, we must address the problem of unsustainability at its roots: by building a strong and abiding set of environmental values.

In this chapter, we will look at values conducive to building a sustainable society, focusing on the many ways you, as a parent, can help your child develop a strong and sensible environmental ethic — one that helps promote two mutually supportive goals: an enduring human presence and a healthy global ecosystem.

> *Deeply held environmental values that do not waver through the ups and downs of our everyday lives — or downturns in the national economy — are the foundation of a sustainable society.*

SUSTAINABLE VS. UNSUSTAINABLE ETHICS

We begin this exciting and challenging journey by looking at our current system of ethics. Why? Because we must know where we are before we can heal the fractured ethical system that is leading us astray.

FRONTIER ETHICS

Years ago, Kenneth Boulding, a prominent University of Colorado economist, dubbed the dominant value system of American society a kind of "cowboy ethics." What he meant by this was that we Americans operate by the ethics of our predecessors, individuals who encountered the wide open spaces of the continent, a new frontier, where the idea of limits seemed preposterous. Our six-shooter mentality took no prisoners. Everything was fair game and everything was ours for the taking.

I prefer to call this a *frontier ethic*.

Frontier ethics are characterized by several tenets. First is the notion that there is no limit to Earth's resources. That is to say, frontierists hold the belief that there's an abundance of resources. "Don't worry, there's always more," is their answer to threats of resource depletion. This fallacy, in turn, excuses careless behavior like that of the early settlers of the North American continent — and current public policies of many countries. Buoyed by a false belief in limitless resources, we use what we want, recklessly depleting resources, and then moving on to virgin territory to initiate the cycle once again.

Frontier ethics not only subscribes to the idea that the Earth has an unlimited supply of resources, it also maintains that the bounty is all for us. This notion stems in part from the dominant idea that humans are the crowning achievement of evolution, or God's creation —whatever your belief. The ethical system handed down to us over the years says, in short, that not only is our world blessed with unlimited resources, but its abundance is intended primarily for human beings. Put more succinctly, "there's always more and it is all for us." Little thought is given to the countless species that share the planet with us.

Operating under these notions, we not only ask all the wrong questions but propose solutions based on faulty reasoning. Einstein said something to the effect that "you can't solve a problem with the logic that created it." When a resource supply is used up, for example, we ask "Where can we find more?" The response is typically "over there." The true cost of reaping the presumed wealth "over there" — for example, the loss of wild species and disruption of the ecological life support system — is rarely considered. The fact that "over there" will soon be depleted raises nary an eyebrow. The push to develop the Arctic National Wildlife Refuge's possible oil reserves is a good example.

Frontier ethics contains two other fundamental beliefs. Most frontierists, for example, also subscribe to the notion that humans are "apart from nature." We are her crowning achievement, yes, but truly separate from nature, even immune to the laws that regulate life on Earth. This thinking has been passed down to us from prominent philosophers and economists. The 17th century English philosopher John Locke, for example, wrote that we must become "emancipated from the bonds of nature." Translated: to prosper, we must separate ourselves from nature. Writer Thomas Hardy put it even more bluntly when he wrote, "Man begins where nature ends; nature and man can never be friends."

These ideas have been conveyed from generation to generation and remain firmly entrenched in the human psyche in the western world. But they've also been fine-tuned into further foolishness. Locke, for example, also preached unlimited economic growth, an improbable and dangerous idea that persists today.

Notions of separateness cause us to treat the environment with near-total disregard and have led to the careless pursuit of human needs — a joy ride on the planet that has recently crescendoed into mass destruction. This pursuit, in turn, is frequently justified by a third tenet of frontier ethics: the idea that the key to our success lies in the domination and control of nature. We turn to Locke again for his particular brand of misinformation. He wrote that "the negation of nature is the way toward happiness." Matthew Arnold, a 19th century British poet, summed up the modern view even more adeptly, however, when he wrote: "Nature and man can never be fast friends. Fool, if thou canst not pass her, rest her slave!"

Ethics that suggest there is always more; that humans are separate from nature, so what we do to her will have no consequence; and that domination and control are key elements of our success, today continue to guide our thinking, our policies, and our actions, indeed our economies. The fact that they are widely held beliefs does not make them right or even useful to our survival. In fact, they're just the opposite: ideas that could lead to our undoing if we persist in our belief in them.

THE SELF ABOVE ALL OTHERS

When it comes to human values that influence our future, there's more to consider than our views of the abundance or lack thereof of natural resources, whether we are a part of or apart from nature, and the role of domination and control vs. cooperation as a path to success. There's also a deeply erosive ethic that puts self-satisfaction above the whole, self-satisfaction above responsibility to the planet.

This bankrupt national ethic leads to excessiveness and a long string of environmental impacts that we'll discuss in more detail in Chapter 5.

SUSTAINABLE ETHICS

As a parent, a new set of values — a sustainable ethic — is one of the most important lessons you can offer to your children.

Sustainable ethics are the antithesis of unsustainable ethics. Whereas frontier ethics pay little, if any, attention to the health of the world's ecosystems, sustainable ethics recognize that a healthy planet — one with clean air, clean water, healthy soil, and well-functioning ecosystems — is vital to our long-term survival and prosperity.

Sustainable ethics also hold that, while the Earth houses huge supplies of resources, they are nonetheless finite. In other words, it recognizes that the Earth has its limits. That is to say, there

> *Sustainable ethics recognize that a healthy planet — one with clean air, clean water, healthy soil, and well-functioning ecosystems — is vital to our long-term survival and prosperity.*

are very real limits to non-renewable resources, such as minerals, and even many renewable resources, such as clean water, forests, and ocean fishes.

Those who argue in favor of a sustainable ethic suggest that not only are there limits, but the Earth's riches are not just for us. There's a bounty, to be sure, but it must be shared by all living things. Other species have a right to live and to enjoy the bounty.

The second tenet of sustainable ethics is that humans are a part of nature. Any serious student of human ecology knows that the idea that humans are somehow emancipated from the bonds of nature is ludicrous. Nothing could be further from the truth. We are a part of nature; we depend on nature to provide the goods we require to survive and prosper. We rely on natural systems to remove our wastes, too. As pointed out in Chapter 1, the Earth is the source of all our resources and a sink for all of our wastes. Without the Earth and its ecosystems, there can be no human life and no economy. The negation of nature, to be perfectly honest, is a suicidal impulse.

You can help your children appreciate this notion by pointing out that each and every breath they take requires oxygen that is produced by plants and algae. Without plants, the atmosphere would quickly be depleted of oxygen. And without oxygen, we'd perish in a blink of an eye.

Humans not only depend on nature to provide a wide range of life-sustaining resources, we also participate in nature's most vital workings. We are, for instance, part of the great recycling networks that keep the planet alive, replenishing nutrients and other important chemical substances that ensure the continuation of life on a planet of finite limits. The carbon dioxide you exhale today, for example, may be incorporated into a wheat plant in a nearby farm field tomorrow. Here it is converted into starch, which after harvesting is incorporated into a loaf of bread. The starch is consumed by others. When it is broken down, it gives off carbon dioxide, which is free to continue its endless cycle. The tear in your eye, I tell my students, may have been a tear in Napoleon's eye when defeat finally occurred at Waterloo. Before that, it may have been a drop of water in the blood of a dinosaur.

Not only are we part of the ecological fabric of Earth, we also have the ability to alter vital global nutrient cycles. For example, by pumping excess chemicals into the environment we often overwhelm nutrient cycles and alter physical and biological conditions on the planet. The more than seven billion tons of carbon in the form of carbon dioxide we release from the combustion of fossil fuels into the atmosphere each year represents an excellent example. According to mountains of scientific data, our disruption of the carbon cycle may be dramatically altering the planet's climate. Humans are indeed a part of nature, with profound impacts on the fate of nature. "For 200 years we've been conquering nature. Now, we're beating it to death," wrote author Tim McMillan.

The third tenet of sustainable ethics is that rather than trying to control, dominate, and destroy nature, we must work with nature — that is, find ways to meet our needs that do not destroy but rather enhance ecological systems, the soil, the air, the water, and other living things — which together form the planet's life-support system. As writer and educator Barry Commoner once noted, "Nothing can survive on the planet unless it is a cooperative part of a larger, global life."

As abstract as cooperating with nature may sound, there are countless examples of humans meeting their legitimate needs in ways that enhance rather than destroy our future prospects. Organic farming and passive solar heating of homes and offices are two examples. Hydrogen fuel is another, as are solar and wind electricity. The list goes on.

PUTTING ETHICS INTO ACTION: THE VALUE OF GOOD MODELING

Children begin learning values — consciously and subconsciously — during their preschool years, according to psychologists. They learn both good and bad values from a great many sources; for example, from parents, teachers, and religious leaders. As our children mature, friends influence their values positively and negatively, as do life experiences. We also absorb values from our culture through an assortment of media, including books, television, and movies. As you'll learn in Chapter 6, advertisers are particularly powerful purveyors of consumer values.

Despite the multiplicity of sources for our values, a child's parents are perhaps the most significant in most instances. Despite all the other factors, we parents have a considerable head start on the competition — a good five- to six-year jump on others. If we choose to take an active role in our children's lives, this influence stretches even further. As a result, Linda and Richard Eyre observe in their book, *Teaching Your Children Values*, "Parents have the potential to be, during the first fourteen or fifteen years of life, a drastically more influential force on their children than any other person, factor, element, or group." Our influence occurs through our teachings and by the examples we set — how we live our lives, how we act, and so on.

Many individuals I interviewed for this book told me that their parents' teachings and the examples they set influenced their thinking and their way of life. Jim Schley, a writer, editor, and artist who lives on a land cooperative in Vermont said, "Both parents taught us to avoid waste, make prudent choices as consumers, and to think about the consequences of our choices." These and other teachings from parents and others laid the foundation for a life deeply committed to making the world a better place.

Teaching values is one of a parent's most basic responsibilities. Don't abdicate this role to others — especially advertisers. The consequences of laziness can be significant. As the Eyres point out in *Teaching Your Children Values*, when parents avoid teaching children their values, children learn "that values aren't important." They may also grow up in something of a moral vacuum and some may adopt dangerous values that lead them to make all kinds of foolish and sometimes potentially dangerous choices. "If children start from a values vacuum — with none taught, none learned — they will float at the mercy of circumstance and situation, and their lives will never be their own," contend the Eyres. Overall, permissive parenting that avoids values education is a "catastrophic mistake." It is "analogous to setting a tiny, powerless vessel down in the midst of turbulent, destructive currents and hoping that by some chance it will wash into a safe harbor."

> Teaching values is one of a parent's most basic responsibilities. Don't abdicate this role to others — especially advertisers.

Unbeknownst to most of us, we parents teach and reinforce values every day. When we treat a misbehaving child firmly but respectfully, we send the message that we value respect and nonviolence and frown on misbehavior. When we listen to our children tell the truth about breaking the mirror in the bathroom, and do not fly off the handle, they learn that we value their honesty. When we cart our family's recyclables to the nearby recycling center or drop them off at the curb, when we turn off lights to cut down on energy use and pollution, or when we drive the speed limit — our children are watching and learning that we value the Earth. And don't forget: children learn more from our actions than our words.

Many people I interviewed in the course of writing this book stated that parental actions inspired them deeply — and continue to do so. Michael G. Smith teaches natural building and is author and co-author of two books on the subject, *The Cobber's Companion* and *The Hand-Sculpted House*. He lives in an intentional community in northern California and is deeply committed to living an environmentally sustainable lifestyle. He notes, "By the time I was a small child I had a strong environmental consciousness," which he attributes to his family. "Family time often involved taking walks in the woods or other natural settings. My mom used to take me on walks to pick up garbage off the side of the road, starting when I was a toddler."

Learning is especially likely if we parents add a comment or two — nothing too preachy — about why we are doing what we do. For example, when I bend over to pick up an aluminum can in a parking lot or alongside the road, I sometimes say to my kids, "Why do people throw this stuff out? Do you know that by recycling this can, rather than making a brand new one from aluminum ore, you can save enough energy to run a 100-watt light bulb for four hours?" Or if I'm really on a roll, I might add, "Or it could run one of our energy-efficient compact fluorescent light bulbs for over 16 hours!" Or if I feel like emphasizing aesthetics, I might say, "I wish people were more careful. This trash looks pretty ugly, don't you think?" Or, emphasizing pollution: "Recycling this can saves energy and cuts down on air pollution from making aluminum by 95 percent!"

I try to be matter-of-fact or, more commonly, enthusiastic — not preachy, as I mentioned earlier. Although I'm teaching my kids little facts, I'm also showing them that I care. I'm demonstrating that the environment is valuable to me, that clean air matters, and that saving resources matters. I'm helping them to see that "every little bits helps" and that there's nothing wrong with doing your part. There's no shame in picking up an aluminum can or a scrap of paper. Sometimes, we'll pick up a dozen cans along a short section of road, which shows them that the actions of a few can add up pretty quickly. So far, they have never said, "Dad, you're embarrassing us by picking up trash."

Simmons Buntin, a former student of mine, lives an environmentally sound lifestyle and works in the field in an environmentally friendly development in Tucson, Arizona. He serves as the editor of Terrain.org, a journal of the built and natural environments. He also works with local nonprofit groups to fight sprawl and lives in a resource-efficient solar home. His current lifestyle and choice of work were influenced by a great many factors. One of the most significant influences was his mother, who was born in Sweden. Her teachings helped Simmons understand the importance of animals, both domestic and wild, and to appreciate natural systems. She was not preachy, he says, but made sure the family visited wildlife and state and national parks when they vacationed. Their family had many pets over the years, including pheasants, finches, parakeets, hamsters, dogs, cats, ferrets, a skunk, and fish — though generally not all at once! When they watched TV, says Simmons, "It was more often than not a nature show on PBS or even Mutual of Omaha's *Wild Kingdom*."

Through their vacations, their lifestyle and their entertainment, Simmons' mother demonstrated her love for and interest in all living things. She even fueled his curiosity for all things natural by buying the whole set of Audubon field guides. Interestingly, Simmons' dad "was just the opposite." His materialism drove Simmons in the opposite direction. (As you might suspect, his parents divorced.)

Do whatever you can to show your kids that the environment is valuable to you and them — and the whole world. Be sure to walk your talk, and talk as you walk — that is, let your kids know *why* you do the things you do. You'll be planting seeds that could influence their thinking and their actions for a lifetime.

THE VALUE OF GOOD STORIES

What about sustainable ethics, though? How do you teach your kids the tenets of sustainable ethics that I've outlined in this chapter?

One way is to begin by telling stories — real life stories — that demonstrate that there are very real limits, humans are a part of nature, and we can achieve success by cooperating with nature. Granted, this may be difficult. You may not have had any personal experiences that will help you relay these values (which may be part of the reason many people don't subscribe to them).

I assert that most adults have had some experiences that illustrate these tenets. Think hard about your life. When have you seen limits exceeded? How about each time the air in your city becomes blanketed with a brown cloud of pollution? How about a nearby river that is being polluted by runoff and sewage and factory waste? How about a nearby park being so crowded that there's hardly any room to enjoy a pleasant afternoon?

You also may have stories you learned from your readings. Al Gore's book, *Earth in the Balance*, for instance, describes in detail ancient civilizations that, in meeting their needs, slowly but surely destroyed the environment around them. It may come as a surprise, but much of the Middle East was once rich grassland with forested hills. The Romans felled the cedar trees that once adorned the hills of Lebanon to build their warships. Modern Iran and Iraq were once the cradle of civilization with rich farm fields where agriculture got its start. Over the years, the steady pressure of too many people operating with disregard for the environment decimated this once-lush landscape, creating a hot, barren desert. One has to wonder if the massive environmental destruction has not put stress on the people of this region that spills out in ethnic violence.

For younger children, you may want to read the delightful tale of the Lorax and the Once-Ler at the far end of town where the grickle grass grows. What I'm referring to, of course, is the *The Lorax* by the incomparable Dr. Seuss. It's a delightful tale that demonstrates to young readers what happens to the land and air and the delightful species that inhabit our world when human greed runs roughshod over the landscape.

You can also draw on modern examples. For instance, we know that many women in villages in less developed nations such as India, Bangladesh, and Somalia spend most of their waking hours in search of firewood. They may wander 16 to 20 miles (25.6 to 32 kilometers) each day to gather twigs to fuel the cook fire. Why? Over the years, the landscape has been denuded by women seeking firewood, forcing them farther and farther from their villages. Not all examples will come from the less developed nations. There are countless instances of humans exceeding very real limits. Many coastal fishing villages along the northeastern United States and in eastern Canada, for example, have turned belly up in the past decade because of overfishing — the relentless over-harvesting of cod. Some wilderness areas in Colorado have become so crowded that backpackers have to obtain permits to camp in them. Permits limit numbers. Huge areas of the West like New Mexico's Rio Puerco basin, once a rich grassland, were denuded by overgrazing in the 1800s. Many other western grasslands have met a similar fate. In fact, when you drive by acre after acre of sage brush in the wide open West, don't presume that it always looked as parched and scraggly as it does now. Much of it was once rich grassland. The sage was introduced by sheep introduced from abroad as seeds were carried here in their wooly coats. Now sage thrives in the heavily overgrazed land.

A good environmental science textbook should have countless examples that you can study and relay to your children. Again, you might want to pick up a copy of my text, *Environmental Science: Creating a Sustainable Future*. Most of the examples in this and competing titles illustrate frontier ethics in operation: the belief that there's always more, and its all for us; that we're apart from nature; and that domination and control lead to success.

I've included a piece on the world's fisheries in this chapter that you can read to your children. You can use it to discuss the values that have led to this tragedy.

MODELS OF SUSTAINABILITY: MINING HUMAN WASTES TO FEED THE HUMAN POPULATION

Fish are a popular source of protein in many countries. Today, in fact, the world's fishing fleets catch over 110 million tons (100 million metric tons) of fish from the world's oceans each year. This is made possible because of advanced technologies such as sonar, which help fishing fleets find and capture fish.

Unfortunately, commercial overfishing has depleted several dozen of the world's richest fisheries in the Atlantic ocean alone, areas of the ocean that once served up huge fish catches. Many other fisheries are now in danger. In fact, of the world's 15 major oceanic fisheries, 11 are in decline. So heavily harvested are many of these fisheries that if we stopped fishing immediately, it would take them from 5 to 20 years to recover.

Overfishing has had a ripple effect on other species, reducing populations of seals and other fish-eating animals. So not only are we threatening our own food supply, we're eliminating the supply of the many species that share this planet with us.

If you're not convinced, just look at a list of the fish species that were popular in 1970. On the list of the top ten species you will see Peruvian anchovies, Atlantic cod, Alaska pollock, Atlantic herring, Cape hake, Atlantic mackerel, and a number of others.

Twenty years later, however, only three of the ten species are still on the list. The others have been driven into near extinction. In their place is a whole new set of fish, many also being heavily overfished.

Top 10 Species by Weight, 1970, 1980, and 1992 (catch in million tons)

1970		1980		1992	
1. Peruvian anchovy	13.1	1. Alaska pollock	4.0	1. Peruvian anchovy	5.5
2. Atlantic cod	3.1	2. South American		2. Alaskan pollock	5.0
3. Alaska pollock	3.1	pilchard	3.3	3. Chilean jack	
4. Atlantic herring	2.3	3. Chub mackerel	2.7	mackerel	3.4
5. Chub mackerel	2.0	4. Japanese pilchard	2.6	4. South American	
6. Capelin	1.5	5. Capelin	2.6	pilchard	3.1
7. Haddock	0.9	6. Atlantic cod	2.2	5. Japanese pilchard	2.5
8. Cape hake	0.8	7. Chilean jack		6. Capelin	2.1
9. Atlantic mackerel	0.7	mackerel	1.3	7. Silver carp	1.6
10. Saithe	0.6	8. Blue whiting	1.1	8. Atlantic herring	1.5
		9. European pilchard	0.9	9. Skipjack tuna	1.4
		10. Atlantic herring	0.9	10. Grass carp*	1.3

Source: UN Food and Agricultural Organization.

*Raised on freshwater fish farms; all others are wild marine species.

Unfortunately, the story does not end here. Each year, millions of tons of fish netted by commercial fishing operations are thrown overboard because they are the wrong species or sex or are too small. This is called "by-catch," the numbers can be staggering. Each pound (0.45 kilograms) of shrimp captured from the sea, for example, results in 5 pounds (2.25 kilograms) of dead sea life — other oceanic creatures destroyed during shrimp harvest.

International fishing regulations require that by-catch be thrown overboard, to "protect" various species and populations. Why?

Undersized fish represent the future generations — the youngsters that will grow to become adults that will someday replenish their kind. Non-target species such as these are called bycatch.

Throwing them overboard is a good thing, yes?

Well, maybe not.

As it turns out, most of the fish are dead *before* they hit the water.

Some commercial fishing interests believe that they should be allowed to sell the bycatch for food. Fish discarded each year in Alaskan waters, they argue, could provide an estimated 50 million meals.

Sound reasonable?

It may be, but if regulations allowed bycatch to be kept and sold, some critics contend that there would be no way to keep unethical companies from catching whatever they wanted, wiping out important fisheries. The answer, they say, is in developing better fishing gear that eliminates undersized fish.

We can also turn to fish farming — growing fish and shellfish — to increase food production. Fish and shellfish can be raised in artificial environments such as ponds or in natural bodies of water (for example, in bays where they are contained by nets) then harvested for food when they've reached market size. Worldwide, fish farms produce about 24 million tons (22 million metric tons) of food a year.

Important as it is, fish farming is not without its problems. Fish need to be fed, for example, and fish food needs to be grown. That takes resources and a considerable amount of energy. Moreover, fish in ponds produce lots of waste that can pollute the waters into which their ponds are emptied, waters that we may eventually drink from or swim in, or upon which species depend.

There is an environmentally sustainable way to raise fish for human consumption, however. Consider the work of a group called ZERI, an acronym that stands for Zero Emissions Research and Initiatives, founded by Gunter Pauli, a European businessman with a firm commitment to the environment. Pauli's organization is pioneering an ecosystems approach to raising fish — and many other foods as well — for human consumption in ways that do not harm the environment and, preferably, enhance it. His group helps people in less developed nations utilize waste from one activity, for example, brewing beer, to produce fish, fruit, vegetables, and animal food.

At the Monfort Boys' School, a Catholic technical school in the island nation of Fiji, located in the Pacific north of New Zealand, officials use waste grain from a local commercial brewery to feed an entire human-made ecosystem, reaping a huge profit in the process. The waste grain begins its travel through this human-made food chain as a substrate for a commercial mushroom venture. It could be fed directly to livestock such as pigs, but the waste grain is not well digested as is. Enzymes released by the mushrooms, however, render the waste more digestible. So once the school has harvested the mushrooms, the biologically processed waste grain is mixed with pig food and fed to the hogs. Waste grain is also mixed with duck and chicken feed, cutting down the need to purchase expensive feed for them as well.

Hogs are occasionally slaughtered and the meat is sold or eaten by the school's 100 students. But that's not the end of the story. In fact, it is only the beginning.

Waste from the pigpens is washed out twice daily and drains into a huge settling tank. Here, the waste is broken down by anaerobic bacteria, microorganisms that break down organic material in the absence of oxygen. One by-product of this process is methane, a combustible gas that can be burned to produce light and to cook food. The farm produces enough methane for a family of six.

The sludge is drawn off by bucket and used to fertilize crops — bananas and various vegetables — that are then sold or consumed by the students. Liquid waste from the settling tank is then fed into a series of settling ponds where naturally occurring algae consume much of the nitrogen and phosphorus in the waste. The algae-rich water is then delivered to a fish pond containing six different species of fish. The fish consume the algae, living entirely off this free food source. At the end of each year, the fish are harvested and sold for food. Interestingly, ducks and chickens, which are fed waste grain, are raised in pens suspended over the fish ponds. Their waste freely drops into the ponds, adding additional nutrients to the waters. In this ecological production system, all waste is food for something else.

At one time, waste from the hog farm polluted nearby mangrove swamps, killing aquatic life. Today, when the water leaves this facility, it is so clean that the nearby mangrove swamps are showing promising signs of recovery. Species of fish and crabs nearly wiped out by pollution are now returning.

Besides producing food from waste, this farm also generates a fair amount of income. This system, in fact, can produce an annual income of as much as

$60,000 for a family of six, working a half a day a week each! Compare that to the typical income of a worker in the less developed world, averaging about $2,000 a year. Needless to say, this system is being seriously considered by a great many people in other countries.

What can you and your family do to help save endangered fish populations?

One thing that will help immediately is to buy fish whose populations are not in danger. See the Monterey Aquarium's website for a list of fish ("Seafood Watch") that you can eat without guilt. It can be found online at <www.mbayaq.org>.

Another important step you can take is to cut down on shrimp consumption, or avoid it altogether. Shrimp harvesting is one of the most environmentally damaging activities in which humans engage. Trawlers drag huge nets along the bottom of the ocean, scooping up shrimp and a host of other sea creatures. As noted earlier, for every pound of shrimp that is harvested, there are five pounds (2.25 kilograms) of other sea life that are swept up. Most are dead before they are thrown back overboard. Shrimp nets also scrape up the bottom of the ocean, removing plants and leaving the ocean floor in a state of ecological disarray.

Another thing you can do is to purchase fish raised on the farm — fish farm, that is.

Yet another option is for us to eat lower on the food chain. Most Americans eat far more meat protein than they need. By reducing fish and other meats from the diet, or eliminating them, we can reduce our demand on fish farms and natural fisheries. A good vegetarian diet can provide all of the protein one needs.

THE GENTLE ART OF PERSUASION:
LET THEM DO THE THINKING

Another opportunity for teaching values may come when you and your children listen to the evening news. Here, you can help point out the disregard for limits that pervades our thinking. When listening to a news story about energy — for example, drilling in the Arctic National Wildlife Refuge, or attempts to solve troubles such as the blackout that affected 50 million people in the northeast United States and southeastern Canada in the summer of 2003. You might ask, "I wonder if we ought to be looking for ways to save energy rather than trying to produce more?" Let that sink in, then ask, "If we were more efficient in energy use, we could meet our needs without having to open up a wildlife refuge to development. We wouldn't have to spoil the Arctic Wildlife Refuge. Don't those animals have a right to live, too? Where can they go if we destroy their home?" Or you might ask, "I wonder if solar energy could be used to heat homes instead of natural gas or oil?" It's a cleaner way to achieve the same goal, and cheaper, too. We would be able to meet our needs without polluting the air and destroying ecosystems that other species rely on. Solar seems to be a much more planet-friendly way of meeting our electrical energy needs, doesn't it?

In Colorado, severe drought in the late 1990s and early 2000s sent cities and towns in search of ways to meet the state's ever-growing water demands. One proposal Governor Bill Owens advanced was to clearcut huge patches of forest — turning the mountains into a mosaic of clearcuts — to increase runoff. When I talked with my children about this I said, "What if this happened, what would the state look like?" They thought about it for a while and gave me some answers.

"Pretty yucky," my twelve-year-old son said.

I then added, "Maybe this plan would increase stream flow and increase our water supply, but do you think it might also increase flooding during the spring snow melt? And what about the animals that would lose their homes by clearcutting? Wouldn't it be easier if we insisted on planting grass that thrives on much less water than Kentucky bluegrass which needs 50 to 60 inches (127 to 154 centimeters) of rain each year in a climate that gets only about 15 inches (38 centimeters)? Wouldn't it be easier if we found other ways to cut our water usage — like watering early or late in the day? Did you know that watering during the heat of the day can result in half of the water evaporating?"

After the devastating forest fires of 2002, many hard-hit states and the U.S. Forest Service developed plans to prevent future fires, most of which involved efforts to thin forests and reduce undergrowth. Very little thought was given to the root cause of the problem: global warming, which had caused record-breaking temperatures, droughts, and extremely dry forests for five years in a row. You could ask your kids, "Wouldn't it be better if we got to the root of the problem, and found ways to reduce carbon dioxide emissions? What can our family do to help make this happen?"

The key to helping children develop environmental values is to let them do the thinking. Rather than trying to persuade them to believe what you want them to believe through lecturing, let your children ponder potential answers. Let them grapple with ethics and solutions. You become a consultant, of sorts, helping guide them to good ethics and good decisions.

Bear in mind, while many of the ideas in this section have been about inspiring children to think more deeply and to come up with alternative solutions, they are also about teaching children sustainable values. Here are some

> *The key to helping children develop environmental values is to let your children do the thinking.*

questions you can ask to encourage your children to think about each of the underlying tenets of sustainable ethics.

To emphasize the first tenet of sustainable ethics — the Earth has a limited supply of resources to be shared by all species — you can offer in comments like, "Eventually, we're going to run out of oil." Or, "How can we continue to pollute the air? There is only so much of it." Or, "Can we continue to destroy wildlife habitat? If we do, what will be left for the animals?" Or, "Don't other species have a right to clean air and clean water? Don't they have a right to exist?"

To emphasize that humans are a part of nature, you can say, "Polluting the environment hurts us in the long run. People are dying from pollution. Pollution destroys our forests and food crops. What we do to the Earth, we do to ourselves. We need the Earth."

My favorites are: "We only have one Earth," and "Good planets are hard to come by."

To emphasize that we can succeed by cooperating with nature, you can say, "I'll bet there's a better way to do that. What about farming organically? I hear that eliminates pesticide use, but still gets food on our plates." Or, "What if more of us rode the bus or light rail to work each day? What if the buses were powered by hydrogen made from water?" Or, "What about recycling all of our garbage? We'd do a lot less damage to the environment, and it would create many jobs in the recycling industry to replace those lost elsewhere."

HELPING YOUR CHILDREN CLARIFY THEIR VALUES

I recall my early years as a college professor vividly. Although the times were exciting, there were difficult moments. One of them came when, as a teacher of environmental science, I had to grapple with ethics. I was growing pretty comfortable with the science and even the public policy aspects of environmental issues, but had given very little thought to ethics. It became obvious to me, however, that ethics had to be a part of the classroom discussions, too.

The reason for my discomfort came primarily because I didn't think scientists needed to ponder such things. That's foolishness, of course, but I was young and, frankly, I hadn't spent much time ... well ... to be honest ... had spent very little time ... well, okay, I'll be really honest...hadn't spent any time clarifying my own values. The thought of uncovering my value system seemed mind-boggling. I'd never studied ethics in college, nor even heard it talked about. It's a subject avoided assiduously in public schools for fear of stepping on parents' toes or violating the separation of church and state (because so many values have a religious connection, I suppose). As a Boy Scout I had learned to recite our credo: A Scout is trustworthy, loyal, helpful, friendly, courteous, kind, obedient, cheerful, thrifty, brave, clean, and reverent. No one, however, ever sat down with us and said, "Hey, these are values we're trying to teach you. Values we think are important." To me, they were just a bunch of words that rolled off my tongue like saliva in one of Pavlov's dogs after he rang the bell.

You can help your children avoid this problem by talking with them about values as soon as they are able to understand such things. You might say, for example, "Did you know that people have values, beliefs that profoundly affect their actions and decisions?" If your child gives you a perplexed look, you might say, "Well, I notice how well you take care of your parakeet. You must value that bird. It is important that your bird is well taken care of. Living things are important to you, so you take care of them. That's a value."

Or you might approach it through other values. For example, "Your daddy and I value honesty. You know how we always tell you that it is better to tell the truth when you do something wrong than to lie about it. That's because we think it is always important to be honest. We value honesty."

"We value the Earth, too. That's why we recycle and shut off the lights. We don't want to damage the Earth. There are lots of animals and plants that would be killed by pollution, and recycling and shutting off lights helps reduce pollution. So that's why we do it. And you will have a better Earth if we all act responsibly now."

Obviously, the older the child, the more you can ramp up the conversation — moving from basic values articulated simply to more sophisticated values in a language that is appropriate for your child.

"As you go through life," you might tell your child, "you will learn lots of values. Some people value money. They will do almost anything for money. Sometimes they do careless things that can damage the Earth and the many species that live here with us. For example, they might leave the lights on when they're out or buy too many things. It doesn't seem like much, but all of these little things add up."

You get the idea.

As your children grow, work with them on values. Help them understand how values direct our lives, and what values you're trying to teach them. Don't insist that they adopt your values; just tell them what you believe, and why you believe it. Let them know that their values are theirs to create and that they'll learn values from teachers, friends, ministers, and even television and books they read. Some values might be detrimental to them or to the Earth, too.

It's important for children to learn to draw on their values when they make decisions. It's also important that they know that people often have conflicting values. We might value the Earth, but also value our family's recreation and time together. These don't have to be conflicting though. Instead of flying halfway around the world to visit the Galapagos Islands as a family, maybe a camping trip to a nearby state park or a nearby wilderness area might be a better alternative. Your family could tune into a special on the Galapagos Islands on the National Geographic Channel, and curb their desire to actually go there because of the jet fuel that would be required to transport you *en masse* to this marvelous place.

KNOW THYSELF

As a final note on this subject, it may seem preposterous to suggest that before you actually start teaching your values to your child, you spend some time exploring them yourself. Make a list of your values — those standards by which you judge your own and other's behaviors.

When making a list, you may want to look for potential inconsistencies. For example, do you have two standards of honesty? Do you hold one standard of honesty for the family and another slightly malleable version for business transactions or the Internal Revenue Service?

For additional ideas on teaching values to your children, you may want to pick up a copy of Linda and Richard Eyre's *Teaching Your Children Values*. It includes a time-tested method of teaching values that you might like, and some very thoughtful comments on values in general that may be helpful to adults. Jamie Miller's *10-Minute Life Lessons for Kids* is another valuable resource. While both books deal with general values, such as honesty and respect, and fail to address environmental values, these values will surely influence the way your child treats other people *and* the environment. The techniques for teaching values, which both books offer, may be useful to you as a parent. In addition, both books could help you promote values that contribute to sound character development, which in turn helps children resist the barrage of negative influences in our modern lives.

LIVING WITH SUSTAINABLE VALUES

The challenge for all of us who think and act sustainably is that we're a relatively small minority. Despite the polls that suggest our fellow earthlings are solidly behind the environmental movement, we live amongst a vast population of people that don't live environmentally sensitive lifestyles. It's their actions that express how much they care. It's not what they say, but what they do that casts their vote for or against the planet.

Teaching your child sustainable values that oppose mainstream thinking could be a dangerous proposition. As much as we brag about our independence and cherish free thought and free speech, we humans do like to fit in. When given the freedom to do as we wish, we often dance the same dance as our neighbors. Marketers are having a field day with our seemingly insatiable need to be just like everyone else — and they're finding ways to make us feel really special when we are.

Let's face it, mainstream America, despite its protestations to the contrary, doesn't like people who think differently. By instilling environmental values in our children, we could be setting them up to be ridiculed. It all depends on how vulnerable your children are to peer pressure and to what others think. Some kids take pride in thinking differently. I was that kind of child. Fitting in wasn't that appealing. I'm like that as an adult, though maybe not as extreme. For me, holding values that could be characterized as "counterculture" wasn't and still isn't all that difficult (although it does get me into trouble from time to time.) It engendered a sense of pride.

As a parent, you can prepare your children for life in the real world by cueing them in to what they might expect. Let them know that their opinions about alternative ways of living are not widely accepted. You can give them a little pride and hope for the future by quoting Emerson: "Every reform was once a private opinion," and saying, "We're that private opinion that Emerson talked about." Or, "We're on the cutting edge. Someday, they'll all get it. Isn't it great to be on the leading edge?" While kids do like to fit in, they also like to feel different, special. This is one way they can distinguish themselves.

You can also help your child learn ways to express opposing opinions without getting a black eye. Some opinions they may simply want to keep to themselves. I tell my children, "Well, you might not want to get into it with other kids. They come from very different backgrounds. I wouldn't make a big deal out of it. Live the way you want, and let them live the way they want. Don't judge them as bad. They're just living their lives the way they were taught."

Other children may want to be more on the forefront, even confrontational, convincing their peers of the correctness of their viewpoints. Here, the gentle art of persuasion might work best. Teach them to ask questions. "Wouldn't it be better if we recycled these pop cans rather than throwing them by the side of the road?" Or, "Wouldn't it be better if we walked to the skate park, rather than getting a ride from one of our parents?" Or, "We're eventually going to run out of oil, so wouldn't it be better if we found environmentally friendly alternatives now?"

Like many of us, our kids may become impatient with the slow pace of change and the general resistance to the adoption of good ideas. You can help them develop patience with statements like, "We're doing everything we can as a family to make changes, but these things take time. Don't be too impatient with your friends or teachers."

It is important for us to teach our children to be loving and understanding, not judgmental and derisive. From a practical standpoint, we'll win more converts with love and compassion than bitterness and disdain for those who do not subscribe to sustainable ethics. This approach will also make your children's lives easier. They'll be happier in the long run if they're not turned into misanthropes. They'll be far more powerful forces if they approach the task of building a sustainable future with kindness, respect, and tolerance.

ABOVE ALL, BE PATIENT

Albert Einstein was a scientist with values. He understood the importance of living lives directed consciously by values. Environmental values are more important today than at any time in human history, as our population and economy expand and as technology moves forward, advancing rapidly year after year, posing new dangers to the life-support system of the planet. Indeed, we have become the victims of the instruments we've created. Today, as Lewis Mumford writes, "Every gain in power, every mastery of natural forces, every scientific addition to knowledge, has proved potentially dangerous, because it has not been accompanied by equal gains in self-understanding and self-discipline." Self-discipline must come, in large part, from values that we teach our children, values that respect the Earth, recognize the importance of nature, and help us seek to live harmoniously.

> *It is important for us to teach our children to be loving and understanding, not judgmental or derisive. From a practical standpoint, we'll win more converts with loving compassion than bitterness and disdain for those who do not subscribe to sustainable ethics.*

Not all children will respond to your gentle and persistent nudgings, but if you start when they're young, you've got a good chance your kids will adopt the values you hold. At the very least, kids will get the message that certain ideals are important to you, if you remain persistent. As Foster Cline and Jim Fay write in

Parenting Teens with Love and Logic, "Parents often don't know this, but patience is one of the best qualities for enduring a values battle. Long before your teens turn thirty, they will wake up and discover that they hold many of the same values as you do!"

A WORD OF CAUTION

In her book, *Raising Kids Who Will Make a Difference,* Susan Vogt tells a story of two parents who raised their kids to live simply. They modeled frugality, spent lots of time with their children, cooked from scratch, made their own bread, and even went without a TV. Unfortunately, one of the couple's children seemed to reject their values. The parents were crestfallen when their daughter announced that she'd be sure to be rich when she grew up, apparently so she wouldn't have to suffer the deprivations of their family.

> *"Parents often don't know this, but patience is one of the best qualities for enduring a values battle. Long before your teens turn thirty, they will wake up and discover that they hold many of the same values as you do!"*

"Be careful how you express your most dearly held values," warns Vogt in response to this story. "Because of the strength of these convictions, parents are tempted to impose them rigidly, and in an extreme way on their children. During the early teen years, young people often choose to assert their independence in this area."

"As a result of observing our friends," Vogt notes, "we decided to be cautious about how vigorously we enforced countercultural values. It doesn't mean that we gave up on the values, but rather we tried to listen hard to our children's deeper needs and make adjustments where appropriate."

Here's the rub: like many parents, you probably want to raise your children to be independent thinkers. However, independent thinking may come back to you now and again like a bullet ricocheting off a rock. The sting may be profound. You may be left with a feeling of failure. Maybe they're just not getting the message. Remember, though, teenagers assert their independence in part by thinking their own thoughts. A lot of the time all they're doing when they express alternative viewpoints is trying out new values or ideas.

Resist the temptation to "go ballistic" when your children announces they subscribe to a value that differs sharply from yours. Remember: They may simply be trying out a new idea. Remember, too: you probably did it when you were growing up. You read something, thought it was a good idea, then took it for a test-drive. Your new idea may have fallen apart under more intense scrutiny, but you had to give it a test-drive nonetheless. As a young adult, I read a piece in *Scientific American* on nuclear power, and was convinced that this was a wonderful technology. A few years later, as I began to study it, I realized that the troubles of this "remarkable technology" far outweighed its benefits. Today, I view it as one of the most potentially damaging technologies we humans have developed.

Give your kids the same opportunities to experiment with and adopt values on their own. And remember, too, that although they may come up with different values, if you have done a good job, they will have come to their values consciously with a basis for comparison. Who knows, maybe later in life, they'll realize they like yours better.

Unfortunately, we parents often don't know if we have made a difference, if we're doing things correctly, until our children have grown up.

My advice is: do your best, and hope for the best.

Frankly, there's not much more a parent can do.

KIDS WHO ARE MAKING A DIFFERENCE
JUSTIN LEBO: BUILDING BIKES FOR A BETTER WORLD

At age ten, Justin Lebo from Paterson, New Jersey, bought an old beat up 20-inch BMX bicycle at a garage sale and took it home, hoping that he could bring the bike back to life. It would be no small feat. As Phillip Hoose, who writes about the boy's adventure in *It's Our World, Too!* points out, "Everything — the grips, the pedals, the brakes, the seat, the spokes — was bent or broken, twisted or rusted."

Fortunately Justin and his dad were quite familiar with bike repair. Both were fond of bike racing and they had a garage full of tools and bike parts, accumulated from their many hours of working on bikes. The two immersed themselves in this latest project and within two weeks they were done. Justin hopped on the bike and gave it a spin. Although it rode well, it was a far cry from the bikes he raced.

He put the bike aside. The next week Justin bought another bike in similar condition and fixed it up. "After a while," writes Hoose, "it bothered him that he wasn't really using either bike." The thrill, he discovered was not in riding the bikes, but rather in rebuilding them — making them useful.

A short while later, Justin came up with an idea about what to do with the bikes. He decided to give them away to the Kilbarchan Home for Boys. He and his family had lived nearby at one time, so he phoned the director and asked if he could donate two refurbished bikes to the school.

A few days later, he and his mother delivered them. Seeing the joy on the faces of the two boys who rode the bikes and realizing that the rest of the boys in the home might want bikes as well, Justin returned home with a new mission: to build a bike for every boy in the home by Christmas, which was only six months away.

Justin quickly realized the enormity of the task. To get the parts he needed, he would need at least three or four bikes for every bike he would donate. Buying the bikes, even from garage sales, would cost a fortune. So he asked his parents to help with the financing of this project. They agreed to match every dollar of his allowance that he spent on buying used bikes with a dollar of their own.

Justin and his mother spent most of the next two months scouring garage sales and thrift shops looking for bikes for his new venture. By the first of August, though, he had only assembled ten bikes. School would be starting soon and he'd be gone most of the day and at night he would have homework and a lot less free time. Clearly, he was in a jam, but then a neighbor of his wrote a letter to the local newspaper explaining what Justin was up to.

From that point on, the project snowballed. "People would call me up and ask me to come over and pick up their old bike. Or I'd be working in the garage and a station wagon would pull up. The driver would leave a couple of bikes by the curb," remarks Justin. Soon the family's garage, shed, and backyard were jam packed with broken down bicycles.

The press coverage snowballed, too, and soon Justin had offers of more bikes and cash to help purchase bikes as well as parts in bulk to expedite the process. A week before Christmas this ambitious young boy delivered the last of the 21 bicycles he had promised — much to the delight of the boys at the home. After he'd delivered the bikes, the joy of the boys reminded Justin "how important bikes were to him. Wheels meant freedom. He thought how much more the freedom to ride must mean to boys like these who had so little freedom in their lives. So, he decided to keep on building," writes Hoose.

And make bikes he did. Justin went on to make 11 bikes for a foster home his mother had mentioned to him. He made bikes for the women in a battered woman's shelter and then made bikes and tricycles for the children in a home for children with AIDS. He then made 23 bikes for the Paterson Housing Coalition. In four years, Justin rebuilt somewhere between 150 and 200 bikes, all of which he donated. Why?

"Once I overheard a kid who got one of my bikes say, 'A bike is like a book. It opens up a whole new world.' That's how I feel, too. It made me happy to know that kid felt that way. That's why I do it."

Giving such as this is often considered a sacrifice. I like to think of it differently. It is not giving *up*, it's giving *to* the community and ourselves. As Henry Ward Beecher once noted, "It's not what we take up but what we give up that makes us rich." The world would be a whole lot better if we all realized these things.

For a more detailed account, see Philip Hoose, *It's Our World Too!* Farrar, Straus and Giroux, 1993.

POST SCRIPT

One thing I'd like to point out before moving on to the topic of consumerism is that environmental values are often viewed as inimical to the interests of most people. We hear it all the time from people who have a limited understanding of the importance of the Earth's ecosystems to our present and future.

The fact is, values that promote a sustainable future are values that could help us build a stronger country and a better future. They could help create broader prosperity, too. By using resources efficiently, for instance, to honor the limits of nature, all of us will have more money at the end of the month. These funds could be set aside for college educations, vacations with our families, unforeseen medical expenses, or even retirement.

Energy efficiency measures and the values that underlie our interest in these activities — a recognition of limits and a desire to live in harmony with nature — are particularly important as the end of cheap oil is upon us, in large part because global production of oil either has just peaked or may soon peak. Global natural gas production is following quickly in its footsteps.

Environmental values could help us ease our way through potentially devastating economic times. It could make the transition to a renewable future much less painful. It could help foster economic stability *for all of us*.

In contrast, if oil and natural gas prices rise many people will likely suffer. Wealthy individuals, however, are likely to be able to garner the resources they need to continue their prosperity. By practicing frugality and other important principles like recycling, many people can be saved from difficult times that lie ahead. Environmental values — humans are a part of nature, the Earth has a limited supply of resources, and the importance of working with nature — could help promote broader prosperity. It won't be only the rich who survive.

All of this — the values and the activities that put our values into action — is about forging a better future. What could be more in line with people's personal interests than that?

FAMILY ACTIVITIES

Below is a list of possible activities for children of various ages. You will very likely need to tailor some of these activities to your children, simplifying them for younger children, for instance.

1. Over dinner or while taking a family trip, open up the subject of values. Help your children understand that people have values — things they view as right or wrong — and that these values come from many different sources. You may want to share some of your values. You can explain how you learned them.
2. Ask your children what their values are — and what they value. They may not have many ideas if they are young. If so, you can help them clarify their values by asking questions: Do you value honesty? Do you value the environment? Don't be judgmental if you hear values that do not coincide with yours. Remind your children to be thinking about their values as they grow up. They should be able to articulate their values. Explain how a clear understanding of one's values can help them in life.
3. Work with your children to understand how values can get in the way of good decisions. For example, how valuing money can sometimes sabotage decisions about environmental protection.
4. Outline the frontier ethics described in this chapter, for example, over dinner or while in the car. You might read the section on this topic to your child, depending on his or her age. Explore each one individually for the most impact. Ask your child what he or she thinks about these values. Ask him or her how these values might stand in the way of environmental goals.
5. Describe the sustainable ethics outlined in this chapter, one at a time. Ask your son or daughter how these values might change the way our society operates — how we live and how we conduct business.

6. Explore the notion of cooperating with nature, giving examples like solar energy, and asking your child to offer other examples of ways we can meet our needs in ways that do not harm the Earth.

7. Tell stories about limits — how people have exceeded the Earth's natural limits. You might use examples like ozone depletion, global warming and climate change, acid rain, and world hunger. You can even use local examples or personal examples. You may want to read the first chapter of Al Gore's book, *Earth in the Balance*, which describes countless civilizations that have toppled because they have exceeded the Earth's ability to supply resources. You may also want to read the case study in this chapter about the depletion of ocean fisheries.

8. For young children, you may want to read Dr. Seuss's book, *The Lorax*. You can discuss how this happens in the real world, giving a few examples.

9. Describe the critical thinking rules outlined in this chapter to your children, one at a time, over dinner or while on a trip. Then work with them (for example, after watching the evening news) to apply these rules.

10. Talk to your children about their need to fit in with their peers and what values they adopt when doing so. You may want to examine those values with respect to sustainable values. Ask your child how he or she can hold sustainable values, yet still be part of the community of kids or, later as adults, how they can belong to society while holding alternative values.

Excess kills more than the sword.
— The Bible

5 AFFLUENZA, TELEVISION, AND YOUR CHILD

Many years ago, while touring the South Island of New Zealand, I met a delightful ten-year-old boy who was camping with his family. This engaging and talkative lad stuck to my wife and me like a fly to maple syrup, obviously delighted to be in the presence of a couple of Americans.

As we walked along the windy beach that day in December (their spring), he proclaimed proudly, "I know all about you Americans."

"What do you know about us?" I quizzed.

"You've got heaps of money and you all carry guns," was his response.

I laughed, and asked him where he had acquired his insight into American culture.

"From the telly."

"Of course, the telly," I murmured.

"Dallas and Miami Vice," he explained.

I laughed again and showed him that I wasn't packing a gun, and didn't even own one. Then I assured him that very few of us had bucketloads of money in the trunks of our cars.

On that windswept beach on the South Island of New Zealand, I learned a valuable lesson: Television broadcasts images of American culture throughout the world, offering glimpses of what life is like in this massive and diverse nation.

Exaggerated as some images may be, they stick in the minds of others, shaping how they view our nation.

Since then I've learned that television is more than a mere conveyor of our culture; it is a cultural icon. For the lonely among us, television is an electronic surrogate for human companionship. For the frazzled and hassled, it provides solace and soothes raw nerves. And in recent years, it has occurred to me that for businesses like local restaurants, whose many TVs blare day and night, it serves to bring the familiar to strange surroundings, making customers feel at home when they're out to eat. The television is also a whittler of time, as it helps us while away the hours, entertaining us and occupying our minds with its often silly entertainment.

With programming to suit every conceivable taste, made possible by cable and satellite technology, television helps to keep us from wandering into serious thought while we're waiting in airports, tire shops, and bars. Like a cancer, television is metastasizing to every public place you can imagine. I counted 27 televisions in a small sports bar I passed by in an airport not too long ago!

And, oh yes, television is a messenger, delivering us the daily news, keeping us informed of who is killing whom these days.

But TV is more.

It also shapes culture, transforming us — and our children — in ways we're not always aware of, ways that we might not tacitly approve of. Put another way, television shapes our values — and profoundly affects our children — in a variety of ways, as you shall soon see. However, it is the advertising on television — the financial underpinning of all stations — that has the most powerful (some say dangerous) influence on our culture, molding our and our children's values, wants, and consumption patterns.

Don't get me wrong: Television has the potential to deliver much good that could, in turn, lead to a better world, and occasionally it does achieve this laudable goal. From an environmental standpoint, however, television seems to be a lead weight on our society, dragging our culture downward. It does this in at least two ways. First, television fosters a hazardous addiction to economic growth. Second, it promotes reckless spending and levels of consumption that not only erode our pocketbooks but rob us of the planet's true riches. In the process, it is undermining our future with a force as powerful as a chain saw in the flank of an old-growth tree. A dire pronouncement, you say?

Maybe, but not when you pause for a moment to see television — especially the advertising that pays for all of the programming — for what it is: a purveyor of values and ideas that steer our society hopelessly along the path of ever-increasing production and consumption.

Over the years, television has become a finely orchestrated weapon of commerce, parading an endless supply of goods and services before the consuming public through advertisements, shopping channels, and nightly infomercials. It promotes a spendthrift society, while providing ready access to the means to finance the consumption frenzy, notably, credit cards and home equity loans galore that make buying easier and easier by the day. Television is a temptress in a black box, an alluring advocate of heedless spending that provides a convenient outlet for satisfying the consumer passions it stirs.

Advertising preys upon adults and victimizes our children, steering them — and without their knowledge — into a lifetime of high-speed consumption, hyperconsumption, if you will. In the process, television stimulates unsustainable spending patterns that could put many of our children in deep debt before they graduate from college.

> *Television is a temptress in a black box, an alluring advocate of heedless spending that provides a convenient outlet for satisfying the consumer passions it stirs.*

American spending and consumption are driven by continuous population growth and our ever-escalating appetite for the constantly expanding array of goods and services made available to us by corporations and their partners in "consumer crime," the advertisers.

Over a few short decades, consumerism has become a runaway train with potentially devastating environmental repercussions. Uncontrollable consumption, a disease producers Robert de Graaf and Vivia Boe called *Affluenza* in their film of the same name is a frontal assault on the planet and its finite resources. The outward manifestations of this infectious disease spreading through society are the clear cuts and mines that scar the Earth's surface; the toxic pollutants seeping into groundwaters and poisoning drinking water wells; acid rain falling on farms, fields, and forests and percolating into our lakes and streams, killing fish and other aquatic species; holes in the Earth's protective ozone layer; frightening changes in the climate; and rapidly declining species, to name a few. These symptoms of affluenza result from the endless expansion of mining, clear cutting, oil drilling, and a proliferation of factories hell-bent on turning the Earth's natural capital into goods that fuel consumer fever — many of them short-lived products of questionable value.

How does TV do all this?

THE MEDIA, YOUR CHILD, AND YOU, THE UNWITTING ENABLER

Most critics of television and other media — newspapers, magazines, radio, and the Internet — who care about values and the outcomes they generate in our children, focus on the pernicious effects of advertising.

THE ADVERTISING AGGRANDIZEMENT

Our nation is becoming a giant commercial advertisement. Advertisers, it seems, are working behind the scenes with extreme diligence to paste their messages on every square inch of the Earth's surface, from billboards to magazines to newspapers to the floors of grocery stores. Everywhere we look we encounter their carefully crafted enticements, meant to persuade us to buy more and more of their wares. Advertisers have taken over the airways, hawking their goods and services on radio and television. Like other forms of media, radio and television now air a dizzying assortment of commercials custom-made — often with the help of highly paid psychologists — to convince us that our lives would be better, more convenient, more comfortable, and more luxurious, and that we'd be prettier, handsomer, stronger, more respected and well liked, if we'd just buy their products. They prey on our weaknesses — our insecurities — and promise the moon to those who heed their "message." (Stations don't even pause for commercials anymore; they pause for "messages.")

Hard as it is for adults to resist the temptations, it's even more difficult for our children, a vulnerable subset of our citizenry, viewed as a huge potential market ripe for the picking. At least adults can reason that the products whose virtues are extolled in the barrage of TV advertisements might not perform as well as depicted or might not deliver the tangible and intangible benefits implicitly and explicitly stated in this onslaught. Children haven't got a chance — nor, for that matter, has the planet. Especially frightening is the future impact of the young hyperconsumers now being groomed by advertisers for a lifetime of profligate spending. Gullible and highly trainable, children fall victim to corporate America's newest brainchild, "cradle-to-grave advertising." When our children reach adulthood and can fully unleash their consumer passions, the planet will very likely be in a shambles.

How do we know advertising works?

Look in your child's room. Look under the Christmas tree. Look at the aisles in kids' stores. Look at your credit card account. Chances are you're still paying for a present or two that's currently gathering dust in a corner of your child's room. And look at our children: Many of them begin recognizing logos and singing jingles at an extremely young age. Teachers in preschools throughout the nation, in fact, often remark that our children are more likely to know a commercial jingle than a traditional song. Even "Twinkle Twinkle Little Star" and the alphabet song play second fiddle to commercial jingles!

Marketers are working to achieve brand loyalty by the age of two, according to Betsy Taylor founder and president of the Center for a New American Dream and author of *What Kids Really Want That Money Can't Buy*. According to Taylor, more than one in five parents surveyed by her organization reported that brand-name requests began as early as age three. Nearly half of the parents said their children began asking for brand-name products by age five. "Children may not know their letters or numbers yet," says Taylor, "but they can spot a corporate logo from a mile away."

Advertisers stand to gain big by entrapping kids at a young age and converting them into hyperconsumers. Studies show that their efforts are paying off. In 1999, children aged 4 to 12 spent over $31 billion of their own money, according to Taylor. In 2003, teenagers spent a whopping $175 billion on clothes, skateboards, and an assortment of other goods. American children also pry huge sums of money from their parents' dwindling personal wealth — about $300 billion a year — by convincing them to buy the latest fashion or newest toy.

A nationwide poll conducted by the Center for a New American Dream, Taylor notes, found that "the vast majority of parents feel their kids are overly materialistic." The poll also indicates that many parents "feel they are losing ground in the struggle for the hearts, minds, and wallets of their children."

And right they are.

Corporate America is usurping the role of parents, raising our children their way — that is, to become good consumers. Not conscientious consumers, but hyperconsumers, programmed to take in as much as they possibly can in their waking hours, putting whatever they can on our credit cards, so they can acquire more in the immediate present, fulfilling the cultural myth that "he or she who dies with the most toys wins."

Advertisers are brainwashing our children by preying on their needs for acceptance, convincing them that if they buy their products they'll be cooler and more popular and more likely to fit in. Especially vulnerable are our teens, who are in an awkward period of

Corporate America is usurping the role of parents, raising our children their way — that is, to become good consumers.

development. Theirs is a world in which outward appearance, fashion, acceptance, being liked, and belonging are paramount. More than half of the parents questioned in the Center for a New American Dream poll said that they have bought things their children wanted in order to fit in with their peers.

But there's more to this than fitting in. Somehow, advertisers and our culture have convinced kids that possessions make us who we are. According to the same poll, nearly two thirds of the parents interviewed said that their own children define their self-worth by their possessions.

Most parents polled by the Center placed the blame on the shoulders of the advertising industry and businesses who market directly to children. Eighty-seven percent claimed that advertising makes kids too materialistic.

But by the looks of things, we parents are partly to blame. We're caught up in a spending frenzy to meet our children's desires. Not surprisingly, nearly a third of the parents polled by the Center admitted that they are working longer hours to buy things their kids wanted, but didn't necessarily need.

Many of us are also on a spending spree of our own. In 1984, Americans on average saved 8.6 percent of their annual income. Today, we save on average –0.6 percent.

Excuse me?

What this means is that we don't save anymore; we go into debt, spending more than we make to pay for our large new houses, large new cars, big screen televisions, and to pay for our children's supersized desires. In short, we are setting a bad example for our children. "If mom and dad race out to buy whatever they need or want, whenever they need or want it, why shouldn't we?" reason our children. A new car every year or two is a good example. (To learn about alternatives to private car ownership, see the accompanying piece on car-sharing programs.)

Even more disturbing, children are being encouraged and taught to badger their parents into buying for them. In her book, *Living Simply with Children*, Marie Sherlock notes that "Corporations now use psychologists and psychiatrists to perform research on children's developmental process to better perfect their kid-targeted marketing. The results are advertising campaigns designed to promote parental pestering by kids until they get what they want, and other campaigns that attempt to undermine the authority of parents." The goal, says Linda Coco, author of *Children First: A Parent's Guide to Fighting Corporate America*, is "to get past the parent, the 'gatekeeper.'" To do this, she says, "marketers try to separate the parent from the child by nagging or making the parents look stupid."

MODELS OF SUSTAINABILITY: CAR SHARING: AN IDEA THAT'S COMING TO YOUR CITY OR TOWN

Car ownership is an expensive and sometimes frustrating ordeal. It is also a major source of environmental damage. With nearly two cars for every man, woman, and child in America, our cars burn huge quantities of gasoline, producing millions of tons of greenhouse gases that are warming the Earth and changing our climate largely for the worse. Roadways and parking lots needed to accommodate our cars also result in enormous losses of open space, farmland, and wildlife habitat. And, of course, building cars requires huge amounts of steel, aluminum, plastic, and other materials — the production of which causes additional environmental damage.

Like our homes, our cars have a major environmental impact. Because of this impact, and because many people only need a car part time, many families have embarked on a new course. Instead of owning a car — or purchasing a second or third car for occasional use — they're sharing a car with others.

The car share movement began — where else? — in Europe in the late 1980s, among ordinary citizens. The idea was so popular that many car share programs evolved to become professionally run organizations that offer an efficient, flexible, neighborhood-based short-term car rental. Currently, there are over 550 communities with car clubs, with an estimated combined membership of 70,000 to 100,000 in Switzerland, Germany, Austria, the Netherlands, Great Britain, Denmark, Sweden, Italy, and France!

In the mid 1990s, the idea of car clubs spread to Canada, and recently the idea has begun to blossom in the United States. Here, two commercial companies, Zipcar and Flexcar, offer car share programs in more than a dozen cities, including Boston, New York, Maryland, Washington, D.C., Denver, Portland, and Seattle.

Zipcar and Flexcar operate fleets of vehicles in each city. Cars are available to participants any time for one hour to several days. (Special arrangements can also be made to rent cars for long trips.) Businesses, families, and individuals can all participate.

At Zipcar, vehicles are reserved online, a process that requires about 30 seconds. The computer tells you where the car is and its license plate number. You show up at the site and hold your personal Zipcard next to the windshield, where it is read by a scanner. If you've reserved the car and the time is correct, the doors unlock. An electronic signal is then sent from the car's computer to company headquarters, where a billing record is activated.

Car share programs in Europe often offer a variety of cars — small commuters and larger cars for taking the family and a kid's friend to the country. In the United States, options are more limited — you'll mostly find small commuter cars.

In car share programs, members pay a small hourly rate plus mileage, while the companies pay for the car, the insurance, the maintenance, and the gas. In San Francisco's City Car Share program, which is run by a nonprofit organization, users pay $3.50 per hour and 37 cents per mile.

In this program, cars are parked in reserved spaces, typically off-street, conveniently located throughout the city. This way members know where the car is and where it must be dropped off. To ensure that members return the cars on time — so the next person can use them — Zipcar imposes a $25-per-hour late fee with a minimum charge of $25. They also prohibit smoking in the car and only allow pets in appropriate carriers.

For people who don't own a car, car share programs provide access to a vehicle for running personal errands, shopping, visiting a doctor, or attending business meetings. They also cater to those who have one car, but occasionally need another. Car share programs are highly effective in urban settings with good mass transit systems, where people already have other options besides driving. But they are also found in some more rural areas.

Car share programs save money and the hassle of car ownership, and thus reduce private car ownership and reduce car usage. (Most people drive less when they have to pay the per hour or per mile fee. They'll pool trips or walk or take mass transit when it's convenient.) Car share programs promote mass transit use in other ways, too. Many people find it more convenient to ride a bus or light rail to commute to and from work, than to rent a car share vehicle for errands. Many car share programs in Europe are integrated with the mass transit system.

HOW TO GET STARTED

If you are interested in joining Flexcar, Zipcar, or a similar program, you may be able to have a vehicle or two located within your neighborhood, provided the company can generate enough local interest to justify it. For a complete listing of car share programs in the United States, Canada, the UK and Europe, log on to <www.eartheasy.com/live_car_sharinghtm>.

Or you can set up your own program. In Europe, informal groups of friends, neighbors, and colleagues have started their own car share programs using cars already owned by individual members of the group or cars purchased jointly. You will need to establish a booking system, a convenient location to park the vehicle, and agreements on buying fuel, access to keys, servicing and insuring the vehicle, as well as other matters. Drivers usually pay in proportion to their use, or by the hour, or by the hour and per mile. In Europe, car clubs operate using normal insurance, so long as no profit is made by the group or any of the members. Car clubs apply for insurance in the club's name and can list four or five people to a single policy.

Car-sharing offers many benefits to those who are interested in help-ing to build a sustainable future. If you like the idea, why not join a car share program in your area and take the idea out for a test drive?

Adapted with permission from Dan Chiras and Dave Wann, *Superbia! 31 Ways to Create Sustainable Communities,* New Society Publishers, 2003.

Television is the main artery leading from advertisers to our children's brains. Ninety-nine percent of the children in the United States live in a home with one or more televisions, according to the *Journal of Advertising Research.* Nearly one third of all our children come from homes with four or more TVs! On average, children watch two and three-quarters hours of television per day. On average, our children see between 20,000 and 40,000 television commercials every year, or about 500 per day!

Our children are bombarded with ads in other venues as well. With logos on shirts, shoes, hats, and skateboards our kids are immersed in a commercial machine tailored to promote one goal: to sell more product. Our children encounter ads on the Internet, at school, in magazines, on radios, in newspapers, through the mail, and along our nation's highways. All this effort to convince our children to buy also gives kids a lopsided view of what life is all about. It is about buying and owning things.

Advertising is not just selling products, then, it is selling values. In essence, says Sherlock, "Advertisers are peddling a complete value system that preaches that purchasing material items will make an individual happy."

In the process, advertising may be damaging our children's egos, too, say some critics. Nancy Shalek of the Shalek Agency notes that "advertising at its best is making kids feel that without their product they are losers. Kids are very sensitive to that [message]." Shalek goes on to say, "If you tell them to buy some-thing, they are resistant. But if you tell them that they'll be a dork if they don't, you've got their attention. You open up their emotional vulnerabilities and it's very easy to do with kids because they're the most emotionally vulnerable." No matter how hard we try as parents to convince our children that a new pair of basketball shoes, costing $100 or more won't make them popular, they're not convinced. Advertisers have beat parents to the moral lesson: You are what you wear or own or eat or drink.

Thanks in large part to advertising on TV and other media, says Betsy Taylor, our children become "educated to entitlement" — to feel entitled to have whatever they want — and "programmed for discontent" — that is, to never be satisfied with what they acquire. As writer Eric Hoffer once noted, "The search for happiness is one of the chief sources of unhappiness." Moreover, in short order our children become deeply entrenched in the more-is-better culture: good little consumers with a possession obsession bound to keep companies and advertisers happy.

Not only does TV transform our children into lifetime programmed consumers, it may be giving them inferiority complexes and it certainly undermines parental values of frugality, when they exist. It does all this while bankrupting families. And despite all this, we continue to let our children watch television much more than is healthy, sitting alongside them munching popcorn ourselves, ticking off the list of new products we'd like to purchase.

Vicki Robin, author of *Your Money or Your Life*, calls the advertising that promotes consumerism and materialism the "largest uncontrolled psychological experiment on human subjects in the history of the world." One parent interviewed for Marie Sherlock's *Living Simply with Children*, remarked, "I don't want the values I pass on to my kids to be those of Nike or Reebok." Sherlock adds, "If you're raising children in North America today and you're not consciously addressing the effects of commercialism on their psyches and beliefs, then you've essentially handed your child's soul over to corporate America. You might as well say, 'Here, mold this child into another mindless consumer.'"

Fortunately, there are some ways to reduce the negative influence of advertising on our children. Before we examine these solutions, however, we will turn our attention to other influences the media have on you, the parent, and explore how they bias your views in ways that encourage you to support your child's spending habits.

THE NIGHTLY NEWS: AKA "THE GROWTH-IS-GOOD REPORT"

Unbeknownst to most viewers, ordinary programming also contributes values and attitudes that fuel patterns of consumer behavior which, in turn, contribute to the ongoing destruction of the environment. Take the evening news, for instance.

Besides pretty much ignoring the environment, until there's an oil spill or some other newsworthy catastrophe, the evening news, over the years of my adulthood, has become a major purveyor of the growth-is-good philosophy.

How so?

Like other media, such as, newspapers and magazines, the evening news offers to the viewing public a lopsided view of progress. It does this by focusing almost entirely on economic growth as an indicator of our nation's well-being.

Take as an example the evening market report, offered by all major media, even National Public Radio. This report provides a nightly snapshot of the economy based on a handful of indicators — the Dow Jones Industrial Average (DJIA), NASDAQ, Standard and Poors Index, and a handful of the latest government statistics such as housing starts, sales of durable goods, and the like.

Over the years, this parade of indicators is presented to the public as the measure by which we assess our nation's economic progress. We hear the numbers so often that we eventually become convinced that they actually have something to do with our overall well-being.

However, surprising as it may seem, these indices have almost nothing to do with a nation's health and well-being. The truth is, these indicators are about as useful in measuring a nation's economic health as measuring a person's pulse is in assessing his or her health. Sure, they provide some information, but they reveal only one aspect of a complex system. The fact is, what really matters is what these indicators fail to tell us: for example, what we are getting for the increase in economic output. Are we getting a proportionate share of the benefits? Are our lives really better? Does an increase in worker productivity mean we are working harder or that there are more machines doing the work people used to be doing?

The answer to such questions can be disturbing. Numerous studies show that as the economy rises, Americans and citizens of the more industrialized nations are actually receiving less and less benefit. For example, studies show that an increasingly larger share of our wealth goes to treat diseases created by the stress of our hyperconsumer culture, or to clean up wastes. Although the economy may be up, our pulse rates and stress levels are too, and so are stress-related illnesses. The Roman playwright Seneca, who lived over 2,000 years ago, recognized the personal impoverishment that goes along with the "wanting more" syndrome when he wrote, "Not he who has little, but he who wishes for more, is poor." As our stress levels increase, so does stress on the life-support systems of the planet.

Yale University economist James Tobin was one of the first to examine this phenomenon. He charted economic growth alongside the benefits we get from economic expansion. He did so by subtracting the amount of money spent on pollution control, disease treatment, crime, and a host of other negatives, from the total economic growth. He called the beneficial growth our net economic welfare. What Tobin found was that both economic output and net economic welfare were growing, but our net economic welfare, the "good economics," was growing at a much slower rate.

Other researchers have performed similar analyses, and although you can quibble with the methods they used, the consensus is that we're spinning the wheels of our economic machine faster and faster but going slower and slower. One of the most impressive efforts is the Genuine Progress Indicator (GPI)(figure 5.1) from the nonprofit organization Redefining Progress. As you can see from studying this figure, although GNP is rising, real progress (the GPI) is actually declining. We're growing but getting less and less good out of it. That's an indicator that we are doing more and more damage to people and the planet as we supposedly march forward.

But there's more to the evening news than the economic indicators. Just about every story that has to do with cities and towns — outside of murders, rapes and other crimes — focuses on economics. Reclining in our easy chairs each evening, for example, we are regaled with stories about the latest movies,

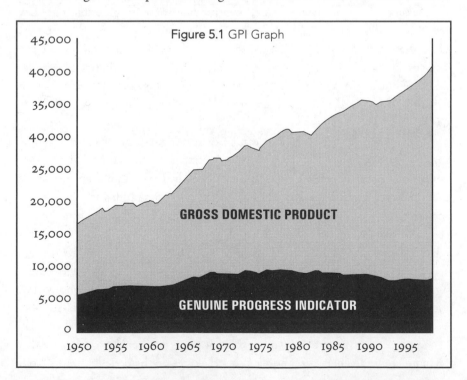

Figure 5.1 GPI Graph

but the main focus seems to be how much each one grossed over the previous weekend. When a local newscaster describes an upcoming convention in our city, we're told how many millions of dollars it will pump into the local economy. When we're told about a company moving to our city or town, it's the same old story: how many jobs the company will create and how many dollars it will infuse into the local economy. All we care about is money. Much of what is valuable to us is pushed aside. As British carpenter and writer Samuel Grafton once wrote, "A penny will hide the biggest star in the universe if you hold it close enough to your eye."

Surely, not all news is bad and not all news is about money. There are promising stories like the tale of young Gina Gallant who has invented recipes to make crackers stay crispy in soup longer, road pavement that puts recycled plastic to good use, and even a safer bicycle helmet. Her story is told in the accompanying piece on "Kids Who are Making a Difference."

KIDS WHO ARE MAKING A DIFFERENCE
GINA GALLANT: MOVE ASIDE MR. GATES!

Bill Gates is a legend in the world of commerce for turning a golden idea into a multibillion dollar international enterprise. His journey from college dropout to a man of vast economic wealth is truly spectacular. But watch out, Bill. You may have to share the spotlight in the not-so-distant future with Gina Gallant, a young inventor from Prince George, British Columbia.

This young superstar entrepreneur, though, isn't any ordinary inventor out to get rich. She's got a social conscience and is, it appears, out to save the world — one invention at a time. Gina's now making big time news throughout Canada and the United States. In 1999, for example, she received national attention from the media and from several major food companies when she invented a recipe to keep crackers in soups from becoming soggy so fast. That was not her first invention though; Gina has been inventing things since she was in first grade. Her first invention, she told me, was — get this — broccoli paper. Broccoli was used to enhance paper fibers. Whether we'll ever see broccoli paper is an open question, but at least the much maligned vegetable might have additional uses!

Crackers that won't get soggy in soup won't save the world, to be sure, but many of Gina's ideas will. They are, for example, designed to put recycled waste to good use, reduce pollution and resource extraction, and improve safety.

While working at the asphalt division of Husky Oil, Gina learned that discarded plastic bottles take up a substantial amount of space in landfills — about one-third of all landfill space. What could be done with all of this plastic?

Gina thought maybe it could be used to make pavement for roads. Mixed with asphalt and crushed rock, the material just might work. So she set about researching the idea. She discovered that glass and rubber had both been tried, but didn't work very well. The materials were considered incompatible. She thought maybe plastic and asphalt might make a better combination.

Gina invented a new product called PolyAggreRoad or PAR for short. After a great deal of experimentation, she found the optimal mix: 6 percent plastic, 6 percent asphalt, and 88 percent crushed rock or aggregate.

Next, she set out to test the product.

Now, how does a teenager test a new asphalt?

She called the mayor and presented her idea. He liked the idea, and they were off and running. The next hurdle, though, was to convince some companies to buy into her idea. "At first, some of [the companies] didn't take me seriously because they thought, you know, a 13-year-old can't do something like this," Gina remarks. "But they finally realized I knew what I was talking about."

In October 2002, the mayor arranged for her to test PAR on a 160-foot (48-meter) strip of local road with the aid of four area businesses. One company provided recycled plastic pellets, another ran tests on the product, still another provided asphalt and aggregate, while a fourth company built the test road.

Engineers expect that PAR will be able to withstand more expansion and contraction — what they call movement — than regular road surfaces. The road, they predict, won't crack as much. Because cracks let moisture in, which expands and contracts as it freezes and thaws, ripping a road apart, engineers think that PAR should last longer and will require less maintenance than conventional road materials.

"My ultimate goal is for a company to pick up my product," she says, "and to see it go all the way around the world to reduce garbage in landfill sites."

How are the tests going?

Amazingly well, says the young inventor, "The road is still holding up and it's been there for just about two years now. It has only a few cracks, which is to be expected."

More recently, Gina's work has not gone unrecognized. Besides considerable press coverage, she was awarded a gold medal and a $2,000 scholarship at the 2002 Canada-wide Science Fair.

Lately, Gina has turned her attention to the bicycle helmet after her brother was hit and injured by an automobile while riding his bike. "The police said if it weren't for his helmet being on properly, he wouldn't have survived," she said.

Whereas most of us would log this piece of information and move on, Gina set about reinventing the bicycle helmet to ensure that kids wear them correctly. She poured 300 hours into the project, using science, electronics, and her ingenuity to come up with a system of lights that click on if the helmet is positioned correctly. It's a kind of alarm system for bike riders to let them know they are protected. Her goal in all of this is to help reduce injuries among younger children.

Gina's enthusiasm and success have propelled this young lady to the forefront, but they have also inspired other children in her school to do better. Gina's enthusiasm is apparently contagious. Other children are spending more than one year working on science projects and constantly looking for ways to improve their projects.

Gina's advice to other children is: "Believe in yourself and follow your heart, because if you can think of these ideas, you can do them."

So watch out, Mr. Gates — and step aside. This young lady is about to rock our world.

In short, just about every story that doesn't have to do with criminal activity is told through the lens of economic well-being, with growth being the dominant goal. If some action promotes growth, it's viewed as a public good — like building a football stadium for the billionaire owner and millionaire players who threaten to leave town if the citizens don't pony up the $300 million required to create a new playing field.

On the nightly news, or in the newspaper for that matter, if a reported activity detracts from growth, for example, by protecting the environment, it's often cast in a negative light. It's as if all we care about is money and growth!

No wonder all of our new stadiums come with corporate logos: In Denver, there's the Pepsi Center. It's not a place to buy a Pepsi, although they'd be happy if you did, but rather a hockey and basketball arena. Then there's Invesco Field at Mile High. It's not a place to invest in your future, but to spend an afternoon rooting for the Denver Broncos. And there's Coors Field, home of the local baseball team. We're all happy to pay to build stadiums, and let corporate sponsors name them: It's good for the economy.

WHIPPING UP NEUROTIC CONSUMERISM

So all along you thought you were getting news about the world each night when you watched NBC Nightly News or ABC News, when in fact you were actually being fed the party line — that growth is good, indeed essential.

Truth is, you were also being whipped into a frenzy, a neurotic consumer state.

How's that?

Nightly reports of economic progress and news reports told through the economic lens with their singular focus on economic growth have converted us into a nation of the economically hypervigilant — a little like nervous new parents, watching over their first-born child. In the process, we've become economic neurotics.

Consider the nightly stock market report. Dutiful to their economic master, the nightly news stations report on the Dow's and NASDAQ's performance. If we're plugged into the world around us, we also see these indices flashed on our computer screens or our local bank's electronic signs: time, temperature, and the DJIA, up or down so many points.

Over the years, this minute-by-minute market vigilance has whipped up a neurosis, an unhealthy impatience or urgency for continued growth. With so many of us whose financial futures depend on the stock market's growth, watching as carefully as we do, our impatient expectations fuel even greater impatience.

> *Over the years, the minute-by-minute market vigilance has whipped up a neurosis, an unhealthy impatience or urgency for continued growth.*

Watching almost anything too carefully breeds impatience and eventually neurosis, except maybe wildflowers, sunsets, and children playing peacefully in the back yard. As a result, impatient stockholders and board members of corporations push for higher earnings to fuel the economic growth machine. To achieve this goal, sales must inevitably rise.

And growth can only occur through the good graces of you and me, the rapacious consumers who are discontent with whatever we have and hell-bent on increasing our personal holdings.

PROMOTION DISGUISED AS NEWS

Another tool in the growth machine of corporate America is the video news release produced by government agencies as well as pharmaceutical, oil, coal, and timber companies and aired on evening news, in part or in total. A video news release replaces mountains of press releases issued by companies to stimulate interest among the media in the trends or events in their business. However, the video news release also contains film footage — footage that companies and government agencies want you to see. News stations like them because it saves the time and expense of sending a reporter and a film crew to a location to shoot a story.

Although the purpose of the video news release is to inform, it may also promote a particular point of view and frequently is designed to help promote a new product. When watching the evening news with your children, be on the lookout for promotional material disguised as a segment of the evening news.

GUILT RIDDEN AND GUILT RIDDING

The media's role in promoting growth and consumption is most obvious when markets and the economy falter. During such downturns, newscasters and analysts offer incessant reminders of the roots of the downturn: less-than-robust "consumer spending." We're reminded by analysts, who feature prominently on the evening news, that if consumer spending could be stimulated all would be well once again. Not too subtly, we're enjoined to perform our "duty" as good citizens of the global economy — to consume more. We're told that we can pull our nation out of the crisis, restoring growth that is indelibly good and desirable, by prying open our pocketbooks. In essence, we're "guilted" into spending. And when we spend, we rid ourselves of guilt. Consumption is guilt-ridden and guilt ridding. "Enjoy the guilt, because everyone's boat is floating higher these days," is the message we're given.

Even tax rebates by the Bush Administration were doled out to encourage us to spend, spend, and spend. It's no surprise that people are no longer referred to as "citizens," which emphasizes our part in a society, but "consumers," which emphasizes our essential role in a consumer culture led by corporations and advertising firms paid to do their bidding.

In sum, over the years we've become a nation of consumers addicted to growth. We uncritically subscribe to the notion that growth is good, indeed essential. And growth is predicated on the consumption of goods by good citizens like you and me. Guilt-ridden when we fail our duty, we relieve our guilt by purchases that make our economy healthy. No matter that our continued acts of consumption lessen the chances of our long-term survival on the planet. What is even more distressing is that we're raising our children on the same logic.

PROGRAMMING PERILS

But the story does not end here. There are other consumer messages to consider, messages we receive from television's other programming.

Let's take a look at this other programming. What do we see?

Besides a mind-numbing array of shows and movies that feed our fascination for crime and violence, we view a cornucopia of programs that parade wealth before our eyes. The Travel Channel and its "Ten Best" series, for example, showcases the ten most luxurious hotels, the best beaches, mansions, swimming pools, and even bathrooms. Imagine, the world's ten most extravagant bathrooms! Now they're even airing a program featuring billionaire toys.

Other educational channels showcase American opulence in other ways. The Discovery Channel, for instance, gives us glimpses of the life of high rollers in Las Vegas, showing the lavish "digs" they're provided with when they fly in on their personal jets for a weekend of high-rolling entertainment.

What started as a "lifestyles of the rich and famous" fascination, a mere curiosity piece, has become a fairly overwhelming barrage of awe for wealth. For some, this glitzy parade of opulence on television is a mere curiosity; they can remain detached and unaffected. For others, however, it breeds dissatisfaction with their lives, a discontentment with the conditions they live in no matter how good. In other words, the opulence of others breeds a yearning for more in those less fortunate, a longing that many people act on, working harder or — more likely —going deeper into debt. In the process of sharing the good life, we're buying large trucks and cars to keep up with the opulent Joneses. And we are making a mess of the planet.

Not only does the opulence parade foster discontent here, it breeds it every-where. We certainly see this when foreigners view American culture on TV. What they have becomes insufficient.

Television shows also display a great deal of disrespect. Sitcoms, for instance, showcase teens who talk to one another and to their parents with extraordinary insolence. Children pick up on this speech and give it a spin in real life, often adopting a sarcastic, "put-the-other-person-down-in-fun" approach. Although it may make for good television viewing, it makes for lousy interactions with others. And if we can't respect one another, how can we respect the environment?

In the next chapter, we'll focus our attention on ways to help you and your child resist the allure of the consumer culture and to develop environmentally and socially conscientious buying habits.

FAMILY ACTIVITIES

1. Obtain a copy of the video, *Affluenza*, and watch it with your family. You may want to pause it from time to time to discuss issues it raises. Be sure to discuss it when you are done. You may want to talk about how the video affected you, how you see yourself falling into consumption patterns. Ask your children to talk about these issues as well, as they pertain to themselves and friends.

2. Talk with your children about ads on TV and in other media when you are watching or reading the newspaper together. Ask them to critically analyze the ads by asking a series of questions: (a) How likely is it that the product being advertised delivers what the advertisers promise? (b) Is the advertiser creating a false need? In other words, are they exaggerating the need for their product? (c) What is the manufacturer trying to sell besides the product? In other words, are they trying to tell you that you will be cooler, hipper, smarter, better liked, prettier, handsomer, or stronger if you purchase their product? These are the subtle messages, the connections they're trying to make with their product. (d) Why do TV and radio stations call advertise-ments "messages"?

3. Read and discuss the essay on car sharing with your children and ask them their thoughts on it. Why would this be a good idea? What benefits would it have to them and to the Earth? What would the downsides of this be?

4. Talk with your kids about logos on products. Why do logos on clothing and other products make them cooler? Or do they? Should they be getting paid to advertise products?

5. Sit down with your children to watch the evening news and see how many times the growth-is-good philosophy crops up. The local news is especially useful when embarking on this project. Why is the evening news so fixated on growth?

6. Ask your kids about growth. Do we need to keep growing economically? Why or why not? What are the pluses and minuses of this?

7. Go online and look up Genuine Progress Indicator, and study this with your children. Why is the GPI declining while the GNP is growing? Talk with your children about good economics and bad economics, that is, expenditures that are not really helping us live better lives and those that truly contribute to a better way of life.

8. Read the story of Gina Gallant to your family, and ask them what they think about this remarkable girl. Ask them what they can come up with to help improve people's lives.

Our necessities are few but our wants are endless
— George Bernard Shaw

6 SWIMMING AGAINST THE MAINSTREAM: COMBATING ADVERTISING AND AFFLUENZA

Many years ago, my young son Skyler and I were dining out with my dad and his wife in a restaurant near their home in Hilton, New York. After we'd studied the menu, the waitress appeared to take our orders. The adults ordered decisively, and then the waitress turned to Skyler — about four years old at the time — and asked him what he wanted. He returned her question with a question, "What do I get with my meal?"

Without blinking an eye, the waitress announced that they had toys for the kids, just like McDonald's. After the dinner, she returned with a box of toys he could pick from. I, of course, was mortified but tried to curb my emotions, thinking that we could talk about the incident at another time.

As our society plunges deeper into affluenza, our children increasingly become the victims of rewards for consuming. We adults also fall victim to this trend that started as a seemingly innocuous marketing strategy back in the early 1960s, when banks started giving toasters and other goodies for opening an account with them. Today, all major fast-food restaurants offer trinkets to young customers in an attempt to cement relationships with potential lifelong consumers, as do doctors, dentists, and an assortment of other businesses. Although we rarely ate at McDonald's (and when we did, I usually insisted that the toys be removed from the kids' Happy Meals), my son obviously liked the getting-a-bonus-for-buying-a-meal philosophy.

If not addressed, the values passed on to children by Nike and Reebok and a swarm of others eager to build their customer base through giveaways and advertisements, will be here to stay for a long time. Swimming against mainstream consumer culture — combating affluenza and the forces like advertising that feed it — may seem difficult, if not impossible. But that shouldn't deter those of us who want to raise children to care about the environment and to live by their convictions. Let's look at some ideas that are helping parents do just that.

MORE FUN, LESS STUFF: WHAT KIDS REALLY WANT THAT MONEY CAN'T BUY

In a nationwide contest, the Center for a New American Dream asked American children to write about or depict through drawings what they really wanted in life — things that money can't buy. Surprisingly, kids' needs were pretty simple. They wanted their parents — our time, attention, and love. They wanted more time and involvement with their extended family — cousins, aunts, uncles, and grandparents. They wanted acceptance and respect from their family and friends. And they wanted more free time, just to hang out. They didn't want to be shuffled around from one activity to the next. They wanted time just to be kids. Less structured time. More play time. Kids also wanted friends to share their lives with, support them, provide understanding, and to just have fun with.

Surprisingly, many children also asked for more time to be outside in nature. And many yearned for a healthy environment. (You can read about three young girls whose zeal for a clean environment led them to national fame in the "Kids Who Are Making a Difference" section in this chapter.) Our kids wanted to discover purpose and explore spirituality. And many kids wanted a better world, especially peace among the world's people.

Focusing on these needs, The Center's Betsy Taylor contends, could ease our children's vain attempts to create happiness and fulfillment through materialism — and could ease pressure on parents to buy things. It won't eliminate the materialistic impulses of children in a consumer society, but it could curb them. Kids will be less likely to continue to feed their feelings of self-worth through the endless acquisition of more stuff. (I've always believed that feeding the emptiness with stuff is like trying to fill a sieve.) In short, says Taylor, we should help our kids have more fun and more fulfilling lives. The more fun and fulfillment they acquire through noncommercial and nonmaterial avenues, the less stuff they'll want. (Sorry, advertisers and corporate executives. Well, not really.)

This philosophy is not just about filling up our kids' time with visits to the grandparents or cousins or about finding ways to get kids outside more, it is about raising more emotionally healthy children — kids who see value in the nonmaterial world. This approach fosters the most valuable emotional assets one can acquire in youth: a sense of being unconditionally loved, of self-respect and, self-love, and feelings of belonging, acceptance, and self-worth. The emotional foundation you help build translates into less need to fill the voids with junk. Put another way, the more emotionally healthy a child is, the less stuff they need to create the image of success or likeability. The more children belong to the larger world around them, the less they need to belong artificially through logoed clothes! Raising emotionally healthy children is a key to success, but that task requires additional parenting advice offered by many excellent books, including my favorites *Parenting with Love and Logic* and the sequel for teens, *Parenting Teens with Love and Logic*.

Providing more fun and more fulfillment outside of the commercial realm may take a little thought, however. We're so used to going to dinner at Chuck E. Cheese's Restaurant or visiting a mall or trucking off to a movie to entertain our families. With a little thought, though, you can probably come up with a dozen or more ideas on

> *The more children belong to the larger world around them, the less they need to belong artificially through logoed clothes.*

how to satisfy your child's needs. I'd suggest you take out a pen and paper and start listing some of the ways to meet the needs just discussed. It may mean an invitation for the grandparents to join your family for a week or a weekend, or simply a family picnic. It may mean a walk in a nearby forest or meadow with a wildflower guide. Or it may mean playing a card game with your kids. The list of possibilities is endless.

If you'd like a little help assembling ideas on ways to meet your children's root-level needs, I highly recommend that you read Betsy Taylor's book, *What Kids Really Want that Money Can't Buy*. It's a fast read, and chock-full of good ideas. Please note: Your kids may groan when you suggest a card game instead of a trip to the mall, but if you end up having a really good time, next time they may be more willing, even eager, to pursue an alternative form of entertainment for the evening. Be sure to play games for fun, and let your kids win. I know I have to fight my urge to always be the winner. (Sorry guys.)

KIDS WHO ARE MAKING A DIFFERENCE
THE DON'T BE CRUDE TEAM TACKLES OIL POLLUTION

In 1997, Kate Klinkerman, Barbara Brown, and Lacy Jones were seated at the kitchen table at the home of Joni Brown, discussing a common practice in rural Texas — the use of waste oil and other fluids from cars, trucks, and tractors as herbicides and pesticides. Farmers like the girls' dads routinely poured these fluids around fenceposts to kill weeds, for instance. "Because the girls were learning in their environmental science class in school that used oil polluted groundwater, they were in a personal quandary," notes Joni Brown, mother of one of the girls. As air quality program coordinator of the city of Victoria, Joni challenged them to do something about the problem rather than just fuss about it.

Each year about half of the oil that pollutes the world's oceans comes from oil disposed of on land. Oil can also seep into the ground where it contaminates groundwater used for livestock and human consumption. It can leak into nearby lakes and streams, damaging aquatic life. A single gallon (4.5 liters) of oil can contaminate as much as one acre (0.4 hectares) of groundwater.

After doing their research, this determined trio decided to find ways to promote waste oil recycling in Victoria County, Texas, where they live. With assistance from their local 4-H program faculty and parent and adult leaders, they launched a Conservation of Natural Resources project in the Victoria County 4-H program to educate their community about the potential hazards of using motor oil as a herbicide and insecticide.

In January 1998, the three young girls, not even teens yet, formed the Don't Be Crude Team. The County commissioners granted the girls rights to locate five fluid recycling sites in rural Victoria County. The sites were established to provide farmers and ranchers a way to properly dispose of used motor fluids, including motor oil, hydraulic fluid, and used oil filters. (The fluids are used to make roadbed materials and the used oil filters are recycled into metal fencing materials.)

Over the next three years, the girls contacted businesses and found five willing corporate sponsors who funded the purchase of recycling units approved by the federal government. They also gave more than 50 presentations throughout the US on youth empowerment in environmental issues. Their goal, they say, is to educate and empower others.

Today, "Don't Be Crude has units serving 54,000 people in seven counties, protecting more than 600 square miles (1,554 square kilometers) of groundwater resources and 500 miles (800 kilometers) of coastline," notes Joni. "All told, there are 21 units with an average of 50,000 gallons (227,000 liters) of used motor fluids collected annually."

The girls, who volunteered more than 1,200 hours per year in their community through this and a host of other projects, have appeared on CNN and other national TV and radio stations. Stories about their activities have appeared in numerous local, state, and national publications, including *USA Today* and *Seventeen.*

The girls have also received numerous awards for their hard work and dedication, including the 2000 Brower Youth Award, the 2001 Environmental Protection Agency Presidential Environmental Youth Award, the 2001 Texas Environmental Excellence Youth Award, the 2001 Prudential Spirit of Community Award, the 2002 Gloria Barron Prize for Young Heroes, and an award from the Texas State 4-H.

"Today we have five corporate and eight government partners who have sponsored the purchase of 21 do-it-yourself recycling units," said Barbara Brown.

"Many people, when given the opportunity to better themselves, or the world in which they live, will take a chance and try with just a little encouragement," notes Brown. "I want to be that encourager … I know that with support and creativity, we can create solutions to the challenges along the way and inspire others to do the same."

THROW OUT THE TV ... OR AT LEAST LIMIT YOUR KIDS VIEWING TIME

You may find this hard to believe, but I actually like my television set and many of the programs. Contrary to the common grumbling we hear about "nothing worth watching on TV," there really is a great deal of good programming for example; on the Science Channel. The problem with television, besides the silly, inane, and sometimes stupid programming, is the messages we receive through the commercials that attempt to brainwash us and our children. I just happen to be immune to most of the brainwashing. It's my children and all of the rest of the children who stare at the TV mesmerized by it that I'm concerned about.

Whatever you do, don't put a television in a kid's room; you'll not only never see your child again, you'll be unwittingly ensuring that your child will be totally brainwashed by the time he or she is five or six. Along this same line, resist the easy-out habit of using the television as a babysitter.

If you are like me, you may want to explore ways to limit your children's exposure to television and its invasive commercials. Let's begin with a dire advance warning: whatever you do, don't put a television in a kid's room; You'll not only never see your child again, you'll be unwittingly ensuring that your child will be totally brainwashed by the time he or she is five or six. Along this same line, resist the too-easy habit of using the television as a babysitter.

To protect their children from television commercials and bad programming, some parents throw it out altogether! If your children are very young, that's easier to do. Some parents simply get rid of the set, giving it away to charity. Others unplug it or banish the set to the basement, using it only when they want to watch something special.

When children become older and addicted to the television, however, getting rid of it won't be as easy. You can expect your children to put up a good fight. The TV won't go easily! My ex-wife unplugged the cable in her house, leaving my boys only the three main channels that came through via the antenna. The boys watched those channels as much as they could or rented videos. And when they came to my house, during my weeks, they were worse than ever — watching every spare minute of the day, late into the night, trying to get their fix.

So be careful; you may create a severe backlash. Denying anything makes the heart grow more desirous. When I was growing up in western New York, one of our neighbors, who was as strict a father as you could get, refused to let his children see TV. When his kids spent an evening with other children in the neighborhood, they usually were glued to the set until they had to go home.

Another option is to limit television time. In my house, there's no television on school days until school work, music practice and chores are done. During the summer, kids have to ask to watch television, and I usually grant their wish, but with a time limit. "How about watching for an hour, then going out to play?" My kids usually respond with alacrity to the offering, and usually find some very entertaining play that occupies the rest of their day.

You can enable your children's choice of more healthy entertainment options by having art and craft supplies, musical instruments, fort-building supplies, sports equipment, bicycles, and other alternatives to television readily available.

Some parents devise elaborate schemes to limit TV time. Kids can watch so many hours a week, and have to then budget their viewing time. And some parents limit the type of television their children can watch. Their children can watch television, but only the educational programs. At my house, I frown on watching garbage, but that doesn't stop it.

With small families, limiting television viewing is relatively easy, but only if there's a parent in the house. I work at home and can monitor not only how much time kids are spending in front of the idiot box, as my dad used to call it, but also what they're watching. If you work away from home, your ability to monitor television viewing is greatly limited. You can block those channels that have programming you don't want your kids to view. But rest assured, kids will cheat. One night, I came home early from jazz band practice. Through the window, I saw my son scurry to turn off the TV set. When I walked in, he was reading a book. I asked if he'd been watching TV. "No," he said earnestly.

I went over and felt the back of the TV, which was hot. "Hmmm," I said, "the set appears to have been on."

"Oh, I watched for a little bit."

"Hmmm," I said, "I would have sworn I saw you switching off the TV right after I drove in."

"Oh, I was just watching a little." Who knows? To a child, half a day in front of the TV might seem like a little.

Watching less television and spending more time doing other things, limits our children's exposure to mind-bending advertising. But let's face it, with the number of commercials shown in a half-hour, our kids are still going to receive plenty of commercial messages urging them to buy this or that to fit in or be cool or to be better looking. And many children will be bombarded with commercial messages at school and in magazines. They will be pressured by their friends who want to know if they've seen this or that doodad on the TV. The pressure is pervasive. You can't escape it. So where does that leave you?

TEACHING CHILDREN TO TURN A DEAF EAR TO ADVERTISING

For some reason, I am a cynic when it comes to television commercials. Maybe I've been burned by ads whose promises go unfulfilled, or maybe I'm just a cynic. Whatever the cause, when commercials come on, my mind wanders off. When I was in graduate school, I was hired to listen to a commercial for Budweiser beer as part of a consumer focus group. A group of us sat in a room (we were paid $20 to do this, which in the 1970s was a good deal of money for a college kid) in front of a TV screen. The commercial played, and then we were taken aside and asked a series of questions. When the interviewer started quizzing me, I realized I couldn't remember a thing about the commercial, except that it had a biplane in it. I must have gone into my oblivious mode when the commercial started.

Fortunately, the guy at the next desk talked rather loudly. His interviewer was one question ahead of mine, so I could hear responses to the same questions slightly in advance, and I shamelessly robbed his answers. (Sorry guys; write me and I'll refund the money!)

I have also learned the art and science of critical thinking, and employ that when viewing advertising. You, too, can hone that skill, and pass it on to your children to help them understand the hidden messages that spur consumerism. I discussed some important rules of critical thinking in Chapter 3.

To help my children understand that they are being brainwashed, I tell them, for instance, that the sound and color intensity of the images is enhanced during commercials. "Why would advertisers do this? Doesn't this make you suspicious?" I ask them. And when my children were young I would ask, "Now, do you really think that remote-controlled truck can do that?" Now that they are near driving age, I ask them, "Do you think that car will really make you more popular with members of the opposite sex?"

Bottom line: If you want your kids to turn a deaf ear to advertising, they need to be aware that they're being masterfully manipulated — even brainwashed. For example, advertisers are barraging them and us with artificially inflated problems — such as the dangers of germs lurking on our kitchen counters and every other solid surface in the house, hiding in ambush ready to strike us dead! — and offering products that are supposed to cure these highly exaggerated dangers, and often don't!

Kids need to know that the advertisers are playing with their emotions, their lack of security, their need to belong, their need to be cool, their need to look good, and their need to be popular. If kids can see behind the hype, they'll end up a lot more well-adjusted and focused than most of the adults alive today, and they'll end up with a lot more money in the bank, having been saved from frittering away their earnings on an endless stream of junk that fails to deliver on advertisers' promises. They may even gain more self-esteem by being able to recognize and avoid scams.

Ultimately, we can help our children learn that it is right to be content with what we have. Moreover, we can't change who we are by our possessions, only through personal growth.

Don't go overboard on your critiques of modern advertising. It doesn't take much to get kids to see through the deception. However, if you harp on and on about it, your kids might turn a deaf ear to you! And don't expect that their adbusting savvy will always work. Even though they may see the lies and deceit, they still may want the new shoes or new pants or new toy. Your role in "hardening" your children to advertising schemes is to assist them in developing a healthy cynicism, a skill they'll be glad you helped them develop as they grow older and have more disposable income (income to throw away on junk!).

TEACHING KIDS THE VALUE OF ASSET INVENTORY AND VALUE ASSESSMENT

When my children were young, they were constantly on the hunt for the latest stuff — Pokeman cards, Furbees, Beanie Babies, and the like — which they purchased either with handouts from me or by shelling out their allowance. I often asked them if they really needed the new acquisition, and their reply was, "Of course, Dad. Everybody's got it!"

Because that didn't work, I tried another strategy. As their inventory of junk in baskets and boxes under the beds and in their closet grew, I would ask, "Remember how badly you wanted the Furbee?"

"Yes."

"Where is it now? How long did you play with it? Do you ever play with it anymore? Do you think this is something you'll really want a month from now?" I might mention a few other past acquisitions that were gathering dust.

The boys responded to this, somewhat reluctantly at first. "Sure, Dad, but this is different." Over time, however, this excuse began to wear thin, and they began to see the problem with their logic. The new stuff wasn't that different. It was just another acquisition that would be of little, if any, value in a month or two. Maybe they already had enough. After a while, they started agreeing with me and passing up purchases because, upon reflection, they appeared to be items of short-term value. I'd won a small victory, and they rarely ask for or buy the junk that they used to buy. It's been one of my most successful strategies, and one I use myself when faced with a purchase decision.

By encouraging your children to assess their inventory of stuff for its longevity and long-term value, helping them understand the meaning of "enough," you too can help children curb their spending passions and develop good habits that will last a lifetime.

TEACHING YOUR KIDS WHERE THINGS COME FROM

Besides helping your children learn lessons about the necessity of new acquisitions and when enough is truly enough, you may want to help them understand where products come from and the impact of producing them. Take disposable chopsticks.

When my children were young, I pointed out that disposable chopsticks come from the tropical rainforest. Tens of millions of them are produced every month to satisfy the needs of the world's people for this short-lived product. "Why are we cutting down rainforests to produce tens of millions of disposable chopsticks every month?" I asked them. "Think of all of the species that lose their home because of this."

Well, it worked.

You, too, can help your children understand and appreciate the source of the materials we consume and the impacts that result from their production and distribution. When you talk about conserving gasoline, for instance, you can trace oil from the well in Saudi Arabia or off the coast of Louisiana to the oil tanker or pipeline to the refinery to the gas station to the car. You can then talk about the pollutants produced when the gasoline is burned. Of course, the level of detail will depend on your understanding and on the age of the child.

Once your child understands the steps in the production of a product, you can talk about the impacts caused along the way, including the social and economic impacts — for example, the two wars (the Gulf War and the war in Iraq) the United States has fought to ensure a steady supply of oil.

An understanding of where products come from and the impacts they have along the way help to create a more environmentally responsible citizenry. The world would be a lot better off if more of us understood such things.

Children can be taught that they vote with their dollars, too. Each time they purchase a product that is environmentally damaging, they're helping to keep the product and the business that made it around. However, each time they purchase an environmentally sound alternative, they're casting their "market vote" in favor of companies working to forge a sustainable future. By consuming, they impact the Earth. It is not something that many of us really understand.

If possible, I suggest you take your kids to visit mines, clearcuts, factories, landfills, and sewage treatment plants to put a face on the impacts you are talking about. Such trips will help your children see for themselves and will very likely have a greater impact than any well-meaning lecture you deliver.

TEACHING KIDS THE VALUE OF MONEY

While on a trip from Missouri with Linda, my significant other, and her children, we stopped to fill up with gas and get a snack from one of those roadside convenience stores. As we were paying for gas, Linda's son showed up at the front counter with some toy he'd picked up off the shelf and absolutely had to have. (We've all been there a few times.) Linda smiled and said, "Sure, you can get that." He beamed. Another victory! Then she added, "With your own money."

You could hear the mental brakes screeching. Her son retreated into thought, as he walked around the store, weighing the pros and cons of using his own hard-earned cash to buy this item. When it was time to leave, he put the item back on the shelf. "I don't think I really need it," he said, and that was that.

It isn't headline news, but our children are inundated with flashy new toys and other novelties, and they want them all now. If you pull out the cash to buy them, they're happy as clams. Your money is play money to them, but ask them to spend their own hard-earned cash on something and suddenly they are forced to ask the same questions you and I pose all the time as adults: Do I really need this?

More often than not, you'll find your children putting stuff back on shelves. It won't always happen, especially with younger children to whom allowance is still play money, but it will occur more and more often as children start to understand the value of money. This technique will be especially useful as your children start to work for their money. Working for $5 per hour puts a whole new perspective on a $30 purchase that is going to end up on the floor of the bedroom closet in a week.

On a related issue, in my home we have a rule that kids pay the extra for items with logos. If a good pair of sneakers costs $60, but the Air Jordan basketball shoes cost $100, we're happy to let the kids make up the difference. Sometimes they shell out the extra cash; sometimes they don't. In any event, my children are learning about the true cost of logos and the support of high-profile sports figures, rock stars, and skate boarders whose endorsements make many products so much more expensive. They're also learning just how much more one must pay for a logo — to provide free advertising for a company. Shouldn't they pay us to serve as walking ads for their products?

TEACHING CHILDREN THE PAY-AS-YOU-GO APPROACH

Like many other kids, my children like to have the new stuff they see when they see it. My older boy is always working angles, trying to leverage money he's expecting from grandma and grandpa for future birthday and Christmas presents, months before they arrive, to finance his present purchases. I have to admit, I fell for this early on. Wanting to be a good parent, I advanced him money for all sorts of things.

After a while, though, it occurred to me that I was doing my son a disservice. I was enabling his desire for immediate gratification and introducing him to the world of easy credit. Both my boys were becoming part of the buy now, pay later culture that is as American as apple pie, hot dogs, and hamburgers. They had little, if any, sense of delayed gratification. If my lending operation continued, they could very well have become part of the many who are in credit card debt up to their eyeballs. My ex-wife had fallen into the same trap.

Realizing the error of our ways, she and I decided to implement a new policy: No more loans with future birthday and Christmas money as collateral unless the boys have earned at least 75 percent of the full purchase price. We've gotten no complaints and, interestingly enough, no requests.

If you have a child, and you've been enabling his or her instant gratification, you may want to enact a similar policy. It will serve your child well in later life, when credit cards start appearing in his or her mailbox. You may also want to spend some time talking about how credit works in the real world; that is, how fast you can run up a big balance and how long it takes to pay off credit card debt, especially if you fall for the monthly minimum balance trap that credit card companies hope will catch you. That's how they make their money.

The minimum monthly payment is the smallest amount you can pay a credit card company and still be a cardholder in good standing. Generally, the minimum monthly payment is equal to two percent of the balance or $10, whichever is greater. Interestingly, though, some statements refer to the minimum as the "Cardholder Amount Due." That's to trick you into believing that this amount represents your payment. It is not the total owed.

The minimum monthly payment is a scheme credit card companies use to keep you in debt for as long as they can in order to make as much money off of you as they can. If you've had experience with this scheme, you know that they also lower minimum monthly payments as the credit card balance decreases.

If you choose to pay the minimum each month, you will pay a lot more in interest than if you pay the card off quickly. Consider an example: A cardholder who makes a minimum payment of $80 on a balance of $4,000 at a 21 percent annual interest rate will take almost ten years to pay off the loan. The cost of the interest is $5,592 with the cardholder paying a total of $9,592 — over twice the cost of the original loan. Making minimum payments results in more finance charges than if the card is paid off quickly. In fact, credit card debt usually takes three times as long to pay off as any conventional loan of the same amount.

Some credit card companies even allow the cardholder to skip a payment or two without a penalty, especially at holiday times. Although this may sound like a grand idea, bear in mind that interest will be charged during this period and even more in finance charges will be owed than before.

In summary, then, the minimum monthly payment is not designed to get you out of debt quickly. It is a way of making the maximum amount of profit from you.

Not that I don't have credit cards. I got my first credit card at age 51, not out of need, but because many car rental companies won't accept debit cards anymore (my usual way of handling such transactions). I use my credit card judiciously, on a pay-as-I-go basis, liquidating the balance each month while earning some free mileage on Frontier Airlines at the same time. I've explained this approach to my children, and let them in on the secrets of my money management scheme, which is very much "buy only what you really need, pay as you go, avoid credit, and if you need a short loan, pay it off as quickly as you can." I told my boys, for instance, that if you make an extra payment each year on a 30-year home mortgage, you can cut the payment period from 30 to about 20 years, saving tens of thousands of dollars in interest! They loved the idea.

SETTING A GOOD EXAMPLE

All this discussion of credit and personal finances brings me to my last recommendation: Set a good example. As in other areas, children learn more by observing what we do than from what we say. I've said it before, as have others: actions speak louder than lectures. If you spend recklessly, must be surrounded by stuff, must have big houses and big cars, and go hopelessly in debt to finance your spending habits, don't expect your kids to listen to your messages of self-discipline, frugality, buying what you need, delayed gratification, the importance of savings, and so on. You've generally lost your audience, although a number of people I interviewed noted that their parents' conspicuous consumption turned them to lives of environmental commitment. Rob Roy, an author and natural builder from the far northeastern part of New York State, lives an environmentally sustainable lifestyle. "I rejected my parents' patterns of conspicuous consumption," he noted. As a young man, Rob had traveled to 45 countries throughout the world. This travel, he said, had "the greatest influence on me, environmentally and in other ways, too. When I came home to the US, I couldn't believe how wasteful we [Americans] are. I also realized that the Earth cannot support every one of its families at the same rate as mine."

More often than not, it was positive examples that led children to make positive choices about their future. Virginia Winter, a Colorado-based facilitator, who has launched a successful career in organization and management development, grew up in the Adirondack Mountains of New York. "Both of my parents were strong role models for reuse and recycling and not creating great amounts of waste from a very early age," she noted. "Both my father and mother were and are extremely active in community and civic life, giving back and living community values." Ginny continues to live her life by these values, giving enormously to the nonprofit community and living a life of environmental responsibility.

Ed Evans, a retired high school chemistry and earth science teacher in Hilton, New York, has spent a lifetime teaching others about the environment. He learned important values from his parents. His parents, Ed noted, "did not have a lot of money, but my father realized at an early age that if he was to enjoy retirement at all, he would have to start saving for it early on. We kids learned to make do, fix and repair, not to waste, save for a rainy day, enjoy the simple things, and to love picnics." He goes on to say, "We were an environmentally friendly family but not because we understood the environment. We were just being frugal and living within our means." Ed's kids have adopted many of the values he learned. His twenty-six-year-old son has a degree in earth science and has decided that he wants to be an earth science teacher, where he too will help kids learn about the environment.

Robyn Lawrence, editor of *Natural Home* magazine, tells a similar story. She grew up in the Midwest. Her parents were not environmentalists; however, she notes, many of the "solid Midwestern values that I grew up with are inherently environmental. My mom always bought our fruits and vegetables at the local farmers' market in the summer. We didn't buy a new car every year. We drove them till they died. And my father made a lot of our furniture."

Today, Robyn and her family own a Honda Civic Hybrid, conserve energy and water in their home, purchase wind power, recycle, buy nontoxic products including organic produce, and purchase local products whenever possible. She and her son actively scoop up litter along city streets. Her story, like Ed's, proves that frugality and other important values, not necessarily environmental in nature, can produce wondrous results in our offspring.

My advice to readers is to practice what you preach. Adopt a policy of buying only what you really need, and then when you do buy, buy responsibly, and be sure to involve your children in the decisions. Buy from environmentally responsible companies. If it is time for a new car, you may consider joining a car club, a car cooperative like Flexcar or Zipcar, where cars are shared by people who subscribe to the service. As noted in Chapter 5, for a membership and user fee you get ready access to a car when you need it. It saves families hundreds of dollars a year. Car clubs work well to meet occasional needs for automobiles, and especially if you have access to good public transportation.

If you want to buy a new car, buy an efficient hybrid vehicle such as a Toyota Prius or Honda Insight, Civic, or Accord. Or you may want to look into a diesel car run by biodiesel. Again, be sure to involve your children in your deliberations, pointing out the benefits of these more environmentally friendly vehicles.

When purchases are necessary, be sure to buy from environmentally responsible companies like those highlighted in the accompanying case study, "I'm Dreaming of a Green Christmas." You can buy clothes at second-hand stores, too, and shop for necessities at yard sales, explaining to your children that you're not only looking for a bargain — to save money for their college education or some other long-term goal — but also trying to put good products back into useful service, saving them from the landfill. Whatever you do, avoid impulse spending — buying things that you don't really need at stores or yard sales just because they're cheap or on sale. Passing up a bargain if you don't really need the item is a good lesson for our children.

You can also buy green products — environmentally friendly products — such as paper made from recycled waste; energy-miserly compact fluorescent light bulbs; non-toxic paints, stains, and finishes; "wood" made from recycled plastic; and carpeting made from recycled pop bottles. Whenever possible, it is a good idea to purchase from socially and environmentally responsible companies. Check out Co-op America's *National Green Pages* for a directory of such companies in the United States.

MODEL OF SUSTAINABILITY
A SMALL BUSINESS PARK IN SWEDEN UNPAVES THE WAY TO A SUSTAINABLE FUTURE

Umeä is a small city in northern Sweden, a country renowned for environmental stewardship. Among its many environmental features, Umeä is home to a remarkable small business park — a model that other cities could emulate. The business park is home to franchises of three multinational corporations: a Ford Motor Company sales and service dealership; a Statoil gas station, car wash, and convenience store; and a McDonald's fast-food restaurant.

Okay, you say, there's no way these three companies could possibly contribute to environmental protection and a sustainable future.

Well, let's take a look.

To begin with all three businesses have green roofs — not roofs painted green, but rather specially constructed roofs that are planted in grass and other forms of vegetation. These roofs help give back to nature a little of the green space taken up by the development itself. They absorb moisture, which nourishes the plants, rather than letting it run off into parking lots, picking up oil and other pollutants that then wash into surface waters. Green roofs also help keep the buildings cooler in the summer.

The parking lot at the Ford dealership is unlike other parking lots you'll find in industrial nations. This one is made from porous pavers, special blocks that allow moisture to seep into the ground where it replenishes groundwater. By letting water seep into the ground, these pavers reduce surface runoff, water pollution, and flooding.

The buildings are made of natural or recycled building materials, too. Moreover, the buildings are built to be efficient — so efficient that they use 60 percent less energy than similar structures. As an example, motion sensors in the buildings turn off lights when the rooms are unoccupied.

Energy demands are met by renewable energy sources, such as the sun and wind. Electricity comes from a wind generator on the coast about 15 miles (24 kilometers) away. The Ford dealership also has solar panels on one side that preheat incoming air, reducing the energy demand on the heating systems. It also has skylights that reduce daytime electrical consumption by 60 to 70 percent. At the McDonald's, waste heat from various processes such as cooking grills, deep fryers and refrigeration systems, is captured and piped to parts of the complex that require heat.

The business park also uses water efficiently and captures and reuses all the storm water onsite. It flows into an onsite water garden. Ninety-nine percent of the water from the car wash is filtered and reused. Sewage from the facility is used for fertilizer in local farming operations.

In addition, the business park reuses or recycles all of the waste it produces. Wood used to build the facility came from local wood lots and was sustainably grown and harvested.

When building the small business park, the developer removed a house located on the site. Rather than demolishing the structure and hauling the waste to the landfill, he lifted it and trucked the building to a new location. Rather than cut down a large oak tree on the site, it too was transplanted elsewhere. The developer left a pine tree that was home to an endangered beetle on the site, too, rather than cutting it down.

The list of environmental attributes of this remarkable facility does not stop here. The gas station, for instance, sells three types of fuels that replace environmentally unfriendly diesel and gasoline. The convenience store sells organic produce and other organic foods. They encourage customers to recycle food containers by including well-labeled receptacles.

The Ford dealership recycles all waste oil and other waste fluids from cars such as brake and radiator fluids. They use vegetable oil, rather than a petroleum-based fluid, in their hydraulic lifts. They even work hard to make this the healthiest and safest possible workspace for their employees. All three businesses provide ongoing education for their employees to ensure the continuation of sustainable business practices.

Now, you say, sure this is all well and good, but the businesses must be suffering.

Wrong.

The fact is, during the first year of operation, revenue from sales at the car dealership and service center shot through the roof. The other businesses are thriving as well, indicating this is clearly not a case of environmental philanthropy, but sound, economically profitable business practice that provides a model for the rest of the world. Over half a million people visit the park every year, and city officials are encouraging other similar development.

Imagine how the world would change if all businesses pursued a similar strategy.

To learn more, see Sarah James and Torbjörn Lahti's book, *The Natural Step for Communities,* 2004, New Society Publishers.

CELEBRATING HOLIDAYS AND OTHER OCCASIONS SUSTAINABLY

Holidays used to be about celebration and honoring the things in life we value, for example, the day of one's birth. Today, thanks to the constant pressure of advertising and the incessant desire of businesses to expand their earnings, many holidays, birthdays, and other celebrations are more about giving and getting things. Affluenza has made us mad when it comes to spending.

Take a middle-class birthday party, for example. Instead of cake and ice cream and games in the back yard, mom and dad now pack the kids in their car and a few friends' cars, then shuttle them to one of a dozen or so birthday venues, like Chuck E. Cheese Pizza, where they gorge on pizza, play games that entitle them to useless trinkets, and climb the walls in a frenetic flurry of activity. A birthday cake arrives and out come the mountains of presents. And when the event is over, each child goes home with a bag full of party favors, largely useless junk that will end up in the bottoms of toy boxes or on the floor. When all is said and done, mom and dad are slightly deafened by the noise, worn out by the commotion, and a few hundred dollars poorer because of the expense.

Happy birthday! More a day to forget than to remember.

Parents who attend or hear about the party then have to try to meet or exceed the festivities, creating something of a birthday party cold war escalation of celebration and expense.

And then there's Christmas, the greatest orgy of spending that ever existed. No longer a religious holiday, Christmas has become a commercial enterprise. Many businesses rely on the Christmas spending frenzy for most of their annual income.

Holidays and celebrations like birthdays needn't be so harried and expensive and so dependent on consumption for fun. For my children's birthdays, we've tried to engage in quieter, more personal celebrations: a dinner at home, a homemade cake and ice cream, and a few thoughtful gifts. For several of my boys' birthdays, I've even made a poster that lists all of the things I like about them and what makes them so special to me. What could be more meaningful than for someone to say, "I'm glad you were born, and here's how you light up my life!"? Give it a try. Your kids deserve to know what makes them special in your eyes.

When it comes to Christmas, we go even crazier. I don't need to tell you the insanity that grips this nation from the day after Thanksgiving until Christmas, so I won't. Suffice it to say, we can do better. We can set a better example for our children by creating a green Christmas, as explained in the accompanying piece, "I'm Dreaming of a Green Christmas."

I'M DREAMING OF A GREEN CHRISTMAS

No longer content to whittle a few toys for our children from wood we gathered from the back forty (because they built a subdivision on it), or knit a sweater for a loved one from wool gathered from our own sheep (which were displaced years ago from the pasture by a brand new K-Mart that was later bulldozed to create a K-Mart Superstore), we brandish our credit cards and head to the mall.

Whatever the case, we plunge into the hordes of Christmas shoppers, in a frantic rush to find a gift — any one will do — for friends, family, and furry pets, because you're certain they're also out there this very moment searching desperately to find the right present for you, even though you haven't talked since last Christmas when you called to thank them for the boot warmer which curled your toe nails last winter. Like hungry sharks in a feeding frenzy, we snatch toys and clothes and all manner of goods off the shelves. And store owners writhe in glee as we head out to our cars laden with packages to show our love and affection for one another, just as long as they're not blocking our parking space when we're ready to leave.

Now, if you're in retail sales, you probably don't want to hear this subversive prattle. Christmas is to retailers what Thanksgiving is to turkey growers. And if you're concerned about doing your part as a consumer to keep the economy from collapsing, you know you have to be out there doing what you have been groomed to do: Buy more stuff.

Anything else is, frankly, quite unthinkable and unpatriotic.

You're probably thinking that I'm, well, just a bit on the "anti-" side of American. And maybe you're sighing in relief, too, knowing you can cross me off your Christmas list!

I'm simply writing this piece to suggest that maybe this Christmas could be a more personal and green affair. This Christmas, why not give a different kind of present — a gift that helps protect the Earth, which is incidentally, the only habitable piece of real estate in the solar system? Why not give gifts that bring us together?

But what can you do?

Fortunately, there's a lot you can do to help create a more personal and greener Christmas. You can select products made from renewable or recycled materials. Or give presents that help promote conservation. Or select gifts that help raise individual awareness. You can also give gifts of yourself.

Below is a list of specifics under each of these general categories. Keep them in mind this Christmas and the next and the next. Use them throughout the year as you select gifts for other occasions. Consider this a gift from me to you.

Gifts made from recycled and renewable materials

• Why not buy a friend or relative a box of recycled Christmas cards for next year or some recycled stationery or recycled wrapping paper? This practical gift not only saves them a trip to the store, it helps promote the use of recycled products and helps protect our forests, reduces pollution, and diverts valuable resources from landfills. Some beautiful designs are available through Earth Care Paper Co., Dept. 232, 100 South Baldwin, Madison, WI. 53703. Tel: 608- 256-5522.

• For children, consider wooden, rather than plastic, toys. Wood is a renewable resource, unlike the oil from which plastic is made. Wood blocks make excellent presents, and a wide variety of wooden toys including animals and trucks — is available in toy stores and area gift shops.

• Glass and clay figurines — of whales, birds, and animals — make a perfect gift for those who love knickknacks. Some wildlife groups sell them to support their programs.

Gifts that promote conservation

• For friends and relatives who love nature, consider a bird feeder or a bird house. They're available locally in many hardware stores. But avoid redwood feeders and houses — there's no sense in cutting down an endangered redwood to house a starling in your backyard.

For a complete catalog of feeders contact Duncraft, in Penacook, New Hampshire 03303-0508.

• For energy-conscious relatives, or ones you want to encourage to be more frugal, consider a compact fluorescent light bulb or two. Although they're a bit pricey ($3 to $10 each), they outlast nine to ten regular incandescent bulbs and save enormous amounts of energy, thus paying for themselves several times over. Because they use less energy, they're responsible for a lot less pollution. You can buy them at hardware stores, grocery stores, and even the large discount stores.

• Why not buy a gift certificate to upgrade friends' and relatives' attic insulation? Your gift will pay huge dividends over the winter months, making them more comfortable and saving them lots of money on energy bills.

• A water-conserving showerhead or plastic dam for toilet tanks isn't a sexy present, but it makes a perfect gift for the practical-minded. You can buy them at most hardware stores and building supply outlets.

• Trees and shrubs also make wonderful gifts. They help provide shade in the summer, cutting energy bills and reducing lawn watering. A gift certificate from a local nursery will be a welcomed gift. You might even consider planting the tree as an additional favor. Your friends will never forget who bought this gift for them.

• How about adopting a zoo animal for a friend? Not to live in their house! Many folks are thrilled to become the "parents" of a bird or mammal from the zoo or a raptor rehabilitation program. Contact your local zoo. They may have a wide assortment of mammals and birds for adoption. Recipients of your gift typically receive an adoption certificate and an information sheet on the animal, and they may be listed on the Parents' Board at the zoo entrance.

• You can also adopt an injured eagle, hawk, or owl from the Florida Audubon Society's Adopt-a-Bird Program, 1101 Audubon Way, Maitland, Florida 32751. Recipients of your gift will receive a photograph of the bird.

You can also support the birds of prey or raptor rehabilitation organizations in your area.

GIFTS THAT RAISE CONSCIOUSNESS AND PROMOTE GOOD STEWARDSHIP

• For the gardener, how about an environmentally safe, biodegradable chemical kit to treat common insects and fertilize house and garden plants? Check out local garden shops or garden supply catalogs. Avid

gardeners not currently using these environmentally beneficial products, will welcome a chance to experiment and see that they really do
work!

• Or what about a gift membership to an environmental group or a
donation to a worthy cause in a friend or loved one's name? If you
don't know of any organizations in your vicinity, you may want to contact Alternative Gifts. They help individuals donate to charities around
the world in the name of a friend or relative and are listed in the
Resource Guide at the end of this book. American Forests plants trees
in people's honor while the Heifer Project International donates agricultural equipment and small animals to peasants in need in less
developed countries.

• For children, why not give a subscription to *Ranger Rick* (elementary
school age) or *My Big Backyard* (pre-schoolers) or
National/International Wildlife (junior high school and older)? These
beautifully produced magazines can give many hours of pleasure, help
raise awareness, and promote reading.

• Dover Press produces a variety of coloring books for children on
plants and animals. These books help youngsters become aware of
the world around them and provide many hours of entertainment.

GIFTS OF YOURSELF

• One of the greatest — and greenest gifts — we can give to those
we love is a bit of ourselves, a piece of our time, a bit of our heart and
soul. Far from resembling the plastic-wrapped goods we usually offer
up at this time of the year, a gift of the self could be as simple as a
walk in the woods, a massage for a loved one, assistance for an afternoon working in the garden or cleaning the garage, or a few hours of
time sitting by a brook.

• You can prepare a simple coupon informing the recipient what he or
she has been gifted and by whom. List your phone number and your
availability.

WRAPPING YOUR PRESENTS

• Each Christmas a mountain of colorful wrapping paper is carefully
applied to packages, then ripped off, hauled to the garbage can, and
thrown out in a frenzy of gift-opening

• In our house, we avoid the cost — and incredible waste — of new
wrapping paper by reusing old paper, year after year after year, until

the paper can no longer be used. We also use colorful newspaper to wrap presents as well, especially for birthdays.

• Reusing paper requires careful unwrapping but we've found that with a little effort and a few reminders, it is no big deal. My boys are pretty well-trained by now.

• By using paper over and over again, you can save money and cut down on waste. You'll need a box to store old wrapping paper, and will need to trim the pieces a bit from year to year. But your supply will never run out — there's always a present or two or three from a relative or a friend, wrapped in new paper, to replace the stock that is retired each year.

• With a little imagination, you can find an incredible number of more personal and environmentally sensitive presents — and ways to wrap them. If your friends and relatives are like mine, you'll find that most are delighted to receive a gift of love that helps protect the environment, and your children will be learning a valuable lesson about enjoying life while respecting it.

For more ideas you may want to read *Simplify the Holidays*, available through the Center for a New American Dream, which is listed in the Resource Guide. You may also want to obtain a copy of Bill McKibben's book, *One Hundred Dollar Holiday*.

Adapted from Daniel D. Chiras, *Environmental Science: Creating a Sustainable Future, 6th ed,* Jones and Bartlett, 2001.

TAKING BACK OUR CHILDREN

If advertisers have their way, our children will become adults with lives full of stuff that is supposed to make them happy, but repeatedly falls short of the false promises of cagey marketers. As adults, your children will have no savings to speak of and will have credit card bills that rival their monthly mortgage payments. We can rescue our kids, or at least give them tools they can use when they become adults to be responsible citizens in a consumer culture. They can be part of the solution, but it is up to us to help them learn the ways of "Earthwise" spending.

FAMILY ACTIVITIES

1. If you haven't seen the video, *Affluenza*, get a copy and view it with your family. Start a discussion beginning with, "Are we, as a family or individually, afflicted with affluenza?"

2. After you have seen *Affluenza*, get a copy of *Escape from Affluenza* and view it with your family. Discuss ways you can use what you learn to help cure your family.

3. Ask your kids to make a list of things they want that money can't buy. You can do this on a family trip or on a weekend. It would be great discussion for the dinner table.

4. Read the "Kids Who Are Making a Difference" piece in this chapter to your children and discuss it. Are there any issues your children feel passionately enough about to start a similar effort?

5. Ask your children to count commercials on TV, then list what they are selling, and how. What emotions are advertisers trying to appeal to? In what ways are they trying to manipulate your children?

6. Develop a television viewing policy with your family to limit time in front of the TV.

7. Start using the asset inventory and asset value techniques described in this chapter when your children ask for new stuff.

8. Talk with your kids about how you pay your bills and manage your money. Do you pay as you go, or are you deep in debt? Talk to them about the pros and cons of each strategy, experiences you have had with money, and ways you think you have learned to handle money responsibly.

9. Talk with your children about the various ways to pay for purchases: cash, check, debit cards, and credit cards. Tell them how each one works and the pros and cons of each one, especially credit cards. You may want to teach them about the dangers of minimum payments by reading the piece in this chapter on the subject.

10. Talk with your partner, if you have one, about the example you are setting for your children when it comes to purchasing and paying for the things you have in your life. This may be a good opportunity for you to revamp your ways.

11. Read the case study in this chapter on the environmentally friendly business park in Umeå, Sweden, and discuss it with your family.

Everybody thinks of changing humanity and nobody thinks
of changing himself
— Tolstoy

7 WALK THE TALK: TEACHING BY EXAMPLE

Years ago, a friend told me a story of an acquaintance with strong environmental leanings who hoped to share his love and respect for nature with his two young children. One day, while riding in the car with them, he was giving a friendly lecture on the value of recycling. When he'd finished, his son asked, "Dad, if recycling's so good, why don't we do it?"

"To know the answer is not always to live the answer," wrote R. J. Sneed.

In several previous chapters, I have emphasized the importance of walking your talk, aka living by your ideals, aka practicing what you preach. If you hope to have an impact on your child's thinking and habits, you'd better act in ways that are consistent with what you're saying.

Sentiment without action will leave kids without a moral compass. Like so many people in today's world, they may subscribe to high values but live lives unaligned with their principles. And the proof of anyone's values is really in the proverbial pudding! Our values are not judged by what we say we believe in, but by how we act. If you're not acting on your principles, your values are really nothing more than window dressing.

Act on your own convictions. Actions speak much louder than your words ever will. Kids can spot hypocrisy a mile away.

MAKE ENVIRONMENTAL PROTECTION AN EVERYDAY ACTIVITY

If you want your children to grow up to be conscientious, caring adults, don't rely on a few token environmental efforts on your part to teach them the value of an environmental lifestyle.

Because they don't.

To have an impact on your children, you have to live your life consistently by the environmental values to which you subscribe.

If you're not acting on your principles, your values are nothing more than window dressing.

Make environmental protection a part of everything you do. Many people I interviewed when researching this book spoke of parents who recycled or lived frugally, either by necessity or by choice.

If you live according to your values, be sure to talk to your kids about them and how they manifest in your family's environmental policies and practices. Chas Ehrlich, who lives in Davis, California, notes that his mother explained the importance of recycling to him when he was a young boy. At age eight, Chas notes, "I started an aluminum can recycling 'business.'" Chas continues a lifetime of environmental commitment. Today, he not only lives in a cohousing community that shares many resources, he also works as an energy consultant. He helped his cohousing community install a solar electric system to supply electricity to the common house.

ASSESSING YOUR FAMILY'S ENVIRONMENTAL PERFORMANCE

Now here's where things may get difficult. How do you make an *honest* and *accurate* assessment of your lifestyle?

To make such an assessment, you'll have to look critically at your life. Remember what Shakespeare wrote in *The Rape of Lucrece*: "Men's faults do seldom to themselves appear." Maybe you have been coasting along thinking you're pretty environmental — and maybe you are, compared to the average family. But comparisons can be pretty meaningless. You can always find someone who performs less well, so you look like a shining star by comparison.

Rather than trying to assess your performance, I suggest you focus on what you need to do. Listen to the voice in your head. My guess is that deep down inside, you know what you need to do. That little voice has no doubt told you more than once that you should be composting your yard and kitchen waste, or recycling more of your family's waste, or even driving a smaller, more energy efficient car or perhaps, and I know this is going to be tough, driving the speed limit. If you are like so many of us, you've probably been rationalizing that you'll do these and a host of other things you know you should be doing when others do them ... or perhaps when they're more convenient ... or perhaps when they are made mandatory ... or as soon as you can find the time.

Why not sit down right now and write out the list that's in your head of the things you have been meaning to do? For best results, you might want to sit down with your spouse and your children and make an environmental to-do list, a no-excuse list of things you know you should be doing. List your ideas by the easiest — the no-brainers — and then include more difficult steps that might take a bit more time and money. Tackle the simple steps first, then move on to the more challenging ones.

WORKING OUT A FAMILY PLAN

If you want some help working out a family plan, I'd strongly suggest you obtain a copy of *Household EcoTeam Workbook* by David Gershon and Robert Gilman. It's a six-month program to make your household more efficient and environmentally friendly. Chances are it won't make your household sustainable, but it is a very good way to start the process of transformation.

This book is meant to guide groups of individuals — EcoTeams — through a thoughtful and deliberate process of change. EcoTeams meet and work together to make meaningful changes in each of their households. They provide ideas and encouragement for one another. Each chapter in the book begins with important information that will help participants understand the problems and possible solutions. The first week is spent assessing your situation, for example, getting a handle on how much trash your family produces. Worksheets are provided to assist you in this process.

During the second week, participants use the "action opportunities" list to look for ways they can reduce their impact. The list includes simple no-brainer actions as well as more involved — and hence sometimes more costly — steps.

During weeks three and four, participants take the steps that they have committed to. Once again, they use the worksheets to determine how much impact their actions have, for example, how much waste is being recycled or composted, rather than being dumped in a landfill.

The book has advice on setting up an EcoTeam, but your family can use it to embark on the process alone, too. After you have completed the six-month program, you will find that you have made great strides. EcoTeams have achieved remarkable reductions in pollution, waste, and resource consumption and netted considerable economic savings in the process. To date, more than 40,000 people in 30 US states and 17 other countries have participated in EcoTeams. On average, families have cut garbage output by 40 to 50 percent by recycling and composting. They have reduced water consumption by 35 percent and have made dramatic decreases in gas consumption for transportation, cutting fuel use by 16 to 20 percent. Home energy consumption was slashed by an average of 9 to 17 percent. (Imagine if everyone in Canada and the United States embarked on this program!)

If you are feeling reluctant, remember that members are not required to adopt any specific actions; it's up to each household to decide which steps they'd like to take. The EcoTeam process is not designed to be threatening. "It offers structure combined with choice," says Dr. R. Warren Flint of Five E's Unlimited, a consulting firm that will help groups set up EcoTeam programs (you can contact them at <www.eeeee.net>). EcoTeams form a support network; individuals can call on others for help or moral support so that new actions become lifetime habits.

These measures are not only good for the Earth and the future of humans and all other species, they save a fair amount of money — between $265 and $389 per year per household.

EcoTeams offer many other, less tangible, but still important benefits. Jennifer Olsen and Per Kielland-Lund who joined an EcoTeam in Madison, Wisconsin, in the fall of 1998, note, "We were able to implement many changes in our daily lives that we, for a long time, had wanted to. ... In addition to these simple, isolated actions, it [EcoTeam participation] transformed our outlook in two ways: We have become much more aware of sustainability issues in general, and are actively seeking out and supporting ways to organize our lives in a more Earth-friendly way. In addition, we have become encouraged and more optimistic on behalf of the Earth and the future of our species." They add, "Through our own direct experience, we see that necessary changes can be made — even by those of us that are not among the forefront ... of sustainable living. It feels good to be a part of the solution and not only the problem."

If the EcoTeam approach seems like more than you'd like to take on, you may want to start your family's program of environmental sustainability with the book *More Fun, Less Stuff Starter Kit*, written by Betsy Taylor of the Center for a New American Dream. This book offers tips on reducing the environmental impact of your life in a variety of ways. It will show you how to live a more economically and environmentally responsible life by addressing a wide variety of issues such as transportation, food, energy use, water consumption, gift-giving, and recreation. The "*Starter Kit*" also offers worksheets and ways to tabulate the beneficial impacts of your actions.

Another good source of information on living a simpler, more environmentally friendly lifestyle is the *Real Money* newsletter of Co-op America. This newsletter is jam-packed with excellent ideas and strategies for making decisions regarding purchases, savings, and investments that contribute to a sustainable future. Additional information can be obtained from their other publications, such as *Co-op America Quarterly*.

HIGH-IMPACT ACTIVITIES: MY RECOMMENDATIONS

If you want to get started right away, and want to tackle those areas of your life that have the biggest impact on the environment, here are twelve steps you can take to dramatically reduce your family's impact on the environment:

1. Install compact fluorescent light bulbs in the most commonly used light fixtures in your house.
2. Beef up the insulation in your home by adding insulation to the attic and walls, if possible, and by installing — and using — insulated curtains or shades. Also hire a professional to run a blower door test. With this information, you can pinpoint cracks and openings in the building envelope that need sealing. Seal them or hire a professional to do the job for you.
3. Turn the thermostat down in the winter to around 68°F (20°C) and up in the summer to around 78°F (25°C). Plant shade trees to keep your house cooler in the summer.
4. Install water-conserving fixtures such as water-efficient showerheads and water-efficient toilets and replace worn out appliances such as washers, dishwashers, furnaces, and air conditioners with energy- and water-efficient models.
5. Water your lawn sparingly, early or late in the day. Replace water-hungry grasses with grasses that need less water, and remove sections of lawn that are hard to water and wasteful of water.
6. Recycle all household waste from newspapers to cardboard to aluminum to glass.
7. Compost all kitchen scraps (except meat and bones) and yard waste. Compost in your backyard and use the compost to enrich the soils in your flower and vegetable gardens.
8. Eat more vegetables and less meat. Buy organic vegetables whenever possible and start your own garden or join a community-supported agriculture program (see "Models of Sustainability" below).

9. Carpool, ride a bike, walk, or take the bus whenever possible. Replace gas guzzling vehicles with fuel-efficient models getting 40 miles per gallon (100 kilometers per 7 liters) or more.

10. Curb consumption. Learn to live more simply. Buy less. Buy used goods. Practice green gift-giving.

11. Reduce the number of pets you keep. Hard as it is to swallow, our pets have a huge impact on the environment, one rarely discussed these days for fear of offending pet lovers. Cats, for instance, kill tens of millions of songbirds each year. Cats and dogs produce mountains of solid waste that may wash into nearby streams during heavy storms. Feeding cats, dogs, parakeets, cockatiels, and other pets also requires enormous acreage, land that was once wildlife habitat, and energy for processing and shipping the food.

12. Lose weight. Weight loss is another important environmental strategy, though never mentioned.

How can I make such a preposterous claim?

Today, an estimated 60 percent of all American adults and 15 percent of all American children are overweight. They take in more calories than they need. In fact, the average American requires 2,200 calories per day, but consumes 3,200 — 1000 calories extra, which accounts for the extra poundage that can lead to diabetes, heart attacks, and other medical problems. Consuming calorie-rich food in excess, which has become something of an American pastime, is not only unhealthy, it requires more resources. The more food we eat, the more land is required, the more energy and materials are used, the more fertilizer is needed, the more pesticides are applied to our land, and the more pollution is produced. Taking care of health problems also requires resources. By eating less and maintaining our health, we can lower our environmental impact quite dramatically.

These twelve steps can make massive inroads into your family's impact on the environment and create a lifestyle that contributes significantly to a sustainable future. Most of the steps are easy, but I'm sure readers can think of a dozen reasons why they can't pursue them. If you put your mind to them, however, and change your priorities, refocus on your values and commit to living by your ideals, well, guess what?

Anything's possible.

And if hundreds of thousands of people in each state follow suit, we can make huge inroads into current problems and help steer our society back onto a sustainable path.

MODELS OF SUSTAINABILITY
COMMUNITY-SUPPORTED AGRICULTURE

Community-supported agriculture (CSA) "is an innovative and resource-ful strategy to connect local farmers with local consumers to develop a regional food supply and strong local economy," according to the University of Massachusetts extension service, whose website <www.umassextension.org> contains a wealth of information on this idea.

The idea began in Japan in the early 1970s and has since spread to other parts of the globe, including North America. Today, there are well over 600 groups and 100,000 members in the United States alone. Although each group is unique, community-supported agriculture gen-erally involves two parties: a local farmer — typically a small farmer who produces food organically — and a group of residents in a nearby city or town who constitute the members. The members purchase produce directly from the farmer. "In most groups," says author Sarah Milstein in an article in *Mother Earth News,* "members pay ahead of time for a full season with the understanding that they will accept some of the risks of production." If the cucumbers produce poorly, so be it. You don't get cukes from the CSA that year. If zucchini grows particularly well, which is almost a given, you'd better learn how to make zucchini bread or dry the things and use them as firewood in the winter.

"In other groups, members subscribe on a monthly basis and receive a predetermined amount of produce each week," she adds.

Produce is either picked up at the farm by members of the group or delivered to a central location by the farmer. Members of each group generally receive eight or more different types of vegetables each week, starting in the spring and continuing well into the fall. However, "some groups offer fruit, herbs, flowers, bread, cheese, eggs, yogurt, beef, honey, maple syrup, and most anything else you can produce on a farm," says Milstein.

CSA programs vary in size. Slack Hollow Farm in Argyle, New York, has a dozen members. They cover only a small percentage of the farm's operating budget. The rest of the produce from their seven-acre (2.8-hectare) farm is sold through a local food co-op. Pachamamma farm in Colorado, just north of Boulder, grows organic produce on 11 acres

(4.4 hectares) of farmland and has 115 members. Across the Hudson River from Slack Hollow Farm in New York is Roxbury Farm, where growers cultivate 25 acres (10 hectares) and sell to 700 members, whose purchases cover about 90 percent of the farm's annual operating expenses.

Community-supported agriculture is a win-win-win situation. Farmers acquire up-front funding, so vitally needed before the growing season starts. By growing a diverse array of crops, farmers reduce pest problems, increase soil fertility, and ensure a decent harvest. You, the consumer, receive an abundance of healthy food at a good price — provided the weather cooperates.

The environment benefits, too. Food produced without pesticides ensures healthy soil and healthy neighboring ecosystems. The birds that frequent the hedgerows surrounding farm fields live healthy lives, gobbling down tons of Pesticide-free insects they harvest from the field, and feeding the rest to their offspring.

In addition, because food is grown only a few miles from members' homes, rather than on distant farms hundreds or thousands of miles from the dinner table, very little energy is required to transport food to market. The less energy, the less pollution. Production at an oil well in the Middle East may decline slightly, but the billionaire sheik who owns it or the millionaire executives who run the big oil companies won't notice the difference. They are too busy trying to decide which model Lear jet they want.

Most, if not all, community-supported agriculture operations are initiated by farmers looking for a secure local market for their products. They recruit members through word-of-mouth, brochures, flyers, media coverage, and other methods. If you're interested in such a program, ask around and do some research on the Web. Attend local farmers' markets and ask if any of the participating farmers also engage in CSA or know farmers in the area who do.

Americans interested in finding a local CSA program can also check with the local US Department of Agriculture extension offices in their states or can contact some of the nonprofit organizations, such as the CSA Farm Network (which lists farms in the northeastern US), for listings of local CSA farms. They are included in the Resource Guide.

If you can't find a local program, you may be able to start one yourself by contacting local farmers. Ads in rural newspapers might help you make contact. Visits to local farm supply stores could prove helpful in identifying potential farmers. You can also contact local and statewide organic farm organizations.

Be sure that you don't enter into this venture expecting grocery store-perfect vegetables. Because organic farmers don't use pesticides, some organic produce may be slightly blemished. And local farmers battle weather, too. In bad years, production can plummet. Some crops may fail entirely. It's not easy producing food, so help the farms you support and understand that they're struggling to do the best they can.

Adapted with permission from Dan Chiras and Dave Wann, *Superbia! 31 Ways to Create Sustainable Neighborhoods*, New Society Publishers, 2003.

LIVING SIMPLY WITH CHILDREN

After completing the *Starter Kit* or *Household EcoTeam Workbook* or my suggested high-impact actions, you may want to explore deeper commitments. Some readers may want to pursue a path to a simpler, more relaxed lifestyle. Others may find the idea of ecologically oriented living like cohousing or ecovillages appealing. Let's explore simple living before we look at alternative communities.

What exactly is voluntary simplicity?

Some people tend to equate simple, ecologically responsible living, engaged in voluntarily, with a long list of negatives, among them poverty, denial, deprivation, inconvenience, and suffering. They see it as a backwards movement that rejects progress.

A life of voluntary simplicity is clearly not any of these things, say advocates. "Voluntary simplicity", writes Duane Elgin, author of a book of the same title, is a "manner of living that is outwardly more simple and inwardly more rich."

Marie Sherlock writes in her book, *Living Simply with Children*, that living simply is "both a means and the end to a meaningful life." She adds, "Simple living is a life focused on the nonmaterial aspects of existence — family, friends, nature, social service, those things that most of us value."

To me, voluntary simplicity means doing less, owning less, and buying less — and having fewer things that break down and need costly repair or replacement. It helps create true independence. "It is not the greatness of man's means that makes him independent, so much as the smallness of his wants," noted William Cobbett, an English political activist of the late 1700s and early 1800s.

Voluntary simplicity is about slowing down the pace of life to have more time to sit with your spouse and your children to talk about the ups and downs of life — or to simply watch a sunset together — instead of racing children around to sporting events or other extracurricular activities in a frantic hurry to fill every second of every day with activity.

"Contrary to some reports, simplicity is not about deprivation. Those practicing simplicity in North America typically are quite comfortable by global standards. The only thing they've given up is the unnecessary and unsatisfying excess that is common in America. In exchange, they receive the luxury of time, peace of mind, and happiness," writes Sherlock. Socrates summed it up best: "He is richest who is content with the least."

OVERCOMING THE COMPLEXITY HURDLE

For most families in countries like the United States, living simply with children may seem to be next to impossible. With moms and dads working full-time jobs, the kids being chauffeured to a long list of extracurricular activities each week, and the incessant rush to buy the latest fashions or newest products, our lives are anything but simple. In fact, family life is extremely complex and stressful. It takes a computer program to keep track of who needs to be where at what time on any given day, and it takes a huge toll on us personally.

So how does life get so complicated? In *Living Simply with Children*, Marie Sherlock notes that "simplicity and childhood are natural counterparts. Left to their own devices, children lead down-to-earth, uncomplicated, genuine lives." Children, she says, are really rather simple creatures. We adults create the complexity — and the stress that burns us up inside.

Contrary to some reports, simplicity is not about deprivation. Those practicing simplicity in North America typically are quite comfortable by global standards. The only thing they've given up is the unnecessary and unsatisfying excess that is common in America. In exchange, they receive the luxury of time, peace of mind, and happiness.
— *Marie Sherlock*, Living Simply with Children

We create complexity for a variety of reasons. For one, we do so because we want our children to excel, to be the best, which means they must go to preschool so they're prepared for kindergarten and all of the challenges it poses (he says tongue in cheek). And when in school, our tiny tots must join the band and play soccer and football and tennis and join the drama club and take acting lessons and ... well, you get the point. We're so worried our children won't compete successfully in the global economy that we push them to engage in activities that weren't even invented in our youth.

Clearly, there's nothing wrong with wanting our children to do their best and be their best and make the best out of their lives. But what does "be the best" really mean? Does it include being relaxed and happy?

Bear in mind that most of us turned out all right without the barrage of extracurricular activities that we force or encourage our children to engage in. And I'm seriously concerned that the stress of all this activity may turn our children into hopeless neurotics.

Complex, stressful lifestyles also arise from peer pressure, advertising, and the culture of excess that produces a broader form of peer pressure to have and do and accomplish and spend along with everyone else, fitting in nicely like a well-oiled cog in the consumer machine. So how do we counter all of these forces?

Living simply with or without children, writes Sherlock, means focusing on the "good stuff in life, which of course is not stuff at all." You may recall from Chapter 5 all of the things that children want that money can't buy. That's part of what simple living is about. By adopting these goals, you can begin a path to a simpler life and help your children see what really matters. In the process, they become less consumeristic. From time to time, my kids and I play board games. We're not frantically wolfing down dinner so we can catch a 7:10 show at the theatre that's a half-hour drive from our home. We're at home, saving energy, using fewer resources. We're together, laughing, and having a good time (except when the scoundrels are beating me, that is).

Living simply, in short, is about weeding out those aspects of your life that are of no lasting value and concentrating on those that are important, to paraphrase Marie Sherlock. Simple living benefits children and adults. Sherlock notes, for instance, that "by living simply and consuming less — you can work part-time or retire early [or both!], freeing up time to focus on those things that matter most to you." And it has personal psychological benefits to parents: "Without distractions, without financial worries, our minds and hearts are released to pursue our true interests." And, lest we forget, "The adoption of simple lifestyles by Western megaconsumers is truly the only way we're going to save the planet. And living simply is also the method we must employ if we care about global economics and social justice."

SO HOW DO YOU LIVE MORE SIMPLY?

The first step to achieving a simpler life is to assess how badly you really want it. Remember, as Clement Stone once wrote, "The foundation stone for any achievement is desire." Next, draw up a list of things that create frustration and headaches in your life. Think long and hard about the activities and possessions that you could do without. What things and activities do you want to get rid of in your life? If your kids are open to the idea, maybe you could create an ongoing process, even a suggestion box for ways to simplify and de-stress your life.

Once you have your list, you'll need to think of alternatives. For example, suppose you have two or three cars. Do you really need all of them? Is there an alternative to owning so many vehicles? Would carpooling help? Could you walk to the grocery store or ask the kids to use their bikes more? Could you use the bus or light rail to commute to work? Could you join a car-sharing program in your city or town?

Maybe you have a pickup truck that only gets used on occasion. Could you rent one or borrow one, or could you buy a small trailer for hauling stuff around? Or would it be cheaper just to pay an occasional delivery fee rather than owning a truck?

What about kitchen appliances? Do you need an electric carving knife? How about an electric can opener? There are perfectly good options that are much cheaper and more reliable — and they won't break down and cost you a lot of money to replace!

Go through your home with a fine-toothed comb and select things you don't need, and then give them to charity. Make it a game with your family.

You may also want to grow some of your own food to simplify shopping and provide really fresh fruits and vegetables more often. Why race to the store for lettuce and tomatoes when you can grow them in your own backyard?

Next, you may want to focus on activities in your family's busy life that are driving you nuts. Do you really need to push the kids so hard, enrolling them in so many activities? Do you really need to push yourself so hard? Can you celebrate holidays more simply and less stressfully? Are there any committees you serve on that eat up your family time, yet aren't producing much good for the community? How can you simplify your work life? Could you work one or two days at home to avoid the commute and free up some time to be with the family?

What forms of entertainment do you engage in? How do you celebrate holidays? What gift-giving patterns are you locked into? What are some alternatives that are simpler, cheaper, and easier on the Earth?

Clearly, there are a lot of ways to make your life and your children's lives simpler. Start small with a few good ideas, and then expand. Remember, too, if you want your kids to relax and enjoy life, you will need to slow down yourself. Just stop doing so many things. As a psychology professor friend of mine reminded me when I was complaining about too many people demanding my time: "Dan, there's a little two-letter word, called no."

For those interested in learning more about living more simply, I'd strongly suggest picking up a copy of Marie Sherlock's book, *Living Simply with Children*. It provides an abundance of good ideas on ways to create a simpler, more economical, more environmentally friendly, and less stressful lifestyle. You may also want to read one of the several books written over the past 20 years on voluntary simplicity. I strongly recommend Duane Elgin's book, *Voluntary Simplicity*. These two books should help immensely in your quest to forge a more sustainable, less hectic, less materialistic lifestyle.

INVOLVING YOUR CHILDREN IN YOUR ECOPLAN

Whatever path you take, whether it is just making your household more environmentally sound or pursuing a lifestyle of greater simplicity, be sure to involve your children in planning and actions. Your successes will be greater if ideas for a greener lifestyle are generated from within, not top down. "Here's what momma or poppa says we're going to do." Furthermore, it is better if new ideas are implemented by consensus. If your kids say, "This is going to be too hard," and put up a fuss, I'd suggest a trial period. "Let's try this for a few months and see how it goes." This may reduce their resistance, and they may find that it really wasn't as difficult as they anticipated, as is often the case when embarking on a new path.

Make this transition fun, not a dreaded chore. Don't yell and scream if your kids slip up. Compliment them when they do things "correctly" and thank them for doing their part.

Obviously, the younger and more compliant the child, the easier the task. Older, more independent children may be particularly challenging. Again, let older children have their say. Involve them in decisions. Don't force them to do anything. Draw them in with your enthusiasm, if possible. If you have been working with your kids on values and love for nature, their buy-in to the changes you're thinking about will be easier — much easier — to acquire. Remember: Don't jump into this cold turkey. Work on the easiest ideas first. Be mindful of the advice of Confucius: "Even the longest journey is begun with a single step."

Remember, too, that dictums from mom or dad out of the clear blue are likely to be met with resistance by older children, especially if they are perceived as counterculture. If your kids are rebellious, don't get into a fight over saving the Earth.

To encourage participation, you might even consider offering incentives. For example, money saved on energy bills could be spent on an environmentally friendly family vacation that they'd all enjoy, or could be spent on evenings out for dinner and a play or a movie. Be creative. Go with their interests, and — whatever you do — seek low-impact, yet enjoyable rewards. You don't want to save energy at home and burn it on a flight to Disneyland. What would be gained? What lesson would your children learn?

Living simply can have a huge impact on your child. Canadian author and natural builder Chris Magwood's parents moved to the country when Chris was a boy to create a self-sufficient lifestyle. "Even though their experiment didn't work out in the end," he observed, "it instilled in me the sense of what's possible. More importantly, I learned that a simpler, more environmentally sound lifestyle is more enjoyable." And, he points out, the benefit of consuming less is calming. "There's a direct link between consuming less and calming down. We expend a lot of personal energy in the drive to consume, and we regain that personal energy when we're not frantically filling our lives with things."

LIVING IN AN ENVIRONMENTALLY FRIENDLY COMMUNITIES

If you want to do more than transform your own household, which is, by the way, quite a lot, you may want to consider moving to a more socially, economically, and environmentally friendly community. Here you'll find three basic options: cohousing, ecovillages, and new urban villages. Although this book is about raising children to care for the Earth, a few words on alternative living are in order. They'll help you realize the options that exist for families to live in communities that subscribe to and practice the values outlined in this book. This material might also be something you'd want to share with your children. It would help them understand some of the options that are available to them.

As you read this material, you might want to ponder the lessons your children would learn about lifestyle options that are good for people, the planet, and the economy. Let's begin by looking at cohousing.

COHOUSING: REINVENTING COMMUNITY

Distressed by the lack of community in modern society, many people have banded together to form cohousing communities. Cohousing communities typically consist of 30 privately owned houses, apartments, or townhouses, clustered around a park-like common area shared by all, and a common house. Kids play freely on the common green and adults use the space to visit or simply relax in the sunshine. The common house is a community-owned building that typically contains a dining room and a large common kitchen. Here, community members assemble each week, sometimes several times a week, to share common meals and socialize. The common house may also have a TV room, play rooms for children, and the like. Many common houses also have laundry facilities available to all members of the community. Guest rooms in the common house can be used for overnight visitors.

In cohousing, pedestrians reign supreme. The automobile is typically relegated to peripheral parking — car ports and parking lots located on the perimeter of the community. Pathways conveniently connect residents to their automobiles, which are usually parked no more than a block or so away from any dwelling. The absence of cars makes cohousing a safe haven for children to play.

The central theme of cohousing is community, a feature that begins to take shape as soon as a group of people organizes to form a cohousing community. The layout of homes, common house, common green, and parking in cohousing also assists in promoting a

> *The central theme behind cohousing is community, a feature that begins to take shape as soon as a group of people organizes to create their community.*

sense of community not available in most neighborhoods. Activities also build on this vital asset. Common meals, for example, help knit members of a community into a cohesive group. However, privacy is also carefully designed into all cohousing, allowing people to balance their need for social interaction with alone time.

Cohousing communities are also built on the principle of shared resources. This feature helps build and maintain community ties; it also promotes environmentally sound living. In Golden, Colorado, at the base of the foothills, is Harmony Village. This cohousing community consists of 27 families who, among other things, share a single lawn mower. Gardens, workshops, and office space are also commonly shared in cohousing communities, saving resources and money. Neighbors often share in yard work, recycling, composting, playground maintenance, and child care.

Shared responsibility is another key element of cohousing. After construction is complete, community members manage their community together with each adult sharing in some aspect of the day-to-day operations. One resident, for example, might chair a committee that plans dinners, while another organizes daycare or manages weekend work projects. The preparation of community meals is a shared responsibility as well, with each individual in the community taking a turn.

Cohousing communities provide many social, economic, and environmental benefits that all contribute to creating a sustainable human existence. For example, the compact, economical design reduces land use. It therefore helps to decrease urban sprawl and protect open space, farmland, and wildlife habitat.

Many other features of cohousing contribute to dramatic reductions in resource use. The guest rooms in the common house, for instance, eliminate the need for a spare guest bedroom in the private dwellings to accommodate infrequent visits by relatives or friends. Kitchens in private dwellings tend to be much smaller, too. If a family is planning a huge meal, they can book the common house to take advantage of its supersized kitchen. Shared laundry facilities, play rooms, workshops, tools, community offices, community gardens, and the common green reduce the resource demand of each household.

Some cohousing communities also purposefully design their homes to be more efficient and environmentally friendly. The dwellings in Nyland Cohousing in Lafayette, Colorado, for example, were designed to be energy efficient and to use solar energy for heating. Some environmentally friendly building materials were used in their construction.

ECOVILLAGES

Most cohousing communities are isolated from amenities. People form communities but must still commute to work by car, drive to the store, and so on. If you'd like to live a more compact, environmentally sustainable existence, walking to work or bicycling to a nearby store to pick up a gallon of milk or a loaf of bread, you may want to pursue other options, such as ecovillages.

What is an ecovillage?

Ecovillages are rural, suburban, or urban communities where people live low-impact, sustainable lifestyles, obtaining a wide range of goods and services within walking or biking distance from their homes. In short, they are more self-contained, ecologically compatible human villages than suburbs. They can be formed from existing neighborhoods or built from scratch in rural or urban areas. Let's look at a few examples.

TRANSFORMING EXISTING NEIGHBORHOODS

LA Eco-Village lies in the heart of what has to be one the most unsustainable cities in the world. Over a decade ago, community activist Lois Arkin and a small handful of friends dedicated to living sustainably in community began to reshape their urban homes to create LA Eco-Village.

They began simply, by publishing a newsletter. As they talked to neighbors about the newsletter, they began asking them to say "hello" to one another, and to make a point of introducing themselves when they passed on the street. Arkin and her friends also suggested that neighbors actively share "positive gossip —

that is, good news about one another rather than traditional gossip — so that residents would be eager to meet fellow neighbors.

In short order, says Arkin, "the neighborhood — where kids kept to themselves; where racism, crime, and drugs were prevalent; where doors were kept locked out of fear; where graffiti sullied the walls; where people walked with eyes down; and where people leaving in droves were commonplace — came alive." People started saying "hello," and often stopped to chat. Children who were strangers before became fast friends.

Arkin and her friends also began to organize street events, for example: "brunch in the middle of the street." She adds, "Neighbors thought we were crazy, but traffic did indeed slow, and some drivers even stopped to join us for a cup of tea!"

Since its beginning, LA Eco-Village has accomplished much more. Today, neighbors often help one another out in their yards or gardens. Neighbors also participate in group projects that benefit the entire community, such as their community garden.

"Working together, neighbors have planted 100 fruit trees throughout the neighborhood and numerous gardens in backyards that now produce organic vegetables," says Arkin. "With almost no money," she adds, "the community has also acquired two million dollars in real estate." She's referring to two multi-family apartment buildings the neighborhood purchased. "Members of the community also recently converted a manicured courtyard in one apartment complex to a productive organic garden," says Arkin. At this writing, they are planning to convert the apartment complex to solar hot water, and they plan to renovate the building using environmentally friendly building materials. Today, neighbors recycle kitchen and yard waste in community compost bins and continue to meet for community meals.

Ecovillages often strive for greater self-sufficiency than traditional neighborhoods, which allows their residents to live better lives for less. LA Eco-Village is no exception. In this urban community of 500, neighbors live within walking distance of many vital amenities, including schools, grocery stores, and mass transit. Many of the 35 active Eco-Villagers have sold their cars, choosing foot power, pedal power, and mass transit over the high-cost, high-impact automobile.

Today, says Arkin, "about a dozen community members make a living at home, offering services to their neighbors, such as maintenance and repair, remodeling, and cleaning. Imagine the joy of working within a few blocks of your own front door. No long hours locked in traffic, breathing filthy air on a daily commute to an office or factory."

STARTING FROM SCRATCH

In Hackbridge, South London, is a relatively new ecovillage, known as Beddington Zero Energy Development, or BedZED for short. Designed by pioneering architect Bill Dunster, this development was built from scratch and consists of 82 residences, community facilities, and office space.

BedZED is designed and "furnished" to promote energy-efficiency, renewable energy use, water efficiency and recycling, environmentally friendly transportation, recycling, and organic food consumption. "BedZED is very exciting because it allows individuals to make a difference in problems such as global warming through their choice of home," says Dunster.

When building this ecovillage, Dunster used many environmentally friendly or green building materials — all acquired within a short 35-mile (56-kilometer) drive of the building site. In addition, Dunster gave preference to building materials manufactured from recycled waste.

Dunster also paid close attention to one of the most important principles of sustainable development: efficiency. For example, the homes were designed and built to exacting energy-efficiency standards. Dunster made sure that energy-miserly appliances and lighting were installed to reduce electrical use. It's estimated that, overall, residents will require 60 percent less energy than those living in comparably sized homes.

Heat demand is a stunning 90 percent lower. Besides building units efficiently, BedZED residences are heated "passively" through south-facing windows that capture the low-angled winter sun. Sunlight that enters the homes is converted to heat, providing gentle warmth.

The community also generates its own electricity from an energy-efficient power plant on-site. Their power plant burns waste wood chips from a local tree surgery — a business that trims and removes trees. The waste had previously been landfilled. The energy system produces as much electricity as the residents of BedZED consume and waste heat from the facility is used to heat homes.

Subscribing to the waste not, want not philosophy, the community also captures rainwater from the roof, which is purified and used in homes. As in the case of energy, water-efficient appliances and fixtures dramatically reduce overall water use within the development. All told, rain captured from rooftops at BedZED is expected to provide about 20 percent of the community's needs.

Not wanting to send waste water to the local sewage treatment plant, Dunster installed an on-site biological treatment facility, known as a "Living Machine." Enclosed in a greenhouse, it contains numerous tanks that house aquatic plants, microorganisms, and animals (snails and fishes) that collectively remove wastes in household wastewater, purifying it as nature would. The effluent is so clean that it is recycled back into the building for flushing toilets.

Energy-efficient and environmentally friendly transportation is another major design feature of BedZED. To reduce demand for transportation, the progressive designer included numerous units that combine living and workspace. In addition, BedZED was designed to house workspaces (offices, for instance) that allow residents to work within walking distance of their residences. BedZED also contains shops, a cafe, and a childcare facility. Combined, these measures reduce the demand for transportation. Working from home means that residents don't have to waste an hour or two each day traveling to their jobs, and it allows whole families to work together. This arrangement saves time, and allows residents to pursue other interests such as gardening and other hobbies.

Limited parking space and parking fees discourage car ownership and encourage residents to seek more environmentally friendly options such as bicycles, foot travel, and nearby public transportation, including trains, buses, and the tramlink. Roads around BedZED were designed to be safer for pedestrians and bicyclists.

In time, BedZED will be served by a handful of electric cars powered by electricity produced in their own power plant from waste wood. Residents who own electric vehicles pay no parking fee and can charge up their cars' batteries for free.

BedZED also sponsors an on-site car club. Mentioned in Chapter 5, car clubs are run by nonprofit or, increasingly, for-profit organizations. BedZED's car club provides residents and businesses access to two cars that are available for rental by the hour or the day.

One resident, Nicola, who lives and works at BedZED and makes use of the on-site car regularly, booking it two or three times a week, says, "It's a real luxury to have comfortable mobility on tap." It gives her satisfaction knowing that "the huge amount of resources needed to make a car are shared among several users."

Katrina, another resident of BedZED who works for a company housed at the facility says, "Since joining the club, we sold the company car," finding it cheaper to rent than to own.

Ecovillages clearly offer convenience and more free time, but also something many of us long for: greater security. "As a woman, I really appreciate the immense feeling of security living in an ecovillage," notes Katrina. Residents can take a moonlight walk without worry. Children can play freely on the grounds, too, in complete safety, as there are many adults who are on the lookout for their well-being.

Several ecovillages are being built from the ground up in rural areas in the United States. They typically consist of two to five cohousing communities like the spokes of a wheel around a central hub — a small, carefully planned village. The village offers many amenities of small town living: shops, stores, offices, and even schools. They're all a short stroll or bike ride along paths that conveniently run by the residents' front doors. Significant amounts of open space are typically set aside to protect open space and wildlife.

At EcoVillage at Ithaca, New York, for example, the residential portion of the community will eventually consist of three to five tightly clustered cohousing communities surrounding a village green. The 176-acre (70.4 hectare) site borders a nature preserve. In the future, residents hope to include a compost-heated greenhouse, a U-pick organic berry farm for income, orchards for sustenance and income, on-site biological wastewater treatment, gray water recycling, and a village cemetery.

Living among like-minded individuals in an ecovillage "has obvious advantages for people who care about the environment in that your neighbours share your basic belief of living more ecologically," says Val Oliver of Crystal Waters Ecovillage in Australia. "For instance, your neighbour won't be nuking the bugs in his or her garden, and toxic fumes won't be wafting across your yard. The food, air, and water are clean throughout our ecovillage and wildlife flourishes." And what a great place for kids to grow up in!

Ecovillage living offers a great many benefits to couples and their children. It is a place where resource consumption is carefully reduced through renewable energy use, recycling, and other measures. Such places foster greater self-reliance — a great lesson for children. Ecovillages help children grow up with a greater sense of community and their part in it.

In Crystal Waters Ecovillage, people look after each other in times of difficulty. Says Val Oliver, "When my husband and I returned from some travels with dengue fever, neighbors rallied round — taking us to the doctor, feeding us, checking up on us — and all without us ever calling for help." What a great model for children!

I'm not here to tell you that ecovillages are a panacea. Albert Bates of The Farm, an ecovillage in rural Tennessee, summed it up when he wrote to me: "Living in an ecovillage is like driving a Tin Lizzie. It rattles and shudders and scares horses, but it will get smoother by and by, as each generation adds its vision."

Moving to cohousing or an ecovillage is not an option for everyone, but if you are inclined to make the change, it will thrust your children into a potentially more sustainable existence — with dozens upon dozens of lessons that will serve them immeasurably for a lifetime.

TRANSFORMING YOUR OWN SUBURB INTO AN ECOVILLAGE

Many people may find the idea of moving to a cohousing community or ecovillage desirable, but can't make the move for one reason or another. Clearly, cohousing isn't an option for everyone. However, if you're ambitious you can create your own cohousing community or ecovillage right where you live now.

How?

In 2000, I joined forces with author, filmmaker, and futurist Dave Wann, coauthor of *Affluenza* and several other thoughtful books, to map out ways to make this happen. Our collaboration blossomed into a list of 31 suggestions for transforming urban and suburban neighborhoods using cohousing and ecovillages as models. We even wrote a book on the subject entitled *Superbia! 31 Ways to Create Sustainable Neighborhoods*. We grouped our ideas into three categories, based on their relative difficulty. Here they are:

Easier Steps

1. Sponsor regular community dinners.
2. Establish a community newsletter, bulletin board, and community roster with bios of community members.
3. Establish a neighborhood watch program.
4. Start neighborhood clubs.
5. Start neighborhood discussion groups.
6. Establish a neighborhood baby-sitting co-op.
7. Form an organic food-buying co-op.
8. Create car or van pools.
9. Create a neighborhood work-share program.
10. Create a neighborhood mission statement.
11. Create a neighborhood asset inventory.

Bolder Steps

12. Open back yards to create a commons for visiting and play space.
13. Plant a community garden and orchard in the commons.
14. Establish a neighborhood composting and recycling facility.
15. Plant trees to produce a more favorable microclimate and wildlife habitat.
16. Replace asphalt and concrete with porous pavers.
17. Establish a more edible landscape — incrementally remove grass in front lawns and replace with vegetables and fruit trees.
18. Join or start a community-supported agriculture program in which neighbors "subscribe" to a local farm's produce.
19. Create a car-share program, purchasing a van or truck for rent to community members.

20. Retrofit homes for energy and water efficiency.

21. Solarize homes.

Boldest Steps

22. Create a community energy system (e.g., solar or wind turbine).

23. Establish alternative water and waste systems.

24. Establish an environmentally friendly transportation system.

25. Purchase a home in the neighborhood and convert it to a common house.

26. Create a community-shared office.

27. Establish a community entertainment program.

28. Narrow or eliminate streets, converting more space to park and edible landscape, walkways, and picnic areas.

29. As the neighborhood population ages and kids leave home, convert garages to apartments to house students or others.

30. Create a mixed-use neighborhood.

31. Foster diversity.

THE BENEFITS OF SUPERBIA!

We don't propose that you undertake these measures all at once. Rather, we suggest that you start with one or two of the easier steps — perhaps by sponsoring regular community meals. A few picnics and potluck dinners would suffice to get the ball rolling. After neighbors start to get to know one another, you might suggest other ideas, like a baby sitting co-op or a discussion group.

Tackling all 31 ideas could take ten years or more. After you have begun the process it may take on a life of its own. If you're persistent and can find allies in the neighborhood, you could create a more tightly knit and more environmentally and economically sustainable neighborhood out of the existing assemblage of families that, in many cases, barely know one another. Your kids will benefit in many ways, too, as their lives will be enriched by new people, new points of view, and new experiences. You and they will have more fun without having to leave the neighborhood. Children will be better cared for and will have a wealth of playmates within safe distance.

You and your children will benefit enormously from shared resources and could live much more economically. One or two nights every week you'll be able to sit down to a meal someone else has prepared.

Superbia! is truly a win-win-win proposition: the environment benefits, kids and their parents benefit; the economy edges a little closer to sustainability. The world will be a better place thanks to your wisdom and courage.

KIDS WHO ARE MAKING A DIFFERENCE
TWO BIG KIDS TAKE ON THE IMPOSSIBLE

"Okay," you say, "I'm convinced. The ideas on creating a more sustainable neighborhood are interesting and perhaps even doable. But surely not the whole ball of wax. You can't convert an entire community. That seems too far out there, too grandiose."

Think again.

In time, anything's possible.

And you don't have to be wealthy to make the transition.

Consider the case of Brad Lancaster, a much older "kid" who is making a huge difference. At age 27, Brad and his brother Rodd purchased a dilapidated home in a run-down neighborhood in Tucson, Arizona. Most people would have razed the house and started over.

But not these two.

Over the years, the brothers have devoted their energy to fixing up the house and breathing life back into this weed-infested, arid lot, turning the grounds into an oasis and the house into a stellar example of urban self-sufficiency.

To reduce heat gain in the hot Arizona summers, they painted the house white. (A white coating reflects sunlight, reduces heat absorption and increases comfort levels.) They also increased the length of the eaves or overhang, providing cooling shade for the walls in the hot summer months. They constructed trellises from salvaged rebar and steel mesh, then planted vegetables that grow on vines. During the summer, squash adorn the trellises, providing food as well as shade. In the winter, snow peas grow there. Because they only grow to a height of three to four feet, they can't block the low-angled winter sun, which heats the house passively.

Over the years, these two remarkable men have planted trees to shade their home and a vegetable garden that's fed by rainwater collected from their small roof. To protect against overheating in the summer, they often cook food outdoors in a solar oven. Because the desert air cools down substantially at night, they open a few windows each night to permit the chilly desert air to purge heat that has accumulated inside the house during the daytime hours. It's a very effective natural cooling technique that has been used for centuries in hot, arid climates.

During the winter, Brad and his brother heat their home with solar energy streaming in through south-facing windows. A small wood stove provides backup heat, but they provide their own fuel using wood from the trees that now grow in their yard. Hot water comes from a solar water heater all year long.

Electricity comes from a solar electric panel with battery storage. In the summer, solar electricity powers a small ceiling fan that helps keep the place cool. "As the fan is powered by the panel, we literally cool the house with the sun," remarks Brad.

Slowly but surely, these advocates of environmentally friendly lifestyles have become more and more self-sufficient. They have also organized the creation of an organic community garden and orchard. Thirty-five members participate in the community garden, growing an assortment of vegetables including tomatoes, chilies, herbs, eggplant, snow peas, lettuces, broccoli, and watermelon. The community orchard, located in the middle of the neighborhood near the playground, produces peaches, plums, almonds, citrus fruits, dates, and apricots. "This has brought more neighbors together, stressed a more sustainable system of local food production, created a gathering place [there are weekly potlucks and regular work parties], and has become a news and gossip hub with a community bulletin board," notes Brad.

They've even created a small nature park in the inner city. "We grow native species once common around Tucson, but now lost to bulldozing and development," says Brad. "It brings a piece of the desert back to the inner city."

These energetic visionaries — clearly the oldest "kids" I've featured in this book — have also established a monthly neighborhood newsletter, mailed out to everyone in the neighborhood. "The city pays for printing and mailing," says Brad, "which is a great service, because the newsletter keeps everyone current and connected. Anyone can submit articles, art, or stories." The newsletter has reaped other benefits as well. It has, for example, "greatly reduced ridiculous rumors, speculation, and backstabbing as folks know what is going on. It has also enabled us to mobilize volunteers for projects and push city and county officials to recognize our issues and positions."

But there's still more. In recent years, the neighbors have established an artist's cooperative in a nearby abandoned warehouse. These low-cost live/work spaces and the creativity of those within them have created an unofficial and vibrant community center with ongoing classes; concerts; workshops; services; art shows; theater, bike repairs; rentals; and sales; and more. Nothing had to be built, it only had to be opened and made affordable.

When asked about the motivation for his efforts, Brad is eloquent. "I want to live in a vibrant community," he says. "I want to live where people know each other, wave to one another, talk to and help each other, work to make things better, and play together. I want to live in a community that encourages and celebrates diversity and creativity. I want to live in a community with a sense of place connected to the local cultures, history, and bioregion. I want to live in a community that leaves the car behind to welcome leisurely strolls and bike rides. I want to live in a community where we grow much of our food and share it through potluck dinners. I want to live in a community that creates rather than extracts resources. As I want such a community, I work to create it and support it." It's hard to argue with success.

THE CHOICE IS OURS—SO WHAT ELSE IS NEW?

Walking one's talk means living consistently with one's ideals. Our ideals are our better selves, the people we want to be. If we want our children to live by their ideals, we must set the example, providing a good, consistent model where every action telegraphs the intentions in our hearts and souls.

We can also create environmentally, socially, and economically sustainable communities and live our ideals to the fullest by joining a cohousing community or creating an ecovillage. Your children will benefit enormously from the experience of growing up in such a community. Or we can revamp the urban and suburban neighborhoods we live in now using the principles of *Superbia!*

The choice, as it almost always is, is ours and ours alone.

FAMILY ACTIVITIES

1. If you haven't already assessed your family's environmental performance, this might be a good time to do it. You may want to begin by making a list of your values. How important is the environment? How important are clean air, clean water, clean energy, and so on? Then assess your activities in areas such as transportation, energy use, water use, waste, food consumption,

material use, and spending. Consider each area separately and describe how you could improve your family's performance. You may want to get a copy of *More Fun, Less Stuff!* and work through its assessment, or you can obtain a copy of *the EcoTeam Workbook* and work through it with your family and interested friends or neighbors.

2. Study the high-impact changes outlined in this chapter and, with your family, create a plan to address each area.

3. Read the piece on community-supported agriculture to your family. If they are interested, you may want to join one in your area. Or you may want to start an organic garden and an orchard to grow some of your own food.

4. Go through the steps listed on pages 177 – 78 to create ideas on ways to forge a simpler lifestyle with your family, and then adopt some of the ideas that appeal to your children and spouse.

5. Read and discuss the section on cohousing with your family. If they are intrigued by the idea, contact a local cohousing community or an ecovillage for a tour. You can locate one by logging on to <www.cohousing.org>. Afterwards, discuss this option to see if it is something you would like to pursue.

6. You may want to obtain a copy of my book, *Superbia! 31 Ways to Create Sustainable Neighborhoods*. Read the chapters on ways you can transform your own neighborhood. Discuss these ideas with your family. If you are intrigued by the idea, talk with neighbors to see if they are also interested. If so, you might begin by planning regular community potlucks.

7. Read the piece on "Kids Who Are Making a Difference" to your family and discuss the wonderful accomplishments of Brad and Rodd Lancaster.

The true test of civilization is, not the census, nor the size of cities, not the crops — no, but the kind of man the country turns out.
— Ralph Waldo Emerson

8 ENSURING SUCCESS

When my children were quite young, I was determined not to let holidays get out of hand — especially not to get carried away with gift-giving. To ensure that our family achieved this goal, I asked my parents not to shower the kids with gifts when we visited them in Florida during the kids' Christmas vacation.

Sure enough, though, the first holiday season, my generous mother, bless her soul, began to regale the children with gifts.

Shortly after we arrived she began hauling presents out of a closet, giving the boys a gift each day starting three or four days *before* Christmas. When Christmas finally arrived, she piled another dozen gifts for *each* child under the tree. Overcome with a feeling of helplessness, I watched as the kids began to tear open their presents. What kind of lesson was this? I wondered.

COMBATING PEER PRESSURE

Living a life that diverges from the mainstream is fraught with difficulty. Don't expect the path to be easy. As you walk your talk, you will encounter many well-meaning individuals, including friends and relatives, who will sabotage your efforts. You and your children will also face seemingly insurmountable peer pressure. Whether it is creating a simpler lifestyle or starting an organic garden, you and your kids will feel unrelenting peer pressure to conform to societal norms, often the same norms that are steering us off a sustainable path.

Needless to say, peer pressure will be a force to be reckoned with. If you are going to feel it, it's best that you first understand this beast that drives us all insane!

WHAT EXACTLY IS PEER PRESSURE?

Peer pressure occurs when another person's beliefs or actions influence or attempt to influence our thoughts and behaviors. Peer pressure is exerted by friends, co-workers, neighbors, family, and the groups we belong to. It is also applied by society at large through messages on television and other media, as outlined in Chapter 5.

Whether it is creating a simpler lifestyle or starting an organic garden, kids and parents will feel peer pressure to conform to societal norms, often the same norms that are steering us off a sustainable path.

Although we may think of ourselves as independent thinkers, it's hard to ignore peer pressure. As writer Eric Hoffer once said, "When people are free to do as they please, they usually imitate each other." In America, home of the free, freedom of speech and independent thinking are lofty ideals, but frankly we're much more comfortable if everyone exerts their right to personal freedom by saying and doing the same things others say and do.

"The need to belong and to identify with a group is particularly strong as a child is growing up and it becomes nearly overwhelming in early adolescence," says Marie Sherlock. Even as adults, the need to belong remains a strong biological urge. While peer pressure influences our lives, it absolutely rules the lives of our children as they get older, and could easily derail your efforts to raise a child who cares for the Earth. In fact, almost anything you do to live a more environmentally sustainable lifestyle could be hindered by this powerful force. Put another way, swimming against the mainstream consumer culture that poses a gigantic threat to the well-being of the planet won't make your life easy.

But all is not lost.

When people are free to do as they please, they usually imitate each other.
— Eric Hoffer

There are ways to overcome this hurdle. I've done it nearly my entire life. I've lived on the fringe, so to speak, doing "my thing" despite the fact that "my thing" and "my neighbors' thing" were so markedly different.

So let's examine ways that you can counter cultural norms and peer pressure.

KNOWING YOUR OWN MIND

First and foremost, you must have a strong sense of purpose, established in part by the knowledge that you are on the right path. If you have studied environmental trends, you will know that we have made a mess of the planet and that conditions are worsening by the minute. You will know that we cannot continue to proceed on this course without further severe backlashes. Beating up the planet is a form of self-flagellation.

After studying the environment, you will know that unrelenting population growth, a lack of solid environmental ethics, and the ugly duo of excessiveness and wastefulness are largely to blame. If you have doubts about these statements, you may want to take some time to study the issue. Read books on the environment till you can't stand it anymore. In order to overcome peer pressure, you must be convinced that our planet cannot continue to support our extravagances much longer. When you understand these facts, you can say with conviction, "I understand the importance of the Earth and its ecosystems to the well-being of humans and all other living things. I need to support conservation, recycling, population control, renewable and sustainable use of resources, habitat protection, sustainable agriculture, and so on and so on. I can do my part by living more simply, in accordance with my values. I need to teach my children the same." With that conviction, you can move forward. Half-baked convictions won't withstand peer pressure.

> *The need to belong and to identify with a group is particularly strong as a child is growing up and it becomes nearly overwhelming in early adolescence.*
> — *Marie Sherlock,* Living Simply with Children

Withstanding peer pressure also requires a clear articulation of your values. As Marie Sherlock points out in *Living Simply with Children,* "Without articulating your real beliefs and having a foundation of what your true values are, it will be very hard to turn your back on our culture's peer pressure."

Know, too, that we can live well without destroying the Earth. We can live sustainably; we can meet our needs without bankrupting the Earth's vast resources. We can even meet our needs while restoring the Earth, ensuring a healthy ecosystem, but we need to change now.

If you need convincing that we can forge a sustainable path, you might want to read books like *Plan B* written by Lester Brown or my out-of-print book, *Lessons from Nature: Learning to Live Sustainably on the Earth.* You may also want to study the publications of the Worldwatch Institute. Their books and reports present solid and convincing evidence that human society can meet its needs while promoting a healthy Earth. Additional examples are found in books such as *Natural Capitalism, Superbia! 31 Ways to Create Sustainable Neighborhoods*, and *The Natural Step for Communities*. These and other similar books offer a clear vision of a sustainable future, and examples to support the authors' visions.

To withstand peer pressure, it also helps to be sure of yourself, even proud that you see the future and are willing to act. Remember the words of futurist Richard Lamm, who served three terms as governor of Colorado: "It is not enough for a nation to have a handful of heroes. What we need are generations of responsible people."

Take pride in your commitment to leave the woodpile a little fuller, and let your kids know that this is a matter of pride. You're a producer, not a consumer. As such, you need not put others down, nor act smug; simply take solace in the fact that you are willing to act proactively.

All of these ideas can help create an unassailable sense of self-esteem; this, in turn, creates something of a thick skin against the slings and arrows or odd looks and comments that may come your way as you swim against the mainstream of our consumer culture. From self-esteem comes courage, courage to do what you believe is correct, despite what others may say or think. My kids' school bus driver derides our solar house from time to time. When they tell me he makes fun of our solar house, I shrug my shoulders and say, "Let him make fun. He probably pays more in a month for utility bills that we do in three years!"

SURROUND YOURSELF WITH LIKE-MINDED SOULS

I travel frequently to conferences and expos, giving speeches and workshops on green building, solar energy, and sustainable development. Although the trips are often demanding, I usually return home energized. On one trip to Sand Point, Idaho, to deliver a series of talks on sustainability, it occurred to me why I feel charged up by these trips: It's because I am surrounded by like-minded individuals. I am meeting and talking with people who are as excited by the prospects of creating a sustainable future as I am, people who are often taking actions to make this dream become a reality. Their enthusiasm and dedication give me hope and hope is energizing.

You, too, can find comfort and support in like-minded souls. If you are feeling alone in your quest to forge a more sustainable path, I'd recommend joining a local environmental group or attending environmental conferences in your area. Or you may simply want to strike up a friendship with people in your neighborhood, city, or town who think like you do. In so doing, you will find many people concerned about the same issues that keep you awake at night. You will find people who have dedicated their lives to solving them. You will discover that you are not alone; there are others swimming valiantly against the mainstream.

Over time, as these associations and friendships blossom, your community will very likely provide positive peer pressure by supporting what you are doing. "Instead of feeling coerced to behave against your convictions, you feel supported to act in accordance with your beliefs, because those around you accept and value them," says Sherlock. Our local organic food co-op provides an avenue for building this kind of support. (See the "Models of Sustainability" piece in this chapter.)

Surrounding yourself with like-minded individuals can also be educational for children. Canadian writer Chris Magwood notes that his "house is always full of natural building types ... so discussions of environmental impacts are ongoing." Chris and his wife live a simple, resource-efficient life. They rely on solar energy and curb their demands so they can live within the limits of their system. They talk to their daughter about their choices and their responsibilities, "trying to impart to her that we must temper our own personal wants against the cost of the greater whole." Exposure to others with similar viewpoints and similar lifestyles supports their own point of view. Of his daughter's exposure to these like-minded folks, Chris remarks, "I'm assuming that she is getting a lot of information by osmosis, too."

As discussed in the last chapter, you may even want to consider creating a cohousing community so you are surrounded by people with similar values. You can start an EcoTeam or start a discussion group to ponder and act on the ideas.

MODELS OF SUSTAINABILITY
ORGANIC PRODUCE AT BARGAIN PRICES

You recycle, conserve energy at home, drive an energy-efficient car, and take short showers. You vote green, and lately you've even been trying to curb your consumer tendencies. You even buy recycled-content toilet paper and write occasional letters to your congressional representatives in support of the environment.

Despite your green lifestyle, there's one obstacle you've never been able to overcome: the high cost of organic produce. While you would prefer to buy pesticide-free lettuce, hormone-free milk, and eggs produced from free-range chickens, the cost presents a huge road block.

In most stores, organic produce and conventionally grown fruits and vegetables are light years apart in cost. Whereas a regular head of lettuce might run 99 cents, maybe $1.50, a head of organically grown lettuce costs over $3.95. A gallon of ordinary milk runs for $2.50 to $3.00 per gallon; hormone-free organic milk costs $5.00. The difference is hard to ignore; and for many, the price barrier is impossible to overcome.

But there's a way around this economic barrier.

PEOPLE OF ORGANIC PRODUCE

In Evergreen, Colorado, in the foothills of the Rocky Mountains where I make my home, one resident, Mary Denham, and four friends joined forces in 1999 to form a community-wide organic food buying co-op. "I started the co-op," says Denham, "out of frustration. It was hard to go into a regular grocery store and see the poor selection in the organic section. They never looked very fresh, and they were way too expensive."

The co-op was set up to reduce the cost of organic produce and make healthy fruits and vegetables more widely available in this small mountain community, and it is still running strong. In fact, it's never been stronger.

They dubbed the group Women of Organic Produce, then when I joined a few years ago, they renamed it to the POOP Co-op, which (forget your sniggering) stood for People of Organic Produce.

For political correctness, its title has been transformed once again, this time to Lovers of Organic Produce, or LOOP. We're lovingly referred to as "loopers," with its various connotations.

Here's how it works.

Each week one member of the co-op volunteers to be in charge of the produce order. That individual places an order at Vitamin Cottage Natural Grocers, a locally owned retailer thirty minutes away by car from our sleepy little town. Vitamin Cottage offers a potpourri of organic fruits and vegetables.

The person in charge each week gets on the phone or his or her computer on Sunday and calls or e-mails each member of the co-op to see who is interested in receiving a box of produce.

The order is then phoned in to the produce manager at the local Vitamin Cottage Natural Grocer on Monday morning. The affable and ever-pleasant J.P. begins by rattling off a list of this week's specials, and then works with the coordinator to secure the best prices from among his various suppliers.

The next day, the coordinator picks up the order, trucks it home, and divides the produce among the participants. Over the next few hours, participants show up, chat, and haul off their boxes of fresh produce. There's no store front, no overhead, and once the boxes have been picked up there's little evidence of our tiny covert operation to make the world safe from pesticides and artificial fertilizers.

SAVING MONEY, SAVING THE EARTH

Vitamin Cottage sells organic produce to our co-op by the case, charging us cost plus 20 percent, saving each family a huge amount of money. I estimate that I receive $40 worth of organic fruits and vegetables each week for approximately $20 — plus or minus a little. Orders typically consist of eight to ten items, a mixture of organically grown fruit and vegetables. When asked if she felt she and her family were getting their money's worth, co-op member Karin Claus remarked, "Absolutely. If you try to buy $20 worth of organic produce on your own, the money just doesn't go very far."

Our co-op also makes it possible for members to place special orders, for example, for a large order of carrots just for their family, say for making carrot juice. The coordinator will pick up the order and invoice that item separately.

The organic co-op is a fantastic way to feed a family. My kids and I eat a much healthier diet — that is, lots more fruits and vegetables — since we joined the group. When asked what he liked most about the co-op, member Tony Stowe remarked, "Meeting the people, and being surprised by different fruits and vegetables that we have never tried before." Karin Claus echoed Tony's sentiments: "Receiving a variety of produce each week — instead of the usual stuff I buy." On a personal level, my children and I have also been introduced to produce we might otherwise not even have considered. This forces us to experiment with new foods and widens our gustatory horizons.

Yet another benefit is that we're no longer ingesting pesticides in our food! Over the long run, this could reduce our chances of contracting cancer.

The organic co-op also helps build community. Over the years, new friendships have blossomed. The day of pickup is always a great opportunity to get caught up on the latest happenings in and around our mountain community. I personally look forward to visiting with several members of the co-op who have much in common with me. It's nice to know there are like-minded individuals around.

Ordering can be fun, too. Claus remarked, "You have complete control to pick out whatever you want!"

Lest we forget, by participating in the organic co-op, we're helping to promote an important economic activity, organic farming. Most organic produce comes from small family-operated farmers. Compared to corporate farmers, the little guys are often better stewards of the land.

Finally, we're no longer contributing to the production of pesticides and artificial fertilizers and the systematic chemical drenching of America's cropland and all the attendant effects of this systematic application of biocides and artificial fertilizers in the name of increasing agricultural production.

NOT A BOWL OF CHERRIES

This system does have some drawbacks, however. It is not all a bowl of cherries. For one, participants are never quite sure what they're going to receive from one week to the next. The order is completely up to the discretion of the coordinator. Those individuals who plan their meals ahead of time find this system unacceptable, and usually drop out within a short time. (Be sure to warn prospective members of this potential downside.)

Another problem is that participants sometimes receive food they don't particularly like — or don't know how to cook. For instance, I like onions, but they don't like me very much. When we receive a large order of onions, I typically give them away to neighbors. There was also a time when we were receiving a lot of pomegranates, and I didn't have the foggiest idea what to do with them.

To solve this problem, you might ask members to write up a list of "undesirables" — fruits and vegetables they detest. You may also want to set up your co-op so that individuals can call the weekly coordinator to make requests for specific food items. Members can also trade for produce they prefer. For example, one member's onions might be traded for another's broccoli. To help those who don't know what to do with unusual fruits and vegetables, members can share recipes or tips on preparing and cooking unusual food items. Recipes also help those who don't quite know what to do with four bunches of spinach. (Over the years, I've learned some great spinach recipes!)

Another minor problem is that some individuals may be unable to keep up with a weekly box of produce. To address this in our co-op, some members (myself included) order every other week — or order half boxes. For vegetarians, the program is a godsend. Co-op member Tony Stowe remarked, "There are times when we get small boxes of expensive produce. Other times we get big boxes of seasonal produce. Being vegetarians, we always eat everything, except the box they come in."

HOW TO GET STARTED

Starting an organic co-op can be a challenge. When our group started, Mary and her friends just sat down and talked about it. They started with about ten families. "But we had no idea of how we were going to select produce each week, what it would cost, how to split it up or distribute it," noted Mary Denham. "We made lots of mistakes at the beginning. We weren't real clear about how much it was going to cost. And the price for each member shot way up when there weren't a lot of people participating some weeks. Sometimes we weren't sure how much food came in a case. We got a case of ginger, for instance, to share among ten people, which was way too much!"

"Members came up with lots of cool ideas at first, too. Some of which we tried. We thought, for instance, that it would be neat if the person of the week could deliver produce to each member's doorstep," laughed Denham. "It was a cool idea, but it didn't work out ... I remember driving around in the dark looking for one member's house."

Thankfully, readers can benefit from the experience of our little group.

If you're interested, I recommend that you start small and be patient. Contact a local organic grocer or, lacking that option, contact the produce manager at a conventional grocery store that sells organic produce to see if they'll work with you. If so, ask if they'll sell you produce by the case at a good price — hopefully no more than 20 percent above their cost.

Once you've established a supplier, you might ask a few neighbors and their friends to give it a whirl. You'll need ten people, give or take a few, to kick-start this effort.

At first, a small group of people can run the co-op. But as those people move on, you may need one leader to provide continuity. "In the beginning," Denham noted, "I wasn't the leader. The group that started it took on that task. But as the old-timers dropped out, we needed one person to keep track of the calendar, talk with new members, and recruit volunteers." Mary's taken on that role. Although it can be frustrating and time-consuming, it's well worth it. I'd suggest, if you have a leader, that that person receive his or her fruits and vegetables free at least once a month, maybe more often. It might cost members of the co-op an extra dollar or two per week, but it's well worth the work of a strong and dedicated leader.

One other bit of advice: "Keep it simple, so it can sustain itself," advises Denham. "Any idea that could make it more complicated or difficult should be abandoned."

As you gain experience, you can recruit additional members by word of mouth or through ads or articles in a local newspaper. Our local newspaper ran a story on our co-op that tripled our membership almost overnight.

To reduce the work load of the organizer, you'll want to prepare a written description of the program and procedures. It can be handed out or e-mailed to all new members or people who are considering joining. This helps newcomers learn the rules and reduces the time required by the organizer/coordinator. Also, be honest and let all new or prospective members know the potential downsides as well as the many benefits.

In a co-op with a dozen members, each member will be in charge four or five times a year, which means they'll have to order, pick up, and distribute the produce four or five times a year. To ease the burden, members can also work in pairs. One person, for instance, can call members and place the order. Another can pick up and sort the produce.

People who want to belong but can't participate in the pickup of produce, for example, because of their employment, shouldn't be excluded. To compensate more active members, though, they could be charged a few extra dollars to make up for the fact that they can't do the pickup and sorting. As noted earlier, you might even consider giving the person of the week his or her produce that week for free, as a small financial incentive — and a token of your group's thanks.

Those who like to buy unusual foods for the co-op on their week might consider providing members with recipes, as mentioned earlier. Joe O'Leary, a member of our co-op says, "Some advance warning of what's being ordered might help, too. That way, I have a day to find out how to prepare chard or kale or green cabbage for the next week. Sometimes this stuff just sits in our fridge and wilts before I can figure out how to use it." Those in need of assistance can go online and ask members for recipe suggestions.

Speaking of "online," our group now uses the Internet to coordinate our program, distribute the schedule, and solicit volunteers. You might consider the same system. It really saves time!

Organic food co-ops take time and patience to get running, and require a persistent leader who is willing to take up the slack and beat the bushes for volunteers from time to time. The benefits are so great, however, that it is well worth your time.

COMBATING PEER PRESSURE YOUR CHILDREN FEEL

The next challenge is to help your children recognize and resist the peer pressure they feel. Your teachings will be helpful, as will your strength of conviction. When your kids complain about feeling odd or not fitting in, listen to them, respect their feelings, and talk with them about peer pressure and your family values. You may need to remind them why your family does things the way they do. I don't pretend for a minute that this is going to be easy.

When your children become adolescents, don't be dismayed if they adopt the values of their peers. They're programmed to diverge from mom and dad at this age, and this is one way they can do it. My teenage son, who turned 16 in 2004, eats, sleeps, and drinks cars. There's nothing in the world he'd rather have than a souped-up "muscle car," despite my teachings and the example I set in my life. (I drive a fuel-efficient hybrid Toyota Prius). At times, I suspect his interest is a rebellion against my values and my way of life. Nonetheless, I listen, even take an interest in his dreams, and secretly hope that someday he'll see that the muscle car isn't all that it is cracked up to be. (I was gratified to see how intrigued he is by the Prius and its phenomenal gas mileage.)

> *Difficulty is the excuse history never accepts.*
> *— Samuel Grafton*

The teenage years bring an irrepressible need to fit in, and sad to say, that means joining the consumer culture that has a stranglehold on our children's peers. Eventually, though, as I have said earlier in the book, it is very likely that your child will return to the values you taught them through word and deed. Don't let a temporary fork in the road upset your equanimity. "The bottom line, say many parents, is that you have to do the best you can — and then hope," notes Marie Sherlock. Remember, if you have taught your child to value and love nature and have instilled environmental values and have lived by your values, and helped your child learn to reject manipulative advertising, and created a more enjoyable lifestyle by living a simpler, less consumerist life, your child will very likely return to good values and an environmentally responsible lifestyle after his or her forays into the "real" world.

Some parents help their kids resist peer pressure by taking their children out of the mainstream; for example, by enrolling them in schools that focus on the arts and environment, like Orca Elementary in Seattle, Washington. Montessori schools may support values similar to yours. Other parents homeschool their children to reduce their exposure to the mini-consumers inhabiting schools.

You can also encourage your child to log on to <www.generationfix.com>, created by Elizabeth Rusch, author of *Generation Fix: Young Ideas for a Better World*, to join in the forums on hunger, environment, and homelessness, among others. This website is meant for children ages 8 to 15, and offers a venue in which kids can talk with other kids their age about the things that bother them and ways to solve them. It is, in essence, a virtual support group.

BEYOND ENVIRONMENTAL PROTECTION

The environment is the lifeblood of human society. It supplies the resources that keep us alive and support our economy. Creating a sustainable society obviously hinges on efforts to protect and enhance the environment. You and your children can play a role in such efforts. However, creating a sustainable society won't be achieved merely by efforts to safeguard and enhance the environment. We must also promote social conditions conducive to a sustainable society. That is, we must strive to eradicate racism, discrimination, and other social injustices. We must also address poverty and disparities in opportunity among peoples of different sexes and ethnic backgrounds. And, of course, we must eliminate the tyranny of dictatorships that suppress freedoms, often with brutality.

War, too, wreaks havoc on people and the environment and steals valuable financial and material resources, diverting vast intellectual capital from the task of creating a sustainable future. If this does not make sense, ask yourself: How can countries plagued with civil strive devote resources to protect the environment? How can they protect endangered species?

Peace is as much an environmental as a social issue. It is absolutely vital to a sustainable future. Consider the wisdom of Chance Ruder, featured in this chapter's "Kids Who are Making a Difference": "What's so great about peace? I'll tell you what's great about peace. With peace, the world can be fed. With peace, the children can be educated. With peace, we will have the resources and interest to care for wild habitats and restore declining populations of wildlife for our children's children. I have learned that if we allow a *lack of peace* to destroy nature, we diminish ourselves and impoverish our children and *rob them* of their capacity to fulfill themselves and to experience the Glory of God's creation."

Let there be no doubt about it: Creating a sustainable society won't be achieved merely by efforts to safeguard and enhance the environment. We must also promote social conditions conducive to a sustainable society.

As parents, we must sensitize our children to the social changes required to build a sustainable future. A few good examples will help your child see that creating a sustainable future requires much more than the environmental measures presented in this book. To learn more, you may want to read Susan Vogt's book, *Raising Kids Who Will Make a Difference*.

PROMOTING SYSTEMS THINKING

Many years ago, I attended a conference in Berkeley, California, designed to bring together individuals working in various aspects of sustainability. The organizers invited individuals like myself who focus on environmental protection, as well as those who work for organizations that address a wide range of social issues, such as poverty and discrimination. The purpose of this event was to help attendees understand the ways in which the various "factions" contribute to a common goal of building a humane, sustainable society.

> *Let there be no doubt about it: Creating a sustainable society won't be achieved merely by efforts to safeguard and enhance the environment. We must also promote social conditions conducive to a sustainable society.*

During the three-day event, attendees met several times in groups composed of a dozen or so individuals, representing a wide array of interests. Conversations focused on what we were doing and how our work complemented the work of others. When the conference was over, however, I'm not certain that many attendees actually achieved the end results the organizers had hoped for.

During the small group sessions, it seemed to me that it was difficult for members of the environmental community to grasp the full importance of the work of those in social movements. So what, why worry about poverty? The world is burning up as a result of global climate change. Without a healthy environment we're all dead. Folks in the various social movements, it seemed to me, were equally puzzled about all of the fuss over the environment. Who cares about global warming? People are living in poverty, and can't find enough to eat.

They're certainly not going to care about US policies to save endangered species when their own lives are on the line. I was reminded of a quote from Gandhi, "To a man with an empty stomach, food is god."

A few years later, I was invited to the governor's office in Denver, Colorado, to meet with Governor Roy Romer and leaders of the major conservation and environmental organizations in Colorado. After a lengthy discussion about an issue (gambling) that he thought was important, the governor asked us to give him a list of the five top environmental issues he should focus on during his term of office.

When the governor made his request, the group looked stunned. They were paralyzed; not one person spoke up.

As president of the Colorado Environmental Coalition, which represented approximately 30 organizations statewide, I volunteered to take suggestions and submit them to the governor.

Still, no takers.

Shortly thereafter, we walked out of the governor's office without a shred of advice on environmental priorities.

Why?

I've never really understood the paralysis that overtook the group. Perhaps they were suspicious of the governor. He wasn't known as an environmental advocate. Upon further reflection, it occurred to me that perhaps the attendees suffered from a problem afflicting many people: lack of big picture vision.

Let me explain.

In the environmental community, most people gravitate to one or a couple of issues about which they feel great passion. To them, it is the issue of greatest importance. In the group, then, there may have been a feeling that naming the top five issues would surely exclude other issues about which some people felt quite passionately. The representative from the Prairie Dog Protection League, for instance, might have sensed that her issue would have been trumped by folks who were trying to save wilderness or promote renewable energy. Frankly, as much as I love prairie dogs, their protection is not as important as creating a society that manages urban sprawl. Could it have been that the members in attendance were afraid that their issues might not have made the top-five list?

These two stories illustrate an important point: Many children grow up to be single-issue adults. They embrace forestry protection, but don't recycle. They fight for wilderness protection but drive a gas-guzzling pickup truck. Many people lack an understanding of the big picture that might afford a better view of the steps needed to forge an enduring human presence.

As parents, you can help your children become systems thinkers, able to see the big picture and the connections between the parts, a topic discussed in Chapter 3 in the section on critical thinking. Understanding the big picture and the connections within the complex maze of cause and effect will help our children grow up to become thoughtful, humane adults. And it will help them understand why we must work together to build a sustainable future.

Whenever possible take opportunities to talk with your children about the complex issues of our time (not all at once, of course). You can help them draw connections, too, for example, why countries that were once self-sufficient in food production now import large quantities of food. (Why? Because they're exporting cash crops such as coffee and tea to countries such as Canada and the United States. These cash crops are grown on land that once supported crops that fed local people. Developing countries are growing cash crops to help pay off debts to more developed countries, debts often incurred to pay for development programs sponsored by, guess who, the industrial nations of the world.) You can explain why people in so many of the less developed nations live in poverty. (Part of the reason is that wealthy nations import resources from their countries, but corporations and middlemen take most of the profit, leaving field workers destitute while others profit from the sale of timber, food, minerals and precious metals such as gold.)

You can help your children develop a balanced view, so they don't fall into the same trap as those individuals in the two stories I just related to you. You may want to read up on some of this yourself. And don't forget to talk about social issues like those mentioned in the previous section.

FOSTERING COMPASSION AND EMPATHY FOR PEOPLE

Environmentalists are sometimes accused of being insensitive to the needs of people. For example, consider the comments made by individuals from families who make a living from forestry when angry protesters block access roads to a national forest to protect trees from being cut. Local townspeople whose jobs are threatened by this action accuse the activists of "caring more for trees than people."

To be honest, I've known a few environmental advocates who were misanthropic. "Humanity, I love you; it's people I can't stand," seemed to be their motto. Some were quite disdainful of people. Even those activists who have compassion for other humans don't always act accordingly. It occurs to me that the label "environmentalist" suggests a unidimensionality — we care about the environment, but are lukewarm at best about people. (Fortunately, we're not all that way.)

Real and presumed antisocial behavior casts a dark cloud over the environmental movement and it hinders us from moving forward in our quest to create a humane, sustainable future that is good for people, the planet, and the economy.

Helping your children learn to care for others — and to express their compassion when engaged in environmental good deeds — is vital. Kids who care about the Earth but who can understand the other dimensions of sustainability will very likely work toward solutions that satisfy the triple bottom line. They may also be better accepted and will be more likely to achieve their goals.

> *Kids who care about the Earth but also understand other dimensions of sustainability will very likely work toward solutions that satisfy the triple bottom line. They will be better accepted and will be more likely to achieve their goals.*

Remember, too, that environmental values and actions — especially those that will help us build a sustainable future — have enormous benefits to people. Far from being subversive to progress, and far from being detrimental to people, our efforts to build a sustainable world are extremely important to people and nations. They will help us build stronger nations. They will help us build stronger economies and stronger communities. They could help us create more effective government — for example, by focusing our efforts on root causes and root solutions, we can effect economical and lasting solutions. Our actions will promote a broader prosperity and create a better future.

RAISING HUMANE CHILDREN

So how do you raise a child to care for people *and* the Earth? By setting a good example. By teaching your child that people are a part of the environmental equation. People need food and water and good jobs and income. So search for solutions that are good for people *and* the environment *and* the economy.

The best source of information on humane education is the book *Above All, Be Kind* written by Zoe Weil, founder of the International Institute for Humane Education.

Weil is a pioneer in humane education, who has also taken her advice to parents, the very first teachers our children are exposed to. In her writings, Weil asserts that a generation of children raised to be humane will help us along a path toward peace, social justice, and sustainability. Such children will not only be valuable and cherished family members, they will also be an asset to the larger community — and perhaps to the future of humankind.

Based on her work with parents, Weil has produced a list of the ten most commonly articulated qualities for living a humane life. They are:

1. Willingness to choose and change
2. Kindness
3. Compassion
4. Honesty and trustworthiness
5. Generosity
6. Courage
7. Perseverance, self-discipline, and restraint
8. Humor and playfulness
9. Wisdom
10. Integrity

In *Above All, Be Kind*, Weil describes each trait and its importance to building a humane, sustainable society. Kindness, for example, she says means "that we attempt at the deepest and broadest level to

> *A generation of children raised to be humane will help us along a path toward peace, social justice, and sustainability.*

assess what does the least harm and the most good in any given situation." Mark Twain once noted that "kindness is a language which the deaf can hear and the blind can read." You can imagine how kindness can improve our interactions with family members, friends, and neighbors, helping to build a more closely knit circle. But kindness need not stop there. It can also be bestowed on people living in other cities, other states, and other countries. In Weil's words, "Not only can we be kind to those with whom we interact, but also to those whose lives we affect, however distantly, through our daily choices."

Kindness can also be bestowed on future generations and the wealth of wild species that share this planet with us. America's first champion of peace, liberty, and equality, William Penn, once wrote, "I expect to pass through life but once. If therefore, there be any kindness I can show, or any good thing I can do to any fellow being, let me do it now, and not defer or neglect it, as I shall not pass this way again."

I have described many of the traits Weil promotes in her book in previous chapters. For example, compassion is discussed in the chapter on fostering love for nature. It is about helping unleash our children's love and compassion for the entire living world. I've touched on wisdom, too, in my discussions of what we really need to know about ecology and human impacts on the planet's life-support systems. The chapters on consumerism talk about self-discipline and restraint. I discussed honesty and integrity in the chapter on walking our talks. I spoke about courage earlier in this chapter — courage to buck the system and to resist peer pressure.

Rather than describe each trait here in more detail, and uncover the benefits to people and the planet, I leave this task to you (see "Family Activities"). Or you may want to read Weil's book when you are done studying and implementing the ideas in this book.

The importance of humane upbringing cannot be emphasized enough. Miyaca Dawn Coyote, who lives a life of environmental responsibility and works with children to create love and appreciation for the Earth, provides an example. She notes that her parents, both scientists, "enjoyed nature, were very frugal, and conscientious." But they also had other influential traits. They held love and regard for all. They embraced humanitarian attitudes and actions. They possessed an unstoppable can-do attitude. "There was no such thing as impossible. There was always an answer, a way. The only question," says Miyaca, "was how long it would take to figure it out." Her parents displayed integrity and pursued excellence. In short, they were excellent role models who had a profound influence on their daughter. Her parents bestowed on her a conviction that "we were caring, tuned in, can-do people."

Bear in mind, however, that none of us is perfect. Very few among us are patient and kind and loving all of the time. We lose our tempers, say things we don't really mean, do things that are inconsiderate. In short, we have inhumane impulses and we sometimes act on them.

When you look over the list of qualities just mentioned, "you will see that most of them, truly embodied, would dramatically change us, our children, and the world for the better," notes Weil. Remember, as I have pointed out before, the best way to teach is to model appropriate behavior. And if you slip up, acknowledge your "mistake," and discuss why you acted out of character. It is important for our children to realize that adults don't always act according to our own internal set of laws. When we are tired, stressed, overworked, or hungry, we may slip up, but we recognize it and endeavor to live consistently according to our ideals. In other words, we can consciously choose to be kinder, more considerate, more compassionate, more loving, and more careful. We can choose to live as closely to our ideals as possible. It's an everyday challenge. Help your children know this early on, so they don't grow up expecting that at a certain age they have to stop growing. As Weil so aptly notes, it is our "willingness to choose and change ... that makes it possible for each of us to become more humane ..."

Zoe Weil, also notes, "When we try to live according to our deepest values, and when we teach our children to do likewise, we do so not by denying vices, but by naming them, acknowledging them, discussing them, and choosing not to act on them."

"Unless we strive to actually live according to our deepest values, they are meaningless," says Weil. A wise person doesn't preach what is right, he or she lives it. We are our message, and our children understand that.

> *"When we try to live according to our deepest values, and when we teach our children to do likewise, we do so not by denying vices, but by naming them, acknowledging them, discussing them, and choosing not to act on them."*
> *— Zoe Weil*, Above All, Be Kind

Fortunately, children are naturally empathetic. Tapping into a child's natural empathy for others less fortunate is an easy task. Be sure to let your child's compassion blossom through actions. If, for example, your child is concerned about the plight of homeless people in your area, you might both volunteer at a soup kitchen or help collect food to donate to the poor. If your child is concerned about the poor in other countries, you might suggest donations to charitable organizations that help sow self-sufficiency, which supports sustainability, rather than simply giving food aid, which is not sustainable in the long run. Although short-term aid may be beneficial, you may want to pass on to your child the advice of writer W. J. Boetsker, "You cannot help men permanently by doing for them what they could do for themselves."

STAND OUT OF THEIR WAY

Not all children require inspiration when it comes to environmental issues and thus not all parents end up in the role of educator. In fact, you may find that your child becomes *your* environmental mentor, teaching you values, facts, and solutions. One such example I ran across in my research was that of Chance and Josh Ruder from San Antonio, Texas, who are featured in this chapter's "Kids Who Are Making a Difference." If you have children who show similarities to these lads, you may have to stand back and let them be your mentors. You won't be sorry you did; You'll very likely end up a better person for having let your child lead you along the path of environmental responsibility.

KIDS WHO ARE MAKING A DIFFERENCE
TWO TEXAS YOUTHS ON A CAMPAIGN TO SAVE
WILDLIFE AND THE EARTH

As a very young boy, Chance Ruder of San Antonio, Texas (right), showed great interest in wildlife and the natural world. Neither his mother nor his father were raised with an extraordinary interest in the environment. "We were both athletes and when we were growing up our family lives revolved around sports," explained Chance's mother, Angela. Then along came Brooks, their second son, who would later change his name to Chance for reasons explained shortly.

Despite encouragement to play sports like his older brother Josh (left), Chance found the living world fascinating. "At age four," his mother told me, "Chance was a watcher and a reader. He was drawn to anything living. He was unbelievably connected to animals. ..." Moreover, animals seemed to have an affinity for him. "Wild ones, injured ones, pet ones, flying ones ... you name it ... they came and they rested with Chance before moving on. It was like living with Dr. Doolittle."

Early on, Chance's mom noticed that virtually everything her son read was about animals. "Not story books but nonfiction books such as the 'Eyewitness' series that deals with anatomy and function." At age four, Chance was lecturing his mother about placental animals, a subject he'd learned from his father's college zoology books.

"Not all kids take such an academic approach to animals and habitats and conservation," observed Angela, "but many, many children have a natural compassion for life and show an inclination in the direction of conservation. If their parents would just listen and follow, they would be surprised at what that kid can do with it."

Wise parents they were.

Angela, an English major in college and coach of a local middle school basketball team, and her husband Craig Ruder, a US Air Force orthopedic sports physician, let their son explore the possibilities. Over the years, Chance has led them on a wild ride I'm certain neither would have ever imagined.

While his older brother was in kindergarten, Chance (who is one year younger than Josh) checked out every book in the library on nature and watched every nature video he could get his hands on.

"And he soaked up every bit of it," Angela remarked.

"When the first day of kindergarten came, I crossed my fingers, sent him in with all the other kids and wondered how long it would take for the teachers to figure him out. Two weeks later, I got a phone call from a school administrator," she told me. The school official said that Chance's interest in nature had taken him beyond anything that they could offer him in elementary school. "I was told he needed a mentor, someone who would work with him once a week and get him out of the regular school environment."

Soon thereafter, Chance and his mom convinced a local raptor expert, who headed up a nearby raptor rehabilitation facility, to be his mentor. During his first meeting with the man, Chance was given a tour of the facility. As he, his mother, and his soon-to-be mentor strolled along the pens housing injured raptors, Chance was able to identify many of the birds. (Remember, he was five years old.) The raptor expert, John, turned to Chance's mother and raised his eyebrows questioningly, asking, "How does this kid know this stuff?" Angela just shrugged because she honestly didn't know.

From that point on John and his protégé met weekly to discuss birds, wildlife, and the ways of nature. Chance worked at the center and attended every one of the public demonstrations the organization put on, if he could get there.

"Birds of prey became his first love," said his mother, and the mission to teach people why raptors are struggling for survival in their natural environment became his passion. "Soon he was handling the exotic raptors during some demonstrations," noted Angela. He was also fitted with a microphone to speak beside John during his presentations, the only person in the organization who held this distinction.

Chance's family moved to Georgia when he was six years old, but Chance stayed in touch with his mentor. In Georgia, Chance entered a public magnet school. Soon after school started, he learned from John that a new red-tailed hawk at the center in Texas needed costly surgery to repair a broken wing. In a matter of days, his teacher, the media specialist at the magnet school, and Chance came up with an idea to raise money for the operation and eventual release of the hawk. They'd sponsor a penny drive.

"But there was a HUGE problem," noted Chance's mom. "The majority of kids attending the school lived in near poverty. Many wore their dad's shoes to school. They didn't have two sticks to rub together, much less pennies to give. Furthermore, they didn't know the first thing about hawks."

It was then that Chance decided to make a video to teach his schoolmates about the value of hawks. "One day the boys asked to use our video camera to go out to the woods behind our house to tape birds. I said okay and at ages six and seven, Spyverius Productions was launched," noted his mother. "The first tape ended up being about owls because they couldn't find a hawk."

The boys turned the owl video in to the teacher and Chance did a live interview on the school TV system about owls and why they are considered birds of prey. He explained their pivotal role in nature.

The boys continued to hunt for hawks in the nearby woods, but eventually gave up. Undaunted, "Chance borrowed the school's mascot costume — a tattered hawk suit," according to Angela. Chance's older brother, Josh, donned the costume and then Chance did an anatomy talk about the parts of a hawk and why hawks are cool. "The school was hooked. Pennies started to show up in the collection jars. With the help of other kids, the boys started filming short commercials promoting the project. All of these aired on the school's TV system, and unknown to us, on the cable station that sponsored the school equipment," said Angela. "Many, many parents and members of the community were watching the videos that were playing over the school system and were learning about birds of prey from six- and seven-year-olds."

"In the course of six weeks, the school raised in excess of $700 in pennies," Angela told me, "to pay for the surgery and to purchase a web camera system so that the students in the magnet school and other schools could interact with the raptor center online."

"The boys got another elementary school in Texas involved with the red-tailed hawk, and when it was time for the bird to be released in the Texas Hill Country, it was the students from the Texas elementary school that attended the release, along with three teachers from the Georgia school who flew out on their own dime," explained Angela. "The project was all over the news in Texas and Georgia. The boys' videos were shown over and over; the boys were interviewed on the news, and with their newfound knowledge of raptors, many, many children's hearts and futures flew free along with hawk #693, that spring."

Chance was awarded the Pioneer Student of the Year Award by Georgia governor Roy Barnes in Atlanta, which drew more attention. He became a finalist in the "Be Kind to Animals" campaign by the American Humane Association and was featured as the Amazing Kid of the month on a website called "Amazing Kids" (<www.Amazing-Kids.com>). In addition, Chance was featured on a show on Zoom television, as a "Zoom a Cum Laud" — basically a short profile on kids who are making a difference.

"At one point," noted Angela, "Nickelodeon television called wanting Chance to come on one of their shows with birds of prey. It was one of those 'guess my line' sort of a thing for kids. But the studio environment would have been loud, the atmosphere on this particular show was near frenzy when slime got dumped on contestants, and though Chance really thought it looked like fun, he declined the offer because he wouldn't feel comfortable bringing a bird into that situation." It took great character and compassion for a young child to turn down the offer to be on national TV for the sake of a hawk.

"Chance did (not said) all the right things to 'convince' his parents to follow him. He loved what he did. He was good at it. He was committed to it. His passion was noble and of high moral intent and he was willing to place himself second, behind the animals' interest," said Angela. "This little kid was getting ready to take on the world all alone, on behalf of his own future and for the futures of those creatures that could not speak for themselves." What choice did his parents have? "You can bet that Craig and I got behind Chance. Josh, of course, came along because he was part of the off-screen force that was making things happen. Suddenly, we were all believers with him," his mother explained.

Chance's story does not end here. His family moved back to Texas after a year in Georgia, and with his trusty sidekick Josh, Chance went on to make many more videos, filming bats, their favorites, but also snakes, which Chance loves too. "These films were short … maybe 6–8 minutes each. The boys gave the tapes to grandparents and friends and teachers and we often times sent them back to Georgia to their former classmates. Chance had turned seven and was now in second grade. He promoted another penny campaign with his new school to adopt a lanner falcon named Rocket that is used for educational demonstrations. It was also successful," Angela said.

While on a trip to their local SeaWorld, a friend's daughter and Chance wandered to the opposite side of the sea lion enclosure where they struck up a conversation with an employee. When Angela arrived, the employee looked her in the eye and said, "You need to call the education department and see if you can get this kid hooked up there. He knows a lot. I've never had a little kid correct me on the pronunciation of the Latin name for a California sea lion before."

Angela decided to give it a try. Luckily, one of the most senior managers in the department picked up her call. Angela described her son's zest for animals, his knowledge, and his projects. "At the end of the conversation, she (Shannon) asked me to document the things I had told her, and put it in the mail. She would talk to her boss and they would see what they could come up with."

Skeptical that anything would come of this, Angela hand-delivered a packet with Chance's and his brother's work. Much to Angela's surprise, the woman called for Chance a few days later. After meeting with the boy, she agreed to mentor him, even though he was only seven. During the meeting, "Chance committed himself to being a guest presenter for Camp SeaWorld through the summer. As we walked out of the offices, I just looked at him and asked him what he was thinking. Guest presenter? What do we know about presenting? Nothing. Athletes do not present. We play. Ok … I'll follow you."

Five weeks later, at the age of seven, with nothing but information and bucketloads of courage and conviction, Chance "stepped up onto a stage that dwarfed him, took the microphone and, in front of 250 kids, presented one of two 30-minute conservation lectures he had written and memorized," his mother told me.

Chance presented his lectures two times a day every Wednesday for the entire summer. "When I look back at it now," Angela continued, "it seems incredible that he was doing it at age seven. Last month (August 2004), Chance completed his fifth summer of teaching at SeaWorld."

A year later, SeaWorld asked Angela if she would be willing to help out in the education department. "Because of Chance, I knew a lot of the animal information, and what I didn't know, they would teach me," she explained.

"Being there as an employee shed some light on what a miracle it was that Chance was there at all," she added. Angela discovered that the education department takes approximately 50 telephone calls each month from parents who say their child is gifted with animals and would like to have some special attention from a trainer or animal specialist. "SeaWorld pretty much has a standard answer for these parents because they rarely take on mentor students at SeaWorld ... mostly seniors in high school who are in the gifted and talented program. They are usually limited to one semester, I think. Certainly not seven-year-olds."

As the years went on, Angela told me, Chance and Josh started to get "big ideas about their video work. It was no longer 'let's go outside and tape bugs' but rather, 'Mom, can you get us to California so we can film sea lions in their natural environment?'"

And she did. "I took them to Catalina Island twice to film sea lions." They had almost completed that video when Chance decided that he wanted to add manatees to the tape. "Could I please get them to Florida too?"

When Angela told the boys that they needed to raise money for such a trip, they did. As his mom explained to me, "Chance read in a *National Geographic Kids* magazine that they were looking for 'Habitat Hero Kids' who are trying to impact the world for nature. The winner gets a trip to Florida — Disney, a hotel, and airfare. He showed it to me and said 'I'm going to try for this.' I tried to explain to him that a zillion kids read this magazine and many of them are out there doing great things for the Earth. He should not get his hopes up too high ...

but go for it."

"Of course, he enters at the last minute and even tells them that he's only entering because he needs a lift to Florida to tape manatees."

And, of course, he wins.

Why?

"For the same reason that he, the most unathletic person in our whole family tree, can beat us all at bowling ... because he's at peace with the Universe. I'm not kidding ... he just throws stuff out there without a clue, and doors open and opportunities present themselves, and pins fall down," noted Angela.

So off they went to Florida to film manatees in the Crystal River. "The boys couldn't do the filming themselves because they didn't have a waterproof housing for their video camera, but the divemaster brought his and took direction from them on what to shoot and when they were all done, he handed them the entire tape with a written release to use it," said Chance's mom.

"Most recently they completed two more tapes. They had the opportunity to tape the emergence of bats from the world's first man-made bat cave designed for viewing wild bats and they spent weeks on a raptors video, using footage they shot of wild eagles, hawks, vultures, falcons, and owls," said Angela.

Chance and Josh do more than make videos, though. They also give live animal presentations to several schools in the city each year to help kids learn about animals.

While this narrative may make the boys' story seem like a walk in the park, there have been many disappointments. Many times they have been turned away and have been forced to find another way to meet their objectives. They've not always been treated kindly by adults, either. But they've persisted, thanks in large part to Chance's deep and abiding passion for animals and the Earth, his brother's willingness to assist in getting the message out, and his parents' amazing support.

"Because of their video work, they asked for press passes to cover a visit Jane Goodall was making to San Antonio," noted Angela. They spent three days traveling with the esteemed scientist and attending all of her lectures as her guests and being the subjects of parts of her lectures. "She is now a dear friend," Angela added.

At age eleven, Chance submitted an abstract to the Association of

Zoos and Aquariums Docents (AZAD) national convention, and presented a lecture to hundreds of our country's zoo educators on teaching kids about endangered species.

A few years ago, Chance and Josh were featured in a video for SeaWorld. They've developed close relationships with individuals such as Robert Kennedy Jr. and organizations like the International Fund for Animal Welfare.

Chance and Josh are truly remarkable children. It was, however, not their parents who fostered the EcoKid in them, but the other way around. They've become EcoParents. As Angela explained to me, "Chance has been a tremendous education for us. He has challenged our most basic philosophies toward wild, living things. In fact, this is something he has done to nearly every teacher and parent of a friend with whom he has had contact. We hear about the kind but firm lectures he gives to people about their attitudes toward spiders, snakes, vultures, bats, etc.! Lives around the entire neighborhood have changed.

"Though I started out completely clueless about environmental issues, I learned 'nature stuff' at breakneck speed. As a person, a wife, a mother, and student, I went through tremendous growth along with my sons. My attitudes matured and my understanding about the natural world around me grew as I followed Chance around," said Angela. "As a female, the 'ewwww' factor about natural things (bugs, poop, chick pieces that got flicked onto me by a falcon, road kill, etc.) decreased dramatically."

During the time Angela worked at SeaWorld as an instructor she, like her son, excelled. She was typically chosen to show VIPs around the facility. She also managed the gifted, and blind, and deaf groups. During her tours and other educational duties, she helped explain each person's profound responsibility toward these marvelous animals and their habitats.

"Why all the big changes in me? Because I believed in my son. Because he is dedicated to shaping his own future, because I have spent endless nights listening to his valid concerns for wildlife and questioning the reason behind decisions our government and our leadership have made in regard to our natural resources."

Don't think that dad has played a passive role in all of this. "Besides supporting the boys' efforts financially," Angela explained, "Craig has operated on bald eagles, fitting them with modified human external fixators to expedite healing. He has gotten other medical professionals to donate medical supplies." Furthermore, "Because Chance is seen all over the city, and certainly the neighborhood, people show up at our house with injured animals. Craig helps to get them stabilized and prepared for release or to go on to a rehabilitator. At work they call him the 'Croc hunter' because of the adventures Chance drags him through. Believe me, no one in the house has escaped Chance's enthusiasm and mission," Angela said.

"Craig and I both fell in love, like Chance and Josh, with birds of prey and we are studying to get our federal permits in order to care for and hunt with two red-tailed hawks next year," Angela said. Not only because we love it, but also because our boys love it ... and they are still too young to get their own permits. Our lives have *completely* changed, and our home environment now reflects the gifts of *both* of our boys."

Chance may be changing lots of adult lives. But, says his mother, "he doesn't seek out opportunities to teach adults. It is not that he doesn't like them ... he loves adults. He just considers it as sort of a waste of time. I think he's secretly, respectfully annoyed that they let this Earth get into the condition it is in, and as far as he's concerned they have already wasted their tomorrows ... and quite possibly his."

I couldn't have said it better.

"Adults who come to hear him speak in a public forum often start out with their arms crossed because they don't particularly care to be taught by a child," Angela told me. "But when he does speak to them or when they are in the audience, I always hear them say 'Wow, I didn't know that,' about something he's said because, frankly, his studies have been both broad and deep, focusing not only on the animal but also on its environment."

"Every parent should be so lucky to have a child like Chance or Josh. I think you would call Chance an EcoKid who cares for the Earth, but I'm pretty sure that you now understand who raised who," Angela said. "In our case, the child raised the parents. We have been trying to keep up with him ever since."

When I asked Chance what he is learning about wildlife, he answered, "I don't know how to answer that because there's so much we've learned. I'm interested in ethology [animal behavior]. I like learning about the minds of animals. I like studying their behaviors and subtle things they do to communicate."

I also asked Chance what he could tell us about wildlife.

"Mr. Bamberger is this really cool guy out in the hill country who has this huge conservation ranch and he told me one time that you can't just study one thing. If you want to know about animals you have to know about it all. You have to know the whole ecosystem, the geography, the geology, the plants ... everything. Wildlife is a lot more than just the living animals that people think of when you say that word," Chance said. He added, "If you think of it like that, then we learn all sorts of stuff like how important native grasses and native trees are to an ecosystem.

"You know what else we learned?" he continued. "That you can't put 'humanness' on animals. We have a lot in common with them, and they have a lot in common with us, but they do things exactly the way they are supposed to, and sometimes that's not how humans would do it. I guess what I'm saying is that they aren't really 'moral' beings. They shouldn't be judged by human standards. For example, when a shark attacks someone, everyone wants to blame the shark ... like sharks actually would like the taste of a ground-dwelling human. Blech. They like fish and things that are fishy smelling.

"When they eat the fish, they aren't bad or mean or vicious. And when they mistake a person for a food source because the person is in their territory acting like a food item or interfering with their reproduction, it's not their fault that they bite. If a lion walked into a grocery store someone would shoot it. When we invade their spaces, they react, too. I have learned to not judge wildlife by human standards."

"Once you let that go, then you see so many really cool adaptations and abilities that the animals have that you'd give anything to have, too," he added.

Chance tells another lesson he learned. When he was five, three birds of prey were brought to the rehabilitation center where he was volunteering and studying under a master falconer. The birds were autopsied to determine the cause of death. "It's kind of gross," remarked Chance, "but since birds of prey are indicator species at the top of the food chain it's vital that when one comes in dead you figure out what killed it.

"Well, the first two birds we posted [autopsied] were hawks that were killed by I think a cactus and a car. The third was a barred owl.

There wasn't anything wrong with it that you could see and its eyes were wide open and shiny," he noted.

"I hadn't ever seen that kind of owl before and I remember thinking when we unwrapped it, wow this was a really pretty bird. And it was big. The thing is that it flew smack into a house that had been built right in the middle of its habitat. It hit a window and BAM, it was gone.

"I remember all the bright examination lights over our heads shining down on the bird and I bent over it because I was standing on a milk crate. I could see myself reflected in its eyes. It kind of freaked me out to see myself there, in death. But the more I thought about it the more I realized it was sort of a message. I was alive in the bird's eyes. His body was dead but his spirit (or maybe it was my spirit; I don't know) came right at me. I could see through his eyes and I felt really bad about how such a great bird was killed because of people not caring about it needing a safe place to live," said Chance.

"That was when it all hit me like SLAM! I get it now. If you want to have animals on this Earth, then you better care about where they live because it's getting hard for them to survive around the humans. I said I was really sorry to the owl in my spirit and I promised it that I would be his voice. I would try to talk some reason into the humans, sort of like a translator for the bird. For all of the animals. That's what I'm going to do somehow. And that's mostly why I make videos and speak at events and teach at SeaWorld. I know some people think it's boring, but I think there are kids like me who would care and want to do something about this problem. There are other translators out there who don't know what to do. And if we could just find each other and join forces, we could be world leaders."

And that's why he calls himself Chance.

He changed his name on a trip to Georgia from Brooks to Chance. "I was thinking that Brooks was a pretty neat name," said his mom, "but he explained that he was a chance for wildlife and that is the only way he sees himself. It was hard to deny his passion and so, guessing that this was probably just a phase, I agreed to try to remember to call him Chance."

This was about two weeks before he turned six.

It's been six years and he hasn't gone back.

THE PROMISE OF A NEW GENERATION

In this book, I've outlined ways to help raise children who care for the Earth. I started with ways to foster a deep and abiding love for nature and all living things. I then discussed things you and your child should know about nature: how important nature is to us, how it functions, how we affect it, and ways in which we can live sustainably in harmony with natural systems. I then looked at ways to instill environmental values and combat consumerism. Next, I described the importance of walking our talk and making our life our message. We ended with a discussion of ways to help ensure success.

Through all of this, we've been pinning our hopes on future generations to right the wrongs, but we cannot leave this mess to our children. The future begins today. We adults must also change our ways if we are going to create a sustainable future. While the task is enormous, sometimes seemingly impossible, we can't use that as an excuse not to try. As author George P. Burnham once noted, "'I can't do it' never yet accomplished anything; 'I will try' has profound wonders."

So do not despair for lack of hope. You and your children are the hope. Every time you look in the mirror, you stare hope squarely in the eyes.

FAMILY ACTIVITIES

1. Whenever you can, talk with your children about peer pressure. What is it? What forms does it take? How does it influence them to make decisions that may not be beneficial to the planet? Ask your kids to give you examples. You may even want to give a few yourself to show how peer pressure affects you.
2. Spend time with your children talking about values, if you haven't done so already, and then talk about ways your children act and how consistent their actions are with their values. Ask them if peer pressure is causing them to act in ways that conflict with their values.
3. Working with your family, make a list of things you can do to live more in harmony with your values. Ask your children how they can avoid peer pressure when taking on actions that others might frown upon.
4. Go to meetings of local birdwatchers, gardeners, environmental organizations — anything that you feel passionately about. If they have children's programs, enroll your children. Go regularly to those you are interested in and start making friends. They will be part of your support group.
5. Start your own support group. You might want to place an ad in a local newspaper or post flyers for a meeting you will lead at a local school or library that will provide an opportunity for people like yourself to meet to

discuss environmentally friendly lifestyles. You may even want to start discussions around books such as *Affluenza* or *Superbia! 31 Ways to Create Sustainable Neighborhoods*.

6. Encourage your children to log on to <www.generationfix.com>, created by Elizabeth Rusch, author of *Generation Fix: Young Ideas for a Better World*, to join in the forums on hunger, environment, and homelessness, among others. You might want to ask them to share their ideas over dinner.

7. Be sure to talk with your children about the pressing social issues of the time as they grow older. Help them understand what the problems are, perhaps by doing research at the library or through the Internet. Don't overload kids with too much, but be sure to help them understand how solving social issues is vital to creating a sustainable future.

8. Study the list of values on page 199 and ask your family what they think about each one and how these values would help create a better world. You might also ask them if they are practicing these values and, if so, how.

9. Read the "Models of Sustainability" piece in this chapter on organic co-ops to your family and ask them if they would like to form a co-op or sponsor a meeting with neighbors and friends who might like to join together to form an organic food-buying co-op.

RESOURCE GUIDE

There are mountains of books and other resources that I could recommend to those inter-ested in becoming better parents, instilling values, learning about the environment, and tak-ing positive actions. I have culled from the list those resources I think are the most valuable to readers. Many of these resources have been quoted or mentioned in this book.

BOOKS ON PARENTING

Cline, Foster W. and Jim Fay. *Parenting with Love and Logic: Teaching Children Responsibility*. Pinon Press, 1990. A must-read book for all parents.

Cline, Foster W. and Jim Fay. *Parenting Teens with Love and Logic: Preparing Adolescents for Responsible Adulthood*. Pinon Press, 1992. A fabulous book that will take the sting out of parenting teens while helping them learn responsibility.

Hunt, Jan. *The Natural Child: Parenting from the Heart*. New Society Publishers, 2001. A dynamite book that *all* adult couples should read and study — before they have children and as their children grow up.

Miller, Jamie. *10-Minute Life Lessons for Kids: 52 Fun and Simple Games and Activities to Teach Your Children Honesty, Trust, Love, and Other Important Values*. HarperCollins, 1998. The subtitle tells it all.

Reder, Alan, Stephanie Renfrow Hamilton, and Phil Catalfo. *The Whole Parenting Guide: Strategies, Resources, and Inspiring Stories for Holistic Parenting and Family Living*. Broadway Books, 1999. I haven't read this book myself, but it comes highly recommended from people I respect.

Taylor, Betsy. *What Kids Really Want That Money Can't Buy: Tips for Parenting in a Commercial World*. Warner Books, 2003. Read this book if you want to explore additional ways to raise your child to be emancipated from rampant commer-cialism.

Vogt, Susan V. *Raising Kids Who Will Make a Difference: Helping Your Family Live with Integrity, Value, Simplicity, and Care for Others*. Loyola Press, 2002. This book covers a wide range of issues important to parents and their children such as nurturing values of honesty and integrity, how to get along with others, sim-plicity, and health.

Weil, Zoe. *Above All, Be Kind: Raising a Humane Child in Challenging Times.* New Society Publishers, 2003. A dynamite book that all parents should read, starting when their children are young.

BOOKS THAT INSPIRE ACTION

Center for a New American Dream. *Tips for Parenting in a Commercial Culture.* Center for a New American Dream, 2002. Available online as a free download or as a pamphlet from the Center.

Chiras, Daniel D. *The New Ecological Home.* Chelsea Green, 2004. This book describes all of the things we can do to build environmentally friendly homes.

Chiras, Daniel D. and David Wann. *Superbia! 31 Ways to Create Sustainable Neighborhoods.* New Society Publishers, 2003. This book contains numerous suggestions for ways we can make our neighborhoods more livable and more environmentally sustainable. A good resource for children and their parents.

De Graaf, John, David Wann, and Thomas H. Naylor. *Affluenza: The All-Consuming Epidemic.* Berrett-Koehler Publishers, 2001. An insightful and hard-hitting exposé of American consumerism and its impacts on us.

Dominguez, Joe and Vicki Robin. *Your Money or Your Life: Transforming Your Relationship with Money and Achieving Financial Independence.* Penguin Books, 1999. A very popular book that could, if you follow its advice, revolutionize your life.

Elgin, Duane. *Voluntary Simplicity: Toward a Way of Life that is Outwardly Simple, Inwardly Rich,* rev. ed. William Morrow, 1993. A revised version of the 1981 book that is, in my view, largely responsible for the upsurge of interest in voluntary simplicity.

Eyre, Linda and Richard Eyre. *Teaching Your Children Values.* Simon and Schuster, 1993. A valuable guide for those who want to teach their children honesty, self-reliance, and other important values.

Gershon, David and Robert Gilman. *Household EcoTeam Workbook: A Six-month Program to Bring Your Household into Environmental Balance.* Global Action Plan for the Earth, 1992.

Hoose, Phillip. *It's Our World, Too! Young People who are Making a Difference.* Farrar, Straus and Giroux, 1993. Inspiring stories about children who have taken a stand or have taken action to build a better world.

Sherlock, Marie. *Living Simply with Children.* Three Rivers Press, 2003. A highly readable book full of great information for those who would like to create a simpler, less stressful lifestyle with their children.

Taylor, Betsy. *More Fun, Less Stuff Starter Kit.* Center for a New American Dream, 2001. A great place to start if you want to live a more environmentally conscious lifestyle.

Books on the Environment and Environmental Education

Chiras, Daniel D. *Environmental Science: Creating a Sustainable Future*, 6th ed. Jones and Bartlett Publishers, 2001. This textbook, like others in the field, offers a wealth of information on environmental issues as well as solutions aimed at creating a sustainable society.

Sussman, Art. *Dr. Art's Guide to Planet Earth: For Earthlings Ages 12 to 120*. Chelsea Green, 2000. If your knowledge of ecology and environmental issues is weak, start with this very basic book. You'll learn a lot very quickly.

Van Matre, Steve. *Earth Education: A New Beginning*. The Institute for Earth Education, 1990. This book is written for environmental educators, but parents can learn a great deal too about the ways ecosystems function, how they contribute to our lives, and how we can create a more sustainable relationship with nature.

Books for Children and Educators

Andreas, Joel. *Addicted to War: Why the U.S. Can't Kick Militarism*. AK Press, 2004. A high-impact cartoon book that reveals the naked truth about wars. A must-read for all kids and their parents. Will stimulate lots of discussion.

Brody, Ed, Jay Goldspinner, Katie Green, Rona Leventhal, and John Porcino, eds. *Spinning Tales, Weaving Hope: Stories, Storytelling and Activities for Peace, Justice, and the Environment*. New Society Publishers, 2002. A wonderful collection of stories and activities to help children think about and learn valuable skills and ideas. Great resource for elementary school teachers, too.

Center for a New American Dream. *Good Times Made Simple: The Lost Art of Fun*. A 30-page pamphlet that lists many creative ways of having fun with your children without spending money.

Grant, Tim and Gail Littlejohn, eds. *Greening School Grounds: Creating Habitats for Learning*. New Society Publishers, 2001. This book provides ideas for students and teachers who want to green their grounds and expand student understanding of nature, and would be a valuable resource for kids who want to make changes at their schools. Many of these ideas could also be applied to the home.

Grant, Tim and Gail Littlejohn, eds. *Teaching About Climate Change: Cool Schools Tackle Global Warming*. New Society Publishers, 2001. This book is full of valuable information for parents and teachers who want to teach about global warming. It also contains numerous activities to help kids and their families reduce their contribution to the problem.

Needham, Bobbe. *Ecology Crafts for Kids: 50 Great Ways to Make Friends with Planet Earth*. Sterling Publishing, 1998. A terrific collection of ideas for projects for teachers, parents, and children.

Weil, Zoe. *So, You Love Animals: An Action-Packed, Fun-Filled Book to Help Kids Help Animals.* The American Anti-Vivisection Society, 1984. This book is filled with facts about wild and domesticated animals, advice on ways kids can protect them, and projects to teach children ways to treat animals better. An excellent resource for elementary school teachers, too.

BOOKS ABOUT COMMUNITY

Chiras, Daniel D., and Dave Wann. *Superbia! 31 Ways to Create Sustainable Neighborhoods.* New Society Publishers, 2004.

Fodor, Eben. *Better Not Bigger: How to Take Control of Urban Growth and Improve Your Community.* New Society Publishers, 1999.

Hallsmith, Gwendolyn. *The Key to Sustainable Cities: Meeting Human Needs, Transforming Community Systems.* New Society Publishers, 2003.

James, Sarah, and Torbjorn Lahti. *Natural Step for Communities: How Cities and Towns can Change to Sustainable Practices.* New Society Publishers, 2004.

Leafe Christian, Diana. *Creating A Life Together: Practical Tools to Grow Ecovillages and Intentional Communities.* New Society Publishers, 2003.

ScottHanson, Chris, and Kelly ScottHanson. *The Cohousing Handbook: Building a Place for Community.* New Society Publishers, 2004.

Walker, Liz. *EcoVillage at Ithaca: Pioneering a Sustainable Culture.* New Society Publishers, 2005.

IMPORTANT MAGAZINES AND NEWSLETTERS

All Round Magazine, P.O. Box 10193, Eugene OR 97440. This quirky magazine, published twice a year, focuses on specific topics of interest to children such as shelter, trees, and inventing, and contains a wealth of information in a format that many children love. The magazine has a strong environmental bent.

Co-op America Quarterly. P.O. Box 109, Upper Fairmount, MD 21867-9989. Tel: 1-800-58-Green. Covers many important topics related to living a sustainable lifestyle.

Enough! Published by the Center for a New American Dream. 6930 Carroll Ave., Suite 900, Takoma Park, MD 20912. A quarterly that covers issues related to consumption, quality of life, and the environment.

Kids Discover. An advertising-free magazine just for kids ages 6 to 12 that invites them to explore their world. Full of good information. 149 Fifth Avenue, New York, NY 10010. Tel: 212-677-4457. Website: www.kidsdiscover.com

Mother Earth News. 1503 SW 42nd Street, Topeka, KS 66609. Tel: 1-800-678-5779. This truly excellent magazine covers a wide range of topics of concern to those who want to live simpler, more environmentally sound lives. Check out their website, too at www.motherearthnews.com

Opportunities in Public Affairs. Tel: 301-571-0102. This bimonthly newsletter contains listings of jobs and internships in the public sector, primarily in Washington, D.C. Website: www.brubach.com

Ranger Rick. Published by National Wildlife Federation, 1100 Wildlife Center Drive, Reston, VA 20190-5362, Tel: 703-438-6000. Excellent source of information and games related to wildlife.

Your Big Backyard. Also published by National Wildlife Federation listed above. Excellent source of information for children ages three through seven.

Wild Animal Babies. Published by National Wildlife Federation, listed above. A great publication for very young children, ages 12 months to four years.

IMPORTANT VIDEOS AND DVDS

Affluenza. An insightful and entertaining look at our consumer culture and the effects it has on us and the environment. Produced by KCTS videos. Tel: 1-800-957-5387.

Escape from Affluenza. An insightful and entertaining look at ways we can opt out of the consumer culture. Produced by KCTS videos. Tel: 1-800-957-5387.

The Cost of Cool. This video, produced by Population Communications International, discusses the harmful impacts of advertising on teenagers. PCI–Headquarters, 777 United Nations Plaza – 5th Floor, 44th Street and 1st Avenue, New York, NY 10017. Tel: 212-687-3366. Website: www.population.org

The End of Suburbia: Oil Depletion and the Collapse of the American Dream. A shockingly frank DVD that forecasts the imminent decline in oil and natural gas and the impacts this will have on human existence in more developed countries. To obtain a copy log on to www.endofsuburbia.com

IMPORTANT WEBSITES

Amazing Kids. A nonprofit organization dedicated to helping children reach their full and totally amazing potential. Their website contains many inspiring stories of children who are making a difference in the world. Website: www.amazingkids.com

Chinaberry. This company produces age-specific books, tapes, toys, and other products that support families in raising their children with love, honesty, and joy and to be reverent, loving caretakers of each other and of the Earth. Website: www.chinaberry.com

EcoKids. This is not our website, but rather a site sponsored by Earth Day Canada's environmental education program. This site contains a wealth of information on science, nature, and environmental issues; learning activities; and games that encourage children, parents, and teachers. The site is designed for kids, parents, and teachers. It encourages children to form their own opinions, make decisions, and take actions. Website: www.ecokids.ca

Electronic Environmental Resource Library. This searchable website will connect you to a variety of carefully selected websites for information on a range of environmental issues. Website: www.eerl.org

Environmental Kids Club. The Environmental Protection Agency's website offers information on a wide range of environmental issues for students and teachers. This site also contains information on class projects, careers, internships, activities, environmental leadership awards, and more. Website: www.epa.gov/kids/

Henry J. Kaiser Family Foundation. At this website, you can find extensive research data on the effects of media on our children. Website: www.kff.org

Idealist.org for Kids. This was started by children for children. It highlights local, national, and international volunteer efforts that are helping to make the world a better place to live in. Website: www.idealist.org. Click on "orgs by kids."

National Wildlife Federation. This website contains a wealth of information, games, and activities on wildlife for children. For older children there's information on environmental careers. Website: www.nwf.org Be sure to check out their Earth Tomorrow Network. Website: www.nwf.org/kids/

NIEHS Kid's Page. This contains a wealth of information on the environment for children as well as numerous activities, games, songs, jokes, and links to other sites. Print out the jokes and tell them to your kids. Website: www.niehs.nih.gov/kids/home.htm

Sierra Club Youth Services. This website offers programs for youth of all ethnicities, cultures, and backgrounds to enhance participation in club programs, in the outdoors, and in the environmental movement. Website: www.sierraclub.org/youthservices/

Important Organizations

Alternative Farming Systems Information Center. This website offers a wealth of information on community-supported agriculture, including a link to a site that you can use to locate a farm near you: www.nal.usda.gov/afsic/csa/

Alternative Gifts. P.O. Box 2267, Lucerne Valley, CA 92356. Tel: 1-800-842-2243. This organization will help you give gifts to charities around the world in the name of a friend or relative. Website: www.altgifts.com

American Forests. P.O. Box 2000, Washington, D.C. 20013. Tel: 202-955-4500. This organization plants trees in American forests in honor of individuals. A great idea for a gift for birthdays and holidays. Website: www.americanforests.org

Amnesty International. If you are interested in plugging your child into social issues, this organization is a good start. They provide information and programs for high school children. Go to their website to contact an office in your country. Website: www.amnesty.org

Center for a New American Dream. 6930 Carroll Ave., Suite 900, Takoma Park, MD 20912. Tel: 1-877-68-Dream. This organization focuses its attention on ways we can live simpler, happier, more environmentally friendly lives. Website: www.newdream.org

CSA Center. For a list of community-supported agriculture farms in your area check out this website: www.csacenter.org/csastate.htm

CSA Farm Network. Steve Gilman, 130 Ruckytucks Rd., Stillwater, NY 12170. Tel: 518-583-4613. Promotes CSA in the northeastern United States.

Co-op America. P.O. Box 109, Upper Fairmount, MD 21867-9989. Tel: 1-800-58-Green. Offers several valuable publications on green shopping, green investment, and green lifestyles.

Earth Force. 1908 Mount Vernon Ave., 2nd Floor, Alexandria, VA 22301. 703-299-9400. Website: www.earthforce.org

Environmental Career Opportunities, 6535 Broad Street, Bethesda, MD 20816. Tel: 1-800-315-9777. For older children who are interested in pursuing an environmental career. Website: www.ecojobs.com

Habitat for Humanity International. 121 Habitat St., Americus, GA 31709-3498 USA. Tel: 229-924-6935, ext. 2551 or 2552. E-mail: publicinfo@hfhi.org. This organization builds homes for the needy using volunteers. It's a great place for children to plug into the social movement, and to do good work. Many high schools have Habitat for Humanity programs. Website: www.habitat.org

Heifer Project International. P.O. Box 8058, Little Rock, AR 722203. Tel: 1-800-422-0474. This organization donates farm equipment and animals to peasant farmers in less developed countries. Website: www.heifer.org

Kids for a Clean Environment. The world's largest youth environmental organization with more than 2,000 clubs in 15 countries with more than 300,000 members. It provides information on environmental issues, encourages and facilitates youth involvement, and attempts to recognize those who are doing good work. Check out their website at www.kidsface.org

Roots and Shoots. The Jane Goodall Institute, P.O. Box 14890, Silver Spring, MD 20910. This program was established to inspire youth of all ages to make a difference by becoming involved in their communities. A great place to go for projects in your state that involve youth. Website: www.rootsandshoots.org

Union of Concerned Scientists. 2 Brattle Square, Cambridge, MA 02238-9105. Tel: 617-547-5552. This amazing organization helps bring good science and creative thinking to the issues of the day. Their web site and publications offer a wealth of information for parents and teachers. Website: www.ucsusa.org

INDEX

SELECTED TITLES BY THE AUTHOR

The New Ecological Home

Superbia! 31 Ways to Create Sustainable Neighborhoods

The Solar House: Passive Solar Heating and Cooling

The Natural Plaster Book: Earthen, Lime, and Gypsum Plasters for Natural Homes

The Natural House: A Complete Guide to Healthy, Energy-Efficient, Environmental Homes

Lessons from Nature: Learning to Live Sustainably on the Earth

Beyond the Fray: Reshaping America's Environmental Movement

Voices for the Earth: Vital Ideas from America's Best Environmental Books

Environmental Science: Creating a Sustainable Future, 7th ed.

Natural Resource Conservation: Management for a Sustainable Future, 9th ed.

Human Body Systems

Human Biology, 5th ed.

Biology: The Web of Life

Study Skills for Science Students

Essential Study Skills

ABOUT THE COVER

The two children you see on the cover are living, breathing EcoKids. Serena, on the left, was eight years old when this photo was taken in 2004. She is homeschooled and also attends the Aurora Learning Centre on Gabriola Island, British Columbia, a unique center for home-learning children. Serena likes being outdoors and enjoys sailing, swimming, biking, hiking, and exploring ponds and tide pools.

Since Serena was very young, she has cared about global and environmental issues. In the fall of 2002, Serena suggested to the kids at the Aurora Learning Centre that they invite Ryan Hreljac (see <www.ryanswell.ca>) to come to Gabriola. Ryan is an amazing Canadian boy who, since the age of six, has been raising money for wells and sanitation projects in Africa. Serena's plan spearheaded a five-month campaign by the elementary school children of Gabriola to raise money for drinking water wells in Africa and to teach people about the importance of water conservation. The community raised $13,300 for water projects in Uganda and Tanzania.

In the spring of 2004, Serena learned about Monterey Bay Aquarium's "Seafood Watch" which lists seafood choices for healthy oceans (see <www.montereybayaquarium.org>). Serena was alarmed that some of the fish sold locally were on the "Avoid" and "Caution" lists. She wrote to the President and CEO of a major grocery store chain in the region requesting that they follow the Seafood Watch guidelines in their purchasing.

Serena has volunteered over the past two summers at a large organic farm on the island, preparing the vegetables for sale. Additionally, each year the Aurora kids participate in beach cleanups and Serena is an enthusiastic participant.

She attends Amnesty International meetings with her mother and knows quite a lot about human rights issues. She and the other kids at Aurora started the "Maple Leaf Freedom Bear" campaign last year (<www.mapleleaffreedombear.ca>) in which teddy bears, each one representing a "prisoner of conscience," travel around the world spreading a message about human rights. The bears have traveled to five continents.

Alex is a seven-year-old homeschooled boy. He also lives on Gabriola Island with his mother, two dogs, and a cat. He has shown great interest in environmental issues since he was old enough to comprehend them. He's aware of the impact we humans have on the Earth, and tries wherever he can to minimize his impact. He and his mom try to keep their garbage generation to fewer than one garbage bag every two weeks; he's become very good at reusing things that normally would be put out with the trash. He has always been a litter-picker-upper, and has been known to approach strangers to hand them back the garbage they've recently dropped. Alex has participated in beach cleanups. Alarmed by the stench of a nearby pulp mill, he has decided to use as little paper as possible.

Because he lives, for the most part, outside the media mainstream (no television, no chain stores, no outdoor advertising), Alex isn't terribly focused on buying and acquiring new things like many children in the modern world these days. Instead, he spends a great deal of time outside, hiking, walking, and bicycle riding. He's an avid reader, and loves books about animals, both fiction and non-fiction.

Alex is currently learning about local economies, and despite a wary relationship with vegetables, is trying to eat more seasonally.

Through the alternative learning centre to which he belongs, he has participated in a major fundraising project for Ryan Hreljac's "Ryan's Well Foundation," helping to raise an unprecedented amount of money from the tiny community of Gabriola Island. This year, he's also working on the freedom bears project (mentioned above) with the learning centre, in association with Amnesty International.

Alex dreams of building a house with straw bales one day; his mom would even be willing to help, I'm told! He'd like to grow up to be a veterinarian; or if not that, a doctor, so he could go and help kids in poorer countries be healthy.

ABOUT THE AUTHOR

Dan Chiras is best known for his many popular books on natural building, solar energy, and sustainability, including *Superbia! 31 Ways to Create Sustainable Neighborhoods*, *The New Ecological Home*, and *The Solar House*. Dan is a visiting professor at Colorado College and has been teaching about environmental issues, environmental literacy, environmental values and a host of related topics to a wide range of audiences since the mid 1970s.

Dan is also father of two boys and lives in a state-of-the-art environmental home in Evergreen, Colorado.

If you have enjoyed *EcoKids*,
you might also enjoy other

BOOKS TO BUILD A NEW SOCIETY

Our books provide positive solutions for people who want to
make a difference. We specialize in:

**Environment and Justice • Conscientious Commerce
Sustainable Living • Ecological Design and Planning
Natural Building & Appropriate Technology • New Forestry
Educational and Parenting Resources • Nonviolence
Progressive Leadership • Resistance and Community**

New Society Publishers

ENVIRONMENTAL BENEFITS STATEMENT

New Society Publishers has chosen to produce this book on Enviro 100, recycled
paper made with **100% post consumer waste**, processed chlorine free, and old
growth free.

For every 5,000 books printed, New Society saves the following resources:[1]

28	Trees
2,500	Pounds of Solid Waste
2,751	Gallons of Water
3,788	Kilowatt Hours of Electricity
4,545	Pounds of Greenhouse Gases
20	Pounds of HAPs, VOCs, and AOX Combined
7	Cubic Yards of Landfill Space

---

[1]Environmental benefits are calculated based on research done by the Environmental Defense Fund and
other members of the Paper Task Force who study the environmental impacts of the paper industry.

For more information on this environmental benefits statement, or to inquire about environmentally
friendly papers, please contact New Leaf Paper – info@newleafpaper.com Tel: 888 • 989 • 5323.

For a full list of NSP's titles, please call **1-800-567-6772** *or check out our web site at:*

www.newsociety.com

NEW SOCIETY PUBLISHERS